D0073247

UNDERSTANDING SOVIET
SOCIETY

UNDERSTANDING SOVIET SOCIETY

Edited by

Michael Paul Sacks
Trinity College

and

Jerry G. Pankhurst
Wittenberg University

Boston
UNWIN HYMAN
London   Sydney   Wellington

Allen & Unwin, Inc.
8 Winchester Place, Winchester, MA 01890, USA.

Published by the Academic Division of
Unwin Hyman Ltd
15/17 Broadwick Street, London W1V 1FP

Allen & Unwin Australia Pty Ltd,
8 Napier Street, North Sydney, NSW 2060, Australia

Allen & Unwin (New Zealand) Ltd, in association with the Port
Nicholson Press Ltd,
60 Cambridge Terrace, Wellington, New Zealand

Library of Congress Cataloging-in-Publication Data

Understanding Soviet society.
Bibliography: p.
Includes index.
1. Soviet Union – Social conditions – 1970–
I. Sacks, Michael Paul.   II. Pankhurst, Jerry G.
HN523.5.U53   1988   306′.0947   87–18707
ISBN 0–04–445036–2
ISBN 0–04–445048–6 (pbk.)

British Library Cataloguing in Publication Data

Understanding Soviet society.
1. Soviet Union – Social conditions – 1970–
I. Sacks, Michael Paul   II. Pankhurst, Jerry G.
947.085′4   HN523.5
ISBN 0–04–445036–2
ISBN 0–04–445048–6   *Pbk*

Set in 10 on 12 point Garamond by Nene Phototypesetters Ltd
and printed in Great Britain by Biddles of Guildford

Contents

Preface

Understanding Soviet Society has grown out of our experience as sociologists researching and teaching about the Soviet Union. It began as an update of our earlier volume, *Contemporary Soviet Society: Sociological Perspectives* (New York: Praeger, 1980), but developed well beyond a normal revised edition. This was the case not only because of the addition of six new authors, but also because of the major changes occurring in the USSR today that in many ways necessitated new approaches. Nevertheless, *Understanding Soviet Society* has profited from the many helpful comments on the earlier collection. Both professional colleagues in the social sciences and students in our classes have played an important role in determining the direction this work has taken, and we acknowledge their contributions.

More specifically, as this manuscript began shaping up, we both used some of the essays in our classes and received useful responses from our students, for which we are grateful. We also wish to thank the anonymous reviewers who, at two stages in the preparation of this book, provided us with very helpful reactions.

In the midst of rapid and important social change, one cannot hope to compile in a single volume a total, accurate picture of a complex society like the USSR. We have had neither aspiration nor pretense to be definitive in this volume, but it has nevertheless been both perplexing and exciting to make an effort in that direction. Hence, we dedicate the book to the so-called reformers who have made our task so difficult over the last couple of years. May their influence be only positive.

Introduction

Imagine the contents of a book covering the essential characteristics of the American society. Even if it were restricted to aspects of primary interest to a sociologist, such a book would be a formidable undertaking. Indeed the vast majority of American sociology is really the sociology of the United States. Entire courses are devoted to the family, gender roles, ethnic relations, religion, politics, law, large organizations, education, social stratification, social problems, and more; and each course can assemble a multitude of books with diverse and sometimes conflicting interpretations and explanations.

The diversity of views held by the American public might best be illustrated from a review of the vast array of material, such as surveys of public opinion, in depth interviews with citizens, newspaper accounts, and editorials. Other aspects of the culture might be captured through describing contemporary novels, plays, and movies. These sources would reflect the regional differences, class differences, and changes over time that are often manifested in the differences between generations. Considering this you might quickly conclude that it would be absurd to believe that a single volume could achieve any kind of comprehensive understanding of the United States, especially for someone lacking experience living in the society.

When considering Soviet society, however, we tend to see the subject as much more manageable, and many books are available with titles suggesting that a relatively brief account can suffice. Western news accounts about particular events in the Soviet Union often contain broad generalizations to show the reader how the new information fits a broader (and usually quite familiar) picture. These generalizations tend to emphasize the overarching role of the state and are meant, often implicitly, to draw a sharp contrast with the United States. As Hough (1977, 226–28) has pointed out, when comparisons are made between the West and the Soviet Union there is a particularly strong tendency to oversimplify both systems and to neglect information that does not conform to this image.

The recently established Center for War, Peace and the News Media at New York University has been studying the distortions and stereotypes regarding the Soviet Union that appear in the US media. Among other aspects considered, the Center exposes "para-information" that subtly embodies interpretations about the nature of Soviet and American societies and is "encoded in the stories." The Co-director of the Center, Robert Karl Manoff (1986, 3), provides three illustrations: (1) an article in the *New York Times*, in which Philip Taubman concludes his account of a press conference with a high political official by noting that "there was a willingness to talk about almost any subject – but not to challenge basic Soviet values"; (2) a report from the *Los Angeles Times – Washington Post* that Premier Ryzhkov had spoken about the problems of the economy after Brezhnev's death "in the Kremlin tradition of assigning blame to predecessors"; and (3) the comment by Betsy Aaron in an ABC television program that a "dedicated Party member . . . knows the rules: Never criticize the system, criticize the circumstances"; the story regarded a worker who said, "we never blame, we criticize" when asked about blame for river pollution.

Manoff (1986, 3) contends that the assumptions about Soviet society in each case

> might become clear if readers were to interrogate the texts. . . . They might ask the *New York Times*, which was disappointed that a high Soviet official did not challenge basic Soviet values: When has an American done the equivalent, kept his job? They might ask the *Los Angeles Times*, which viewed criticism of predecessors as a Kremlin tradition: What was President Reagan up to the week before when he faulted previous administrations for weakening the country's strategic forces. . . ? Or, they might ask ABC, which found Communist cant in the preference for criticism over blame: What is to be made of Esalen or the self-help books that offer the same advice from every paperback counter in America? And they might also ask ABC, since Aaron found it a Party rule to criticize only circumstances: Is [it] really the American way to criticize the system?

Understanding Soviet Society stresses the complexity of Soviet society and the obstacles to understanding it. The picture sketched here is clearly partial; only selected aspects of the society can be examined, and one obstacle unquestionably has been the limitation on information about the society. (The detail in each chapter shows, however, that this problem should not be exaggerated.) In the end the reader will find that summary assessments of the characteristics of the society are far from easy and unambiguous. Although the authors differ in their assessment of the most significant factors shaping Soviet society, the chapters should foster a deeper appreciation of the problems and fruitfulness of comparing Soviet society with other modern industrial nations and applying to the Soviet case social science theory that has been valuable in explaining and understanding trends elsewhere in the world.

The importance of comparative study and application of social science theory is stressed and illustrated in the chapter by Lewis. We strongly support his view that assuming that the social processes in the USSR are unique can lead to distorted and inaccurate understanding and an inadequate evaluation of empirical data on the society. Careful comparative study is the way to appreciate what aspects of the society are truly distinctive, that is, what aspects cannot be explained without modification of the theory that has been tested or formulated based on the experience of other societies.

The focus of *Understanding Soviet Society* on its diverse aspects necessarily places considerable limits on how exhaustively each subject can be investigated. Some perspective on the scope of the chapters can be gained by examining Berman's classic study, *Justice in the U.S.S.R.: An Interpretation of Soviet Law* (1963). This book represents in our view a model of an especially comprehensive study of an aspect of Soviet society. Berman (4–7) shows how the Soviet legal system is shaped by three sets of factors: (1) an ideological commitment to "Marxian socialism" – "the needs and interests of the socialist state"; (2) a distinctive history and cultural heritage that require examining the trends over as much as the past thousand years; and (3) the requirements for operating a large-scale industrial economy and for implementing centralized political authority that are characteristic of modern societies.

The first set of factors leads to a comparison between capitalist and socialist systems. The third set leads to comparisons of Soviet society with other modern industrial societies to appreciate common factors. Within the context of careful comparative analysis, Berman also stresses the importance of the second set, a culture and history that have had a distinctive influence on the USSR.[1] Looking at the long tradition of legal development in the West and Russia, Berman (1963, 268) shows that "Russian law proves that the different national legal systems of the West are in reality variations on a single theme." But a paragraph later he also notes that "Soviet rulers are not the ultimate masters of Russia's fate; on the contrary, Russia is the ultimate master of Russia's fate" (1963, 269). Berman's book is a masterful treatment of the complex interplay between the three sets of factors and how different aspects of the legal establishment are more strongly shaped by one than by the others. Throughout the book Berman refers to the similarities among and differences between Soviet and Western institutions and how by looking at the Soviet case we can better understand our own society. It is our hope that the chapters here will also contribute to such an understanding.

Conversely, understanding also requires an appreciation of how our own society shapes our perception of Soviet society. In *The Rise and Fall of the Soviet Threat: Domestic Sources of the Cold War Consensus*, Alan Wolfe (1984) shows how strong forces rooted in the domestic political situation of the United States foster cycles in the perception of the USSR as belligerent and a growing threat to national security. The important point here is that the assessment may not be the product of a careful examination of Soviet society but rather it may derive from the need to portray an external threat. Wolfe ultimately sees a very different connection between our objectively looking at the USSR and the genuine threats to democracy in the United States:

> Time after time, elites that possess relatively unpopular ideas – such as a strong executive, an expensive public sector, an inflationary program, an emphasis on large-scale production, and a demand for domestic sacrifice to stabilize the world economy – have managed to stifle the strong opposition to their vision by manipulating the Soviet threat. The task, then, is to take off the husk of the Soviet threat, which does have mass appeal, so that the kernel of an undemocratic and monopolistic program, which does not, will be revealed. (1984, 135)

Berman (1963, 5) expresses a similar sentiment: "It is not true that if the Soviet Union did not exist we would have no serious problems. Indeed, the tensions latent in our social order might flare up with far greater intensity if we could not externalize and objectify them as issues of foreign policy."

Domestic politics have had a direct impact on scholarship. Cohen (1984, 16–19) has noted the fear and harassment of scholars studying the Soviet Union during the McCarthy era. The Cold War profoundly influenced the conduct of inquiry: "Academic Soviet studies became, by the 1950s, a highly politicized profession imbued with topical political concerns, a crusading spirit, and a know-the-enemy raison d'etre" (1984, 10–11). Not surprisingly, a totalitarian model of Soviet society came to dominate the field and, in Cohen's view, greatly stifle objective study.

> More was obscured than revealed. Historical analysis came down to the thesis of an inevitable "unbroken continuity" throughout Soviet history, thereby largely excluding the stuff of real history – conflicting traditions, alternatives, turning points, multiple causalities. Political analysis fixated on a regime imposing its "inner totalitarian logic" on an impotent, victimized society, thereby largely excluding the stuff of real politics – the interaction of govermental, historical, social, cultural, and economic factors; the conflict of classes, institutions, groups, generations, ideas, and personalities. Sovietology – an intellectual profession founded on the potentially rich idea of multidisciplinary area study – committed

an act of self-impoverishment. It eliminated everything diverse and problematic from its own subject. (1985, 7)

Cohen believes that significant change was evident in studies published by the 1970s, but this perspective still continues to have a strong influence within the field.

The more commonly considered obstacle is the limitation on information about the society. It is not possible for a Western scholar to conduct a survey of public opinion in the USSR. There are also restrictions on the kind of simple observation of social activity that an outsider can undertake. Consequently, in Soviet studies it is necessary to rely heavily on a wide range of statistical sources and on other material, such as press reports and literature.

Soviet emigres also represent an important source of information, though over time the availability and reliability of such material have varied. There is a methodological problem in generalizing from an emigre sample to the nation the emigres have left, but major studies have tried to overcome this obstacle with careful analysis and interpretation. In fact, the sociological study of the USSR was given a major boost by the Harvard University Refugee Project of the 1950s, the object of which was to learn about the Soviet Union by studying the wave of emigres associated with World War II. A massive new project in the 1980s, the Soviet Interview Project, has sought to study the more recent emigres (Millar and Donhowe 1987). Based on a survey of some 2,800 former Soviet citizens, the publications from this study are just becoming available and will continue to enhance our perception of Soviet society. In addition, the data from the survey have now been made available for analysis by those who were not part of the study team itself.

At this writing the changes initiated under Gorbachev raise the prospect of the availability of much more published information from the Soviet Union and perhaps eventually of greater opportunities for direct research in that society, in collaboration with Soviet scholars. New statistics have already begun to appear on such subjects as the consumption of liquor, the size of grain harvests, and the level of infant deaths (Schmemann 1986, A7), and strong criticism of past practices has also been published.

The President of the Soviet Sociological Association, Tat'iana Zaslavskaya, states that a primary task of the Party is "to persistently overcome the widespread habit of half-truths, which in this case are worse than lies. We must learn anew to look the truth in the eye..." (1987, 3). In Pravda she has recently written, "If we continue to keep from the people information about the conditions under which they live – say, the degree of environmental pollution, the number of industrial accidents or the extent of crime – we cannot expect them to assume a more active role in economic or in political life.... People will trust and support you only if you trust them" (quoted in

Shabad 1987, A10). Under the policy of *glasnost* (or Openness) not only the Soviet people, but also foreign researchers should become apprised of much more substantive information about Soviet life.

However, even the data that have been available in the past have in many ways been extremely rich. The chapters in this volume show the detailed information available on a wide range of subject matter and also point to the deficiencies. It is interesting that even on such a sensitive matter as problems encountered among soldiers serving within the military, Jones (1984, xvii) has found the Soviet press to be a very valuable source: "The picture that emerges from emigre evidence is not all that different from that which emerges from a careful reading of the press. . . . The most dramatic examples of corruption, cover-up, and abuses of the disciplinary regulations are found not in the memoirs of former Soviet soldiers, but on the pages of *Red Star,*" an official Soviet army periodical.

Plan of the Book

Common ideas about the Soviet Union too often restrict our vision rather than deepen our perceptions of that nation and its people. Each chapter in *Understanding Soviet Society* seeks to go beyond the stereotypes, to overcome prejudgments in order to foster cleareyed knowledge. As well as assembling accurate and relevant facts, two other characteristic strategies in these essays are aimed at improving our ability to perceive the important workings of Soviet society. First, each chapter provides some comparative baselines for understanding, and, second, each tries to exploit major theoretical and analytical approaches rather than to treat the USSR as a case without theoretical relevance, a society apart from all others. The payoff from the latter strategies is not only to put the Soviet Union in a context of comparison that will improve our knowledge of that society, but also to make the analysis of the Soviet Union relevant to the ongoing revision (i.e., perfecting) of theories of society, which is at the heart of social science itself.

Even though all of our contributors are not sociologists, the essays stress a sociological approach to their topics. Western macro-level sociology tends to view all societies as lying somewhere on a range of positions for various important variables, such as urbanization, level of literacy, level of industrialization, and standard of living. Certain consequences are thought to flow from a society's position on these variables even though it has a unique social, political, and economic history, and even though it currently seeks to fashion itself in certain intentional ways (like being socialist or capitalist). Hence, in approaching Soviet society sociologically one goal is to test the alleged universal outcomes of major variables and assess how substantial and unique are the effects of peculiar historical and ideological factors. In obvious or more subtle ways, each essay in the volume does so.

This approach to the study of Soviet society is most clearly elaborated in the essay by Lewis, which concludes Part I. The preceding chapters help provide a more concrete illustration of the comparative application of social science theory that Lewis advocates. The chapters in Part I consider issues in the realm of stratification. Starting with ethnic differences (Clem's essay), and moving through social class (Connor), urban–rural society (Humphrey), and sex or gender inequality (Sacks), the reader is introduced to major notions about the hierarchical aspects of social organization in Soviet society. This first part also conveys a great deal of basic information about the background and current structural characteristics of the society. Underlying our conception of this section is the question of how to see the social solidarity of Soviet society, even with all of the centrifugal strains that are evidenced in the diverse patterns of stratification.

More than any other institution, the Soviet state and party regulate the centrifugal tendencies in Soviet society. Part II deals directly with the important connection between the Communist Party of the Soviet Union (CPSU) and the Soviet people and social institutions. In the two essays by Field and Remington we see the crucial role of the Party in shaping the future of Soviet society. We also see, however, that the Party's role is neither unlimited nor omnipotent. It is intimately engaged in interrelations with Soviet society that make its successes and failures dependent *not* on how it drives the Soviet people, but on how it manages the drive of that people.

The four essays in Part III examine several areas in which everyday life and social problems come to prominence in our quest for understanding Soviet society. Under a Marxist–Leninist system, some behaviors that were once acceptable take on deviant definitions. Pankhurst discusses ways in which the Soviet system creates new deviancies associated with religion, an ideologically negative phenomenon in that society, and Shelley explores new versions of criminality found in the USSR. Lane considers the implications of the political commitment to full employment, and Jones evaluates the mutual influences of Soviet society and the military. However, while each author points out peculiarities of the Soviet situation, each also places Soviet patterns in the context of universal functional issues. The essays examine ways in which Soviet society has adapted to the requirements to define and manage the sacred and the secular, to formalize a system of social control, to mobilize the economic resources of the people through employment, and to defend the country by using its own human resources in the military. Although such efforts do not make the Soviet Union a society just like any other, they do put it in a comparative position vis-à-vis other societies, which enhances our perception of the relative strengths and weaknesses of each.

Knowledge and Understanding
of a Changing Soviet Union

While preparing this book we have seen the Soviet Union experience one of the most disjunctive periods in its seventy-year history. Within five years, four different leaders have stood at the helm of the ship of state in Moscow, and each leader has had a distinctive orientation to the options for change in that society. Mikhail Gorbachev now appears to be the most reformist-minded of these leaders. He has embarked on a program that, in its stated intentions at least, involves massive alterations in patterns we have come to take for granted in the USSR. By careful analysis, we can more clearly see the options and limitations the new Soviet leadership faces.

Above all, Gorbachev seems intent on improving the productivity of the Soviet worker, reorganizing the bureaucratic machinery so it operates more efficiently, and thereby improving the overall performance of the Soviet economy. For understanding the pursuit of these and related goals, the sociological analysis of the situation has great value. In the area of employment and labor, the essays by Connor and Lane address the dilemmas of economic reform. In both cases, it is important to note that the Party and its leader must engage in a difficult "negotiation" with the society in order to pursue their reformist goals. Such a negotiation involves not merely economic factors per se, but also cultural and societal factors. In a similar way, the other essays in this volume serve to remind us that, as we assess the potentials for reform in the Soviet system, important influences derive not only from Politburo politics, pure economics, or ideological goals, but also from the Soviet people, their preferences, habits, traditions, and resources. In short, Soviet society is much more than an intellectual curiosity.

Perhaps the most important development in our understanding of the Soviet Union, since the semidiscipline of Soviet studies emerged during and after World War II, is the realization that society matters. The notion that society, even in a totalitarian nation, has great importance for both social control and social change had long been accepted by a few Sovietologists; but traditional "kremlinology," which sees all the important happenings taking place only in the highest political councils of the land or at least within the Communist party, tended to be the focus of the field.

The realization that society *really* matters struck Soviet studies scholars with significant effect sometime in the late 1960s and has spread among them throughout the 1970s and 1980s. Soviet studies previously had been devoted largely to analyses of the political and economic elite of the USSR, with the few scholars investigating the Soviet people regarded as involved with cultural curiosities and peripheral issues. Now no responsible student of the Soviet Union can ignore the importance of consumer demands; educational and training factors in economic production; the roles women hold in the society; varied ideological or, at least, policy views; and numerous other ways in which Soviet society, the Soviet people, and Soviet social patterns affect the direction of change in that nation, politically and economically, as well as "merely" socio-culturally.

This book seeks to improve our knowledge of Soviet society and, especially, our sensitivity to ways of studying that society that will help us go beyond facile stereotyping and easy conclusions in our analyses. We believe that some honest ambiguity is preferable to baseless assertions of only mythical "facts." As a consequence, although there is less than total agreement among the contributors on several issues of interpretation, we have tried not to homogenize the essays in order not to portray premature closure on any disputed versions. Even with some ambiguities in place, we believe these essays help further real *understanding* of Soviet society.

Note

[1] If any of these influences has been neglected relative to the others in the essays in this volume, it is the second set, historical and cultural factors. However, the goal here is to remain sensitive to the work of these variables while not permitting the unique historical and cultural circumstances to become the end of analysis itself.

References

Berman, Harold J. 1963. *Justice in the U.S.S.R.*, rev. ed. Cambridge: Harvard University Press.

Cohen, Stephen F. 1985. *Rethinking the Soviet Experience: Politics and History Since 1917.* New York: Oxford University Press.

Hough, Jerry F. 1977. *The Soviet Union and Social Science Theory.* Cambridge: Harvard University Press.

Jones, Ellen. 1985. *Red Army and Society: A Sociology of the Soviet Military.* Boston: Allen and Unwin.

Manoff, Robert Karl. 1986. "The Media's Moscow." *American Association for the Advancement of Slavic Studies Newsletter*, 26 (3): 1–3.

Millar, James, and Peter Donhowe. 1987. "Life, Work, and Politics in Soviet Cities – First Findings of the Soviet Interview Project." *Problems of Communism* 36 (1): 46–55.

Schmemann, Serge. 1986. "Kremlin Resumes Issuing Key Data." *The New York Times*, October 28, p. A7.

Shabad, Theodore. 1987. "Soviet Sociologist Candid about Official Disregard of Her Science." *The New York Times*, February 20, p. A10.

Wolfe, Alan. 1984. *The Rise and Fall of the Soviet Threat: Domestic Sources of the Cold War Consensus.* Boston: South End.

Zaslavskaya, Tat'iana Ivanovna. 1987. "Rol' sotsiologii v uskorenii razvitiya sovetskogo obshchestva." *Sotsiologicheskie issledovaniya* (2): 3–15.

PART I

Aspects of Social Stratification

1

The Ethnic Factor in Contemporary Soviet Society

Ralph S. Clem

One of the most important features of contemporary Soviet society is ethnicity.[1] The fundamental importance of ethnicity as a social and political force in the Soviet Union (USSR) derives first from the fact that the country is one of the world's most ethnically heterogeneous states, in terms of both the number of ethnic groups included in its population and the diversity among them. Further, the Soviet Union throughout its history has been in the throes of massive economic and social change and, at times, traumatic events, all of which have catapulted the ethnic issue to center stage. Since World War II, an ever-increasing interest in the ethnic dimension of the USSR has been apparent, an interest inspired by the rise of the Soviet Union to the status of a major power in international affairs, by heightened consciousness among ethnic emigre communities in the West, by the transnational politicization of ethnicity in issues such as the emigration of Soviet Jews and the treatment of dissidents, and – perhaps most important – by the realization that problems stemming from multiethnicity in any setting are not as transitory as once believed and must therefore command greater attention.

The ethnic composition of the Soviet Population

The Union of Soviet Socialist Republics ranks third among the countries of the world in population size (behind only the People's Republic of China and India); however, it is not the magnitude but the ethnic heterogeneity of the Soviet population that is of particular importance. The 1979 Soviet census listed about one hundred different ethnic groups; although many were quite small in numbers, at that time there were twenty-two groups with populations in excess of one million and another twenty-nine groups larger than one hundred thousand persons (see Table 1.1).

Table 1.1
Population of Major Soviet Ethnic Groups: 1959, 1970, and 1979

| Ethnic Groups | Population (thous.) | | | Average Annual Growth Rate (%) | | Percent of Total Soviet Population | | |
	1959	1970	1979	1959–70	1970–79	1959	1970	1979
Russians	114,114	129,015	137,397	1.1	.7	54.65	53.37	52.42
Ukrainians	37,253	40,753	42,347	.8	.4	17.84	16.86	16.16
Uzbeks	6,015	9,195	12,456	3.9	3.4	2.88	3.80	4.75
Belorussians	7,913	9,052	9,463	1.2	.5	3.78	3.74	3.61
Kazakhs	3,622	5,299	6,556	3.5	2.4	1.73	2.19	2.50
Tatars	4,968	5,931	6,317	1.6	.7	2.38	2.45	2.41
Azeri	2,940	4,380	5,477	3.7	2.5	1.41	1.81	2.08
Armenians	2,787	3,559	4,151	2.2	1.7	1.33	1.47	1.58
Georgians	2,692	3,245	3,571	1.7	1.1	1.29	1.34	1.36
Moldavians	2,214	2,698	2,968	1.8	1.1	1.06	1.12	1.13
Tadzhiks	1,397	2,136	2,898	3.9	3.4	.67	.88	1.11
Lithuanians	2,326	2,665	2,851	1.2	.8	1.11	1.10	1.09
Turkmens	1,002	1,525	2,028	3.9	3.2	.48	.63	.77
Germans	1,620	1,846	1,936	1.2	.5	.78	.76	.74
Kirgiz	969	1,452	1,906	3.7	3.1	.46	.60	.73
Jews	2,268	2,151	1,811	− .5	−1.6	1.09	.89	.69
Chuvash	1,470	1,694	1,751	1.3	.4	.70	.70	.67
Latvians	1,400	1,430	1,439	.2	.1	.67	.59	.55
Bashkirs	989	1,240	1,371	2.1	1.1	.47	.51	.52
Mordvinians	1,285	1,263	1,192	− .2	− .6	.62	.52	.45
Poles	1,380	1,167	1,151	−1.3	− .1	.66	.48	.44
Estonians	989	1,007	1,020	.2	.1	.47	.42	.39
Chechens	419	613	756	3.5	2.4	.20	.25	.29
Udmurts	625	704	714	1.1	.2	.30	.29	.27
Mari	504	599	622	1.6	.4	.24	.25	.24
Ossetians	413	488	542	1.5	1.2	.20	.20	.21
Avars	270	396	483	3.5	2.2	.13	.16	.18
Komi[a]	431	475	478	.9	.1	.21	.20	.18
Koreans	314	358	389	1.2	.9	.15	.15	.15
Lezgins	223	324	383	3.5	1.9	.11	.13	.15
Bulgarians	324	351	361	.7	.3	.16	.15	.14
Buryats	253	315	353	2.0	1.3	.12	.13	.13
Greeks	309	337	344	.8	.2	.15	.14	.13
Yakuts	233[b]	296	328	2.2	1.1	.11	.12	.13
Kabardinians	204	280	322	2.9	1.6	.10	.12	.12
Karakalpaks	173	236	303	2.9	2.8	.08	.10	.12

Ethnic Groups	Population (thous.)			Average Annual Growth Rate (%)		Percent of Total Soviet Population		
	1959	1970	1979	1959–70	1970–79	1959	1970	1979
Dargins	158	231	287	3.5	2.4	.08	.10	.11
Kumyks	135	189	228	3.1	2.1	.06	.08	.09
Uyghurs	95	173	211	5.6	2.2	.05	.07	.08
Gypsies	132	175	209	2.6	2.0	.06	.07	.08
Ingush	106	158	186	3.7	1.8	.05	.07	.07
Gagauz	124	157	173	2.2	1.1	.06	.06	.07
Hungarians	155	166	171	.6	.3	.07	.07	.07
Tuvinians	100	139	166	3.0	2.0	.05	.06	.06
Kalmyks	106	137	147	2.4	.8	.05	.06	.06
Karelians	167	146	138	−1.1	− .6	.08	.06	.05
Karachay	81	113	131	3.1	1.7	.04	.05	.05
Romanians	106	119	129	1.1	.9	.05	.05	.05
Kurds	59	89	116	3.8	3.0	.03	.04	.04
Adyge	80	100	109	2.0	1.0	.04	.04	.04
Laks	64	86	100	2.7	1.7	.03	.04	.04

Sources: 1959 and 1970 figures from USSR, Tsentral 'noye statisticheskoe upravlenie, *Itogi Vsesoyuznoi perepisi naseleniya 1970 goda* (Moskva: Statistika, 1973), IV, pp. 9–11; 1979 figures from USSR, Tsentral 'noe statisticheskoe upravlenie, *Naselenie SSSR* (Moskva: Politcheskoi literatury, 1980), pp. 23–26.

Figure for Komi includes Komi-Permyaki.

The population for Yakuts was reported as 236,655 in the 1959 Census itself.

The cultural diversity among these ethnic groups (or, in Soviet parlance, nationalities) is remarkable, so much so that it is difficult to describe their attributes briefly. For illustrative purposes, we consider in detail only nationalities with more than one million members.[2] Our description focuses on two key elements of ethnic culture: language and religion. It should be noted here that within language groups are different degrees of mutual intelligibility among the individual tongues; also, religious affiliation refers to that belief historically associated with each ethnic group but says nothing about the strength of attachment to the various faiths (Matthews 1951; Katz, Rogers, and Harned 1975; Goldhagen 1968; Aspaturian 1968; Wixman 1984).

The Russians by far are numerically the largest of all the ethnic groups in the USSR; they number slightly more than a majority of the population. Closely related to the Russians linguistically (i.e., all speak Slavic languages) are the Ukrainians (second in size and easily the largest minority) and the Belorussians (fourth in size). In terms of historical religious affiliation, Russians are Eastern Orthodox Christian, and Ukrainians and Belorussians divide between Orthodox and Catholic. After the three major Slavic nationalities, the largest bloc of ethnic groups comprises Muslim peoples: the Uzbeks, Tatars, Kazakhs, Azeri, Turkmen, Kirgiz, Bashkirs, Tadzhiks, and others. With the exception of the Tadzhiks, who speak a language related to Persian, the languages of these people are from the Turkic group.

Two other major Soviet nationalities, the Armenians and the Georgians, are both historically Christian peoples (of different rites) who speak distinctive languages. The three Baltic nationalities – the Estonians, Latvians, and Lithuanians – are generally regarded as the most "European" of the Soviet ethnic groups. Estonians and most Latvians adhere to the Lutheran denomination, whereas the Lithuanians and a minority of Latvians are Roman Catholics. Linguistically, Estonians speak a Finnic language, and Latvians and Lithuanians, Baltic languages.

The Moldavians are akin to the Romanians (whose country adjoins the Soviet Union); they speak a dialect of Romanian and traditionally share the Orthodox faith. Of the remaining larger ethnic groups, the Mordvinians and the Chuvash are both religiously affiliated with the Orthodox Church but have different linguistic origins; Mordvinian is a Finnic tongue, whereas Chuvash is Turkic. Finally, Soviet Jews, Germans, and Poles are foreign groups descended from immigrants or from people living in border territories annexed into the Soviet Union.

The foregoing discussion demonstrates the range of cultural traits found among the Soviet nationalities. However, without going into additional detail, the point must be made that ethnic diversity is much more complex than this simple sketch illustrates. The host of smaller ethnic groups adds even more languages and religious traditions to the mix. Also, and very importantly, wide variations exist among the nationalities of the USSR in terms of phenotype, or physical appearance. In other words, there are noticeable differences of skin and hair color, build, and facial features.

Thus, within the Soviet population one finds ethnic groups as different as the Latvians and the Kirgiz; apart from their numbers, which are about equal, and the fact that each is the titular group of one of the fifteen republics of the Soviet Union, they have nothing in common. Whereas the Latvians by any standard (language, religion, phenotype) would be considered Europeans, the Kirgiz quite properly would be viewed by most people as typically Middle Eastern.

Complicating the ethnic multiformity still further is a considerable heterogeneity of socioeconomic characteristics, as we see later in this chapter.

The Formation of the Multiethnic Soviet State

The Tsarist Legacy: The Geography of Empire Building

An excellent question at this juncture is, how did peoples as dissimilar as the Latvians and the Kirgiz come to be in the same country? A key to understanding this situation is the fact that the Soviet Union, in territorial if not ideological terms, is the direct descendant of the empire of the tsars, an empire that grew by military conquest from a humble principality to a powerful state controlling one-sixth of the land surface of the world. During its expansionist phase, which lasted from the mid-sixteenth century to the first decade of the twentieth century, the tsarist Russian Empire acquired territories in Europe and in Asia that were the homelands of more than a score of major and countless smaller ethnic groups, all of which were ethnically distinct from the Russians (Allworth 1967; Donnelly 1968; Seton-Watson 1967). Two vital aspects of the multiethnic character of the Soviet Union are the geographic centrality of the Russian ethnic homeland and the peripheral location of most non-Russian groups. Whereas the majority of the ethnic Russian population is found in the interior, most non-Russians are concentrated in the borderlands, in their respective ethnic territories. Compounding this Russian–non-Russian, center–periphery dichotomy are several irredentist situations, that is, situations in which members of the same ethnic group live on both sides of the border.

Ethnicity and Revolution: The Transition to Soviet Rule

The imperial government desired social, economic, and political uniformity throughout the state, a uniformity based, of course, on the ethnic Russian norm (Raeff 1971). Until the assassination of Tsar Alexander II in 1881, the regime was largely content to leave the attainment of this uniformity to evolutionary means. However, following the accession to the throne of Alexander III, a period of reaction and repression was initiated, with the repression applied to the non-Russian ethnic groups, among others (Pipes 1968, 1–49). This period of forced Russo-conformity, during which ethnic minority rights and limited autonomy were abrogated, coincided (unhappily for the ancien regime) with the rise of nationality consciousness resulting from the general social and economic development in the Russian Empire during the latter half of the nineteenth century. The growth of educated urban elites among the non-Russian ethnic groups, combined with the natural resistance to tsarist oppression, resulted in the heightening of nationalist emotions and contributed significantly to the collapse of the Russian Empire.

Responding to the increasing ethnic tensions in Russia, various political factions, among them the Marxist Social Democrats, began devoting serious attention to the nationality situation. During the first decade of the twentieth century, most liberal political parties adopted platforms that embodied concessions to the nationalities of Russia, although the extent of these concessions varied widely. In 1903, for example, the Russian Social Democratic Labor party (later to become the Communist party) advocated several important points concerning the nationalities, including measures of regional autonomy, equality of all nationality groups, language and education rights, and the right of nationalities to self-determination (Pipes 1968, 1–49).

The head of the Bolshevik faction of the Communist movement, V. I. Lenin, viewed ethnicity and nationalism, in the Marxist vein, as secondary to the class struggle (Low 1958, 36–94). Emphasizing the economic benefits to be realized in large, centralized states, he was opposed in general to the fragmentation of existing states and to decentralized, federal political structures. Further, Lenin saw the amalgamation of ethnic groups as progressive (with the stipulation that forced measures be excluded), and he had little use for small ethnic groups that, he believed, could be assimilated into larger nationalities. As a shrewd judge of political realities, however, he began to realize the significance of the heightened ethnic sentiments in Russia and saw in the various ethnic nationalist movements potential allies for the proletariat in the upcoming struggle with the tsarist regime.

In order to consolidate his alliance with the non-Russian nationalities, Lenin promulgated his policy of self-determination, which stated explicitly that all ethnic groups of the Russian Empire had the right to secede and form independent states (Connor 1984, 33–4). With regard to criticism from other Marxists that the policy of self-determination would result in historically retrogressive fragmentation, Lenin apparently believed that the nationalities would not secede, and in the event that they should try, sufficient qualifications were included in the principle to justify intervention to prevent secession. Self-determination was a right, Lenin stated, but advocating the right did not mean advocating self-determination itself.

The revolution of February 1917 catapulted the nationality situation into a critical political and military problem. From the outset, the Provisional Government, which was in power from February to November 1917, was unwilling to take determined measures to placate unrest among the nationalities. It did remove formal restrictions against certain groups and decreed equality for all citizens regardless of their ethnic, religious, or racial background. As the internal order of the former Russian Empire disintegrated by degrees into chaos and finally civil war, those ethnic groups so inclined were presented with the opportunity for secession. Other groups that, in the past, had advocated only local autonomy found it necessary, in light of events, to adopt some form of self-rule in order to maintain order and to protect themselves from foreign military intervention or from the designs of neighboring ethnic groups. Civil unrest took on ethnic dimensions in non-Russian areas, particularly in the North Caucasus, Caucasus, and Central Asia, with indigenous groups taking up arms against Russian city dwellers, troops, and agricultural settlers. Many non-Russian nationalities saw in the fluctuating political–military situation the chance to regain lands or privileges that Russians had preempted during the period of tsarist rule (Pipes 1968, 50–113).

The years 1917 and 1918 witnessed the secession from the Russian state of Lithuania, Latvia, Estonia, Georgia, Armenia, and Finland, together with the occupation of Poland by Germany and the annexation of Bessarabia (Moldavia) by Romania. In addition to these areas, large territories (notably in Siberia) were controlled by counterrevolutionary military forces or were under some form of local self-rule (such as Ukraine).

The slogan of self-determination had proved a disaster for Lenin and the Bolsheviks, intent on maintaining a large state territorially synonymous with the previous tsarist empire, and it became increasingly clear that the slogan needed theoretical and pragmatic qualification. Lenin, therefore, together with Josef Stalin (who was emerging as the principal Bolshevik spokesman on nationality problems), began to stress the qualifications built into the original, pre-Revolutionary concept of self-determination. Ethnic self-determination, Stalin wrote in early 1918, could not stand in the way of the development and interests of the proletariat.

With a theoretical justification in hand, the Bolsheviks moved rapidly to establish military and political power in the non-Russian areas. Secessionist or self-rule regimes in Ukraine, Belorussia, the Caucasus, and Central Asia were defeated, and their territories reincorporated into the Russian state through a combination of force of arms, treachery, and the granting of temporary concessions (Conquest 1967, 21–49). The Bolsheviks found it expedient to conclude alliances with certain ethnic groups during the Civil War, particularly since the White forces held the minorities in contempt and virtually forced them into cooperation with the Reds. Following their consolidation of power, the vast majority of the pragmatic concessions granted to the nationalities were unilaterally abrogated by the Bolsheviks (Pipes 1968, 161–68).

The force of nationalism had shown itself to be stronger than Lenin and the Bolsheviks had foreseen. More than a factor to be exploited in the struggle for proletarian hegemony, ethnic nationalism proved to be a phenomenon that required some compromises, or at least the appearance of compromise. The federal concept of government increasingly began to suggest itself as the non-Russian areas were incorporated into the proletarian state, despite the previous outspoken animosity of Lenin and others for this decentralized form of government. Stalin justified the adoption of a federal state largely on grounds of expedience; in light of the outright secessions by some nationalities, federation was a step toward unity, a move toward a centralized state, and a sound tactic in the face of strong ethnic sentiments that the Bolsheviks had underestimated (Pipes 1968, 242–93). Most important, however, was the fact that the decentralized state structure was more than balanced by a Communist party that was highly centralized and, in reality, in complete control of the state apparatus.

The final result of the years of revolution, civil war, and ethnic nationalist insurrection was the creation, in 1922, of the Union of Soviet Socialist Republics. The Soviet Union is, in the political–administrative sense, a hierarchy of ethnic units, each of which represents one or more Soviet nationalities. Although there are exceptions to the rule, the status of a nationality's political unit is largely determined by population size.

At the highest level in the hierarchy are the fifteen Soviet Socialist Republics (SSRs), which together constitute the USSR. Each represents an ethnic group larger (in 1979) than one million.[3] Because one constitutional prerogative of these republics is the right to secede from the union, several major nationalities (Tatars, Chuvash, Mordvinians, and Bashkirs) that otherwise might qualify for union republic status are relegated to the next lower level in the hierarchy – Autonomous Soviet Socialist Republic (ASSR) – owing to the interior location of their homelands, where secession would be impracticable. Also, medium-size ethnic groups (those over 100,000 in number) are represented by the Autonomous Republics, of which there are twenty. There are two lower-level ethnic units, the eight Autonomous Oblasts and the ten Autonomous Okrugs, which serve as political entities for the smaller nationalities, mainly those living in sparsely populated Siberia, the Far North, or mountainous areas. In some cases, ethnic groups have more than one representative ethnic unit because of problems of territorial contiguity. Likewise, many units represent two or more ethnic groups. Individually or collectively, virtually all Soviet ethnic groups enjoy official status in the federal system. Although the status of some nationality units has changed over the years, and some groups have had their titular units abolished altogether, the basic structure remains unchanged since Lenin's time.

Social, Economic, and Geographic Aspects of Ethnicity in the USSR

Soviet Nationality Policy

As a consequence of Lenin's political strategy and the use of military force, the territorial integrity of the tsarist state was ultimately maintained in the transition to Soviet power. Likewise, with only two exceptions (the Finns and the Poles), the large number and amazing assortment of non-Russian nationalities that had been incorporated into the Russian Empire over the centuries since the fall of Kazan' are currently included in the multiethnic Soviet Union.

Despite the fact that the USSR virtually replicates the former Russian Empire across geographical and ethnic dimensions, the Soviet government obviously maintains that a qualitative difference exists between the two. Essentially, this difference can be summed up, according to Soviet theorists on ethnicity, by the simple fact that the "question of nationalities" or "nationality problems" in the USSR have been "solved" by the application of Marxist–Leninist nationality policy.

It should be understood at the outset that it is impossible to extract from Soviet government pronouncements or scholarship on the subject of ethnicity exactly what constitutes Soviet nationality policy. To state, as is usually the case, that nationality policy aims at solving the nationality question avoids the issue and requires some explication of what constitutes the nationality question. It is possible, however, to discern at least one main theme implicit, and at times explicit, in Soviet theory and statements regarding problems associated with ethnicity: Soviet nationality policy is designed to remove the social and economic inequalities among the ethnic groups of the USSR, inequalities that developed during the tsarist period. The principal mechanism to alleviate these inequalities is economic development (Arutiunian 1972). This theme, which is crucial to the entire range of Soviet theory on society, has its roots in the writings of Karl Marx and found its implementation under Lenin.

It has been contended that Marx, who is the source of almost all of Soviet social, economic, and political theory, provided precious little guidance pertaining to ethnic problems for his socialist successors. However, his proposed solution was the elimination of class conflict and economic exploitation of one group by another through the victory of the proletariat (Bloom 1967, 1–32; Connor 1984, 5–20). As applied in the Soviet situation, the means of removing the socioeconomic differences among nationalities was the economic (in most cases, industrial) development of the non-Russian areas of the USSR. Eventually, the indigenous population was to be drawn into the development process. The centrally directed socialist economy was the key to this program, inasmuch as control over investment, technology, and manpower would enable the government to plan and implement the equalization directives (Holubnychy 1968, 51).

The program of raising the level of development in the non-Russian areas of the USSR was officially promulgated in the early years of Soviet power and remains a central tenet of Communist party goals to this day. The Fifteenth

Party Congress (1927), for example, charged with initiating the First Five-Year Plan, stated that special attention would be paid to raising the level of development of all nationality regions, "liquidating their economic and cultural backwardness [*otstalost'*]" (Rutgaizer 1968). If the cornerstone of the edifice of Soviet nationality policy is the elimination of the socioeconomic disparities among ethnic groups that were inherited from the tsarist regime, it is clearly vital to assess the extent to which this goal has been attained.

Ethnic Groups and Development: The Reality

This section addresses two broad questions. First, Have the various non-Russian ethnoterritories reached a level of development roughly comparable with that in the ethnic Russian regions? Two key factors must be understood here: most non-Russians live in their respective ethnic homelands (their socioeconomic development is thus linked to that of their own ethnoterritories), and as detailed earlier, these homelands are recognized as such in the constitution, which makes the situation overtly political. Second, and most important, To what extent have non-Russians been integrated into modernized society, the development of their homelands notwithstanding? This latter point focuses directly on the assumption implicit in Soviet nationality policy that the economic development of the non-Russian areas will lead to the socioeconomic advancement of the non-Russian peoples.

With regard to the first question, the consensus among Western scholars is that most non-Russian areas continue to lag behind the European Russian regions of the USSR in terms of economic and sociocultural development. For example, one study that examined changes in the level of urbanization (a good index of development) from the 1920s to 1970 found that the Russian ethnoterritories urbanized at a higher rate than did non-Russian regions, resulting in a widening gap between the two rather than a convergence, as has been touted by Soviet authorities (Clem 1976). Urbanization is important as an indicator of economic development and of social and cultural development because, in the USSR, urbanites enjoy appreciably higher living standards, better access to educational institutions and services in general, and superior health care.

Beyond the data of urbanization, other indexes of economic development point to the perpetuation of spatial inequalities. Leslie Dienes (1972) studied the economic geography of the USSR in the post–World War II period and found major interregional variations in such indicators of economic development as industrial employment, industrial output, fuel consumption, and national income. In general, his figures revealed a much higher level of development in the Russian ethnoterritory and a few non-Russian areas (notably the Baltic republics and the eastern Ukraine), with contrasting lower levels in remaining ethnoterritories (particularly in Moldavia, the western and southern Ukraine, Kazakhstan, and the Central Asian republics). Likewise, Allan Rodgers (1974, 237–39) investigated regional trends in industrialization from 1940 to 1965 (by focusing on indexes of industrial employment) and determined that most non-Russian ethnoterritories were significantly behind Russian areas (exceptions again being the Baltic republics and the eastern Ukraine).

The impression that one obtains from these and other studies is that although progress has been made toward the goal of equalizing ethnoterritorial economic development, important differences still exist among regions (Bahry and Nechemias 1981; Koropeckyj 1972). There are probably two reasons for this. First, the desire to maximize aggregate economic growth resulted in the allocation of scarce development capital to areas where return on investment would be greatest. Second, military–strategic considerations dictated the location of industry in interior, defensible regions (Koropeckyj 1965, ch. 6).

These spatial differences in the extent to which economic development has taken place in the USSR are important because they are linked to similar variations in standards of living among regions (ethnoterritories) (Schroeder 1973). Broadly speaking, the same grouping of ethnoterritories is exhibited in the data relating to standards of living as in those indicative of economic development, with the Russian Republic and the Baltic republics on top and the four Central Asian republics, Moldavia, and Azerbaidzhan on the bottom. (See also Zwick 1976.)

The second dimension of Soviet nationality policy, as it applies to equalization among ethnic groups, concerns the relative standing of the various ethnic groups (not their ethnoterritories) with regard to economic, social, and cultural development. Historically, the Russians have enjoyed higher levels of development than most non-Russian groups, as measured by such indicators as educational attainment, level of urbanization, and participation in nonagricultural occupations. This is due mainly to their dominant position in the tsarist empire and because many of the earliest areas to develop industrially were in the Russian ethnoterritory.

Exceptions to this generalization are "achiever groups," such as Estonians, Armenians, Georgians, Latvians, and Jews, nationalities that have actually exceeded the Russians in most of these development indexes (Lewis, Rowland, and Clem 1976, 333–42).

In the most extensive study of socioeconomic development among Soviet nationalities, Jones and Grupp (1984) found that considerable gains in access to education and to skilled or professional jobs were made by previously disadvantaged non-Russian groups during the 1960s and into the early 1970s. From the middle to the end of the 1970s, however, Jones and Grupp found that the rate of improvement in minority educational attainment and access to white-collar jobs slowed markedly, and minority higher education enrollment rates actually dropped, due to a decline in the growth of the Soviet economy and the inability of the system to provide spaces in schools and universities for the burgeoning minority population (see the later section in'this chapter on ethnic population growth differentials). Thus, the most recent data indicate that, despite a tendency toward socioeconomic equalization, important differences remain between the relatively privileged Russians and achiever groups on the one hand and most minority ethnic groups on the other (Jones and Grupp 1984, 163–64, 171–72; Silver 1974).

In sum, the massive economic growth and concomitant social change characteristic of Soviet history have had a differential impact in both the spatial sense and along ethnic lines. Thus, some regions of the country – and here it is important to keep in mind that in the Soviet context this means ethnoterritories – have experienced much greater economic development than other areas. The fact that social–cultural development (standards of living) closely follows the economic development pattern gives even more importance to this phenomenon. Last, these development disparities tend to be mirrored in ethnic group terms, with certain groups having attained relatively high levels of modernization and others having lagged behind.

Contemporary Ethnic Issues

Bilingualism and Assimilation
Perhaps no other aspects of ethnicity in the USSR have received as much attention as the interesting and emotive subjects of bilingualism and assimilation. There is voluminous literature on the nature and extent of bilingualism and assimilation (and the relationship between the two) among Soviet nationalities, emanating from both the USSR and the West.

Although serious differences of opinion exist among Soviet authorities on certain features of assimilation, virtually all subscribe to a standard framework within which the process is to be acted out (Kozlov 1969). This conceptualization envisions the simultaneous occurrence of "two tendencies," one involving a "flourishing" (in Russian, *rastvet*) of ethnic awareness on the part of the various nationalities of the USSR, and the other involving a "drawing together" or rapprochement (*sblizhenie*) among the same groups. Eventually, it is assumed, the rapprochement will lead to a "merging" (*sliianie*) or, in other words, to a total assimilation of all groups into a single identity. Even though the future identity is usually portrayed as the ethnically neutral "Soviet people," there is little doubt that the hoped-for merging will entail the assimilation of non-Russians into an essentially ethnic Russian norm.

A key to understanding the seemingly contradictory dualism of flourishing and drawing together is the premise that the advent of socialism imparted a new and distinctive character to the nature of ethnic group relations. Once the juridical equality of all ethnic groups was established by the Soviet regime (to include language and cultural guarantees and ethnoterritorial political rights), it is contended, the nationalities could enjoy the full development of their respective cultures (along Marxist–Leninist lines), unfettered by the harsh Russian ethnocentric policies typical of the tsarist era. Hence, Stalin's famous dictum that the various cultures of the USSR were to be "national [ethnic] in form and socialist in content" came about. At the same time, the overall development of the socialist state would eliminate the divisive socioeconomic and political inequalities and exploitation characteristic of the capitalist epoch, thereby facilitating the rapprochement among nationalities. Thus, whereas assimilation in the capitalist setting would be forced and based on economic and political exploitation (therefore bad), assimilation under socialism would be natural and based on mutual trust (therefore progressive) (Connor 1984, 201–16).

Given this outlook, argument concerning assimilation (in the Soviet literature) centers not on the process itself – which is a given – but on the timing of its stages and the desirability of attempting, through government policy, to move ethnic groups slowly or quickly through the stages. Historically, the Soviet government has pursued assimilationist policies with varying intensity, but evidence in recent years suggests a relatively aggressive posture on the part of the Soviet government in promoting assimilation (Connor 1984, 402–07).

In practice, the maintenance of ethnic identity or the erosion thereof is affected to a large extent (but not completely) by factors that are, to some degree, capable of manipulation by the authorities. By far the most important factor is language policy, particularly the respective role and status of the Russian and the non-Russian languages. The importance of this issue derives partly from the belief among many scholars (both in the West and in the USSR) that the increasingly widespread use of the Russian language by non-Russians is a harbinger of assimilation (Guthier 1977).

Specifically, the direct policy questions concerning the language issue are those related to the use of languages in the schools and in the media. With regard to language use in education, the principal consideration has always been the role to be played by the Russian language and, in the case of schools in non-Russian areas, by the respective native languages as either the medium of instruction or as subjects of instruction (Silver 1972, ch. 2). From the earliest years of Soviet rule, the development of non-Russian language schools was a high priority, mainly in the ethnoterritories of the non-Russian nationalities. During the ensuing decades, the network of such schools was expanded greatly, but the situation remains characterized by substantial variation in the extent to which non-Russian languages are, in fact, an integral part of the educational system. The larger nationalities with union republic status are accorded much more extensive native language medium-of-instruction privileges in their ethnic homelands than are the smaller ethnic groups in the lower-level ethnoterritories (i.e., autonomous republics, autonomous oblasts, and autonomous okrugs) (Silver 1975).

The second direct policy question relating to language matters concerns the media. The Soviet government has direct control over the official media not only in terms of content but also of linguistic format. By controlling the availability of newspapers, journals, magazines, books, and radio and television programs in non-Russian languages, the regime can directly influence the degree to which languages are used in everyday life, and therefore the extent to which retention of these languages continues. For example, Roman Szporluk (1979), in an extensive study of media use of native language in the Ukrainian and Belorussian republics, found that Ukrainian was much more widely used than was Belorussian in their respective ethnoterritories. He concluded that "linguistic assimilation in West Belorussia was being promoted by the Belorussians' exposure to Russian in the press . . . [while] on the other hand in West Ukraine the media, in so far as they had any effect on language maintenance, encouraged loyalty to Ukrainian." Again it is generally the case that the number and range of non-Russian native language publications and broadcasts are a function of ethnoterritorial status.

Related to the issue of assimilation, the phenomenon of bilingualism (which almost always involves a non-Russian language and Russian) has become increasingly widespread among the minorities. The Soviet censuses contain excellent data for studying language affiliation, usually providing information on native language and second languages spoken by members of various ethnic groups (Silver 1986). These data reveal that most members of the non-Russian nationalities remain loyal to their respective native tongue – rather than to Russian – as a first language; in 1979, only 13.1 percent of non-Russians declared Russian as their native language, up slightly from 11.6 percent in 1970. In addition, however, in the 1979 census another 49 percent of non-Russians indicated that they knew Russian fluently as a second language, a significant increase from the 1970 figure of 37 percent. Currently, about two-thirds of all non-Russians speak fluent Russian as a native or second language.

The degree of bilingualism, like assimilation, varies markedly from group to group and generally in the same pattern. That is, fluency in Russian is highest among the nationalities that have the greatest linguistic and cultural affinity with Russians (e.g., Ukrainians and Belorussians) and among ethnic groups with historical ties to the tsarist and Soviet state (e.g., Komi, Mordvinians, Chuvash, Udmurts, Mari, and Tatars). On the other hand, linguistically distant nationalities (e.g., Georgians, Estonians, Azeri, Turkmen, and Tadzhiks) tend to have lower levels of Russian fluency. Other factors that influence bilingualism are the availability of native language schools and the degree of contact with Russians. In the first instance, the attenuated native language schooling for smaller nationalities, which means a shift to Russian language instruction, certainly promotes bilingualism among those groups. Secondly, non-Russian areas with large concentrations of ethnic Russians (which facilitates inter-ethnic contact) typically have a more bilingual population (Jones and Grupp 1984, 176–78). Finally, younger generations of non-Russians are more bilingual – often considerably so – than are older persons.

The view that bilingualism is simply a way station on the road to assimilation is probably outdated. Rather, bilingualism seems to have become a compromise between the assimilation of non-Russians into the ethnic Russian culture and the maintenance of isolated non-Russian identities. Contrary to the theory of ethnic group relations in socialist states, as propounded by scholars and the political leadership in the USSR (which stresses assimilation as the ultimate goal), the Soviet government probably will be content for the time being to promote the teaching of Russian to non-Russians for the sake of economic and military efficiency (Russian is the language of command in the armed forces).

One other perspective on the question of ethnic homogenization in the USSR is provided by data on the extent of intermarriage among nationalities. If anything, the degree to which individuals marry people of their own nationality (endogamy) is an even more sensitive indicator of the retention of ethnic awareness than is language loyalty. Among the non-Russian nationalities there is a remarkably high level of endogamy, with very few individuals marrying outside their respective ethnic group. In the definitive work on the subject, the Soviet scholar L. V. Chuiko (1975) presented data for 1969 showing that of the fourteen non-Russian nationalities of union republic status, in no case did the percentage of individuals marrying endogamously drop below 81.7 percent. To an extent, as pointed out by Wesley Fisher (1977), endogamy is a function of other demographic, social, and cultural factors; but even allowing for the fact that the ethnic composition of many areas remains relatively homogeneous (which reduces the odds of finding a marriage partner outside one's nationality), "the strength of endogamy is quite impressive." (See also Silver 1978).

Federalism and Political Elites

The creation of the Union of Soviet Socialist Republics as a federation of ethnoterritories has been viewed as a clever solution to the problem of centrifugation inherent in multi-ethnic states, in this case facilitating the perpetuation of the territorial integrity of the former tsarist empire while allowing for the overt expression of ethnic political autonomy. Whether this federal ethnoterritorial state structure was established for pragmatic or ideological reasons (or for some combination of the two), and regardless of whether the structure itself was (is) viewed theoretically as transitory, the various ethnic groups of the USSR increasingly see the arrangement as long-term if not permanent, assign importance to it, will resist attempts to alter it in the direction of fewer ethnic prerogatives, and are now making demands on the regime through the ethnoterritorial medium. It can also be argued that the ethnoterritorial structure serves to reinforce ethnic identity and thereby slows the rate of assimilation among the non-Russian minorities. Beyond this, what many once thought to be a fraud may actually be a vehicle for legitimizing ethnic group political and economic interests and protecting these interests vis-à-vis the state.

By linking ethnic groups and their homelands to the very structure of the state, issues that might otherwise have been regional become ethnic instead. Hence, problems connected with the spatial allocation of capital investment for development translate directly into ethnic group issues, with some nationalities contending that their ethnoterritories are being short-changed. In this specific regard, Leslie Dienes (1972) has pointed to arguments made by Ukrainian and Belorussian planners and economists against the continued high-priority status assigned to Siberian development. Their contention is that investment monies would be better spent in European parts of the country and that their own republics have been slighted by the emphasis given to Siberia by federal agencies. More recently, political leaders in Soviet Central Asia (especially Uzbekistan) have taken up the cause of river diversion to bring needed irrigation water to their ethnoterritories, a stance that at times has clashed with the stated recommendations of government agencies to the contrary.

In some cases the ethnoterritorial basis of the Soviet state has allowed the nationalities to express unhappiness about the social consequences of economic policies as they relate to ethnic issues. For example, evidence came to light that indigenous elites in the Baltic republics have argued for less economic growth in their ethnoterritories, because in the past rapid growth produced a demand for labor that resulted in a large influx of Russians and other outsiders into the region, an influx generally viewed with disfavor (*New York Times* 1971; Gwertzman 1972). Although specific complaints voiced in these and other cases differ, the common theme is ethnoterritorial rights.

Thus, whether the issue involves the siphoning off of funds to develop other areas, changes in the local economy that are perceived not to be in the interest of the indigenous population, or the social concomitants of economic policies, the arguments are framed mainly in ethnoterritorial terms.

Perhaps the most dramatic statement regarding the economic position of the non-Russian homelands is that of the noted Soviet Ukrainian dissident, Ivan Dzyuba. In his important work, *Internationalism or Russification?*, Dzyuba (1968) criticized the net fiscal drain from Ukraine to the federal budget (through the turnover tax) on the grounds that such transfers inhibited the development of the Ukrainian ethnoterritory. Even more important, he was sharply critical of the lack of local authority in the decision-making process.

On one hand, the Soviet federal system has been thought of as a device whose manipulation will lead to the continued repression of minorities and to an erosion of ethnic identity among the non-Russians. On the other hand, some see the USSR as a country that will eventually be torn apart by its multiethnicity and the tensions emanating from it. A third view is posited here: The ethnoterritorial nature of the Soviet federation may allow for an expansion of ethnic interests to approximate more closely the constitutional prerogatives of the nationalities. In this regard, Teresa Rakowska-Harmstone (1974: 10), in an article devoted to the emerging ethnic problems confronting the Soviet leadership, concluded, "The nationality-based units of the federal political–administrative system have provided the minority elites with both the bases and the means for pursuing national-group interests."

Likewise, Nancy Lubin (1984) conducted an extensive study of ethnic group relations in Uzbekistan, focusing on the extent to which the indigenous Uzbeks participated in politics and the economy. She found that the Uzbeks in many cases avoided competing with Russians and other outsiders for jobs in the modern sector (i.e., manufacturing and mining) because agricultural and service occupations afforded them the opportunity to earn higher incomes through part-time work or illegal and quasi-legal activities (corruption, diversion of state property, and black marketeering). In other words, the Uzbeks used the system to their own advantage, dispensing jobs through patronage, maintaining many features of their culture and way of life, and benefiting from the improvements in living standards brought about by the Soviet government, while avoiding direct challenges to the legitimacy of the political structure.

Finally, in 1978 the most recent dramatic instance of demands for ethnoterritorial rights occurred when party officials in Georgia attempted to change the constitutional status of the indigenous Georgian language. Scores of angry demonstrators poured into the streets of the republic's capital city,

Tbilisi (Whitney 1978; *New York Times* 1978). Apparently taken aback by the vehemence of the crowd reaction, the government quickly reversed itself and reinserted in the constitution the clause that recognizes Georgian as the native language of the republic.

An important question related to the issue of ethnic federalism is the extent to which minorities are represented in the political elite (i.e., the Communist party and government offices). In the broadest measure of political participation, membership in the Communist party, the non-Russians typically have a lower membership rate than do the Russians, but not exceedingly so; in fact, some minority ethnic groups (e.g., Georgians, Ossetians, Buryats, and Komi) are more highly represented per capita than the Russians (Jones and Grupp 1984, 173–74). Moreover, most minority ethnic groups made considerable gains in Party membership in the 1960s as a result of recruitment efforts and the upward social mobility of these nationalities; higher levels of education and greater representation in nonagricultural occupations are positively linked to Party membership. In the late 1970s and into the 1980s, however, some of this improvement eroded as the Party tightened its admissions requirements (Jones and Grupp 1984, 172–73).

Another major consideration is minority participation in Party and state leadership positions, especially those in the non-Russian republics. For most of the Soviet period, ethnic Russians have accounted for a disproportionately large share of key posts in non-Russian areas, particularly jobs dealing with internal security and economic administration. In a detailed study of the political power structure of the Tadzhik Republic, Rakowska-Harmstone (1970) found a recurring pattern of indigenous nationals in *visible* positions backed by ethnic Russian deputies. (See also Miller 1977.) This arrangement provided for a "representative aspect" for local nationalities and a "control aspect" for the Russians (Rakowska-Harmstone 1970, 96). More recently, other studies have shown a significant overrepresentation of minorities in republic-level Party and state posts; the "affirmative action" policies of the 1960s and 1970s apparently wrought changes in the ethnic composition of the political elite (Jones and Grupp 1984, 174–75; Hodnett 1978, 98–112). However, a retreat from recruitment policies preferential to minorities began in the 1980s, which will lead – if continued through the Gorbachev era – to a decrease in non-Russian representation in the leadership (Jones and Grupp 1984, 174–75). One further point in this regard is that studies of the political elite typically focus on the union republics; the fact is that minorities with ethnoterritories below the republic level are generally less well represented than are the larger nationalities.

Ethnodemography: Migration and Population Growth

Two other aspects of the contemporary ethnic scene in the USSR that may have a long-term impact on Soviet society are (1) the mixing of Russians and other ethnic groups through interregional migration and (2) major disparities in the rate of population growth between the European nationalities of the USSR and the ethnic groups of the Caucasus and Central Asia.

Historically, ethnic Russians have moved in large numbers to non-Russian ethnoterritories and have established a major presence (by 1979, about 24 million persons) in these areas. By 1979, Russians accounted for slightly less than one-fifth of the combined population of the non-Russian ethnoterritories but, more important, for more than one-third of the urban population in these areas in 1970 (the latter figure for 1979 has not been published). Although some changes in this situation may be underway, the characterization of cities in non-Russian regions "as islands of Russian people, language, and culture" is still generally accurate; in 1979, two-thirds of the population of Alma-Ata (capital of the Kazakh Republic) was Russian, and ethnic Russians comprised almost a quarter of the population of Kiev and Minsk (capitals of the Ukrainian and Belorussian republics) and more than a third of the population of Tashkent (capital of the Uzbek Republic).

In the tsarist era, this geographic expansion of Russians resulted from their military and political dominance, which allowed the ethnic Russians to usurp the lands previously inhabited by indigenous peoples. In the Soviet period, Russian language and culture are the universal ones (facilitating relocation to non-Russian regions), and the relatively early integration of Russians into the modernizing sectors of the economy equipped them with the requisite skills for nonagricultural jobs (Clem 1976). For example, in a "classic" study of the ethnic composition of the work force in two large industrial enterprises in the Tadzhik Republic, Soviet scholar V. I. Perevedentsev (1965) found that Russians had a distinct advantage over the indigenous Tadzhiks in the competition for jobs because the Russians possessed the necessary qualifications and because a knowledge of the Russian language was required for employment. Further, factory managers, according to Perevedentsev, were reluctant to initiate training programs for unqualified applicants (mainly, no doubt, Tadzhiks) because this would have involved diverting sorely needed funds from the production process.

According to V. V. Pokshishevskii (1969), another Soviet scholar known for his work on population and ethnicity, the proliferation of Russians in non-Russian ethnoterritories was a "natural" result of the lack of skilled manpower in these areas. In this view, the in-migration of Russians provides a trained cadre that, in a fraternal spirit, assists the local ethnic group in the attainment of higher levels of development. Although it is clearly the case that such development assistance was required in most instances, it is difficult to regard the ethnic Russians who total more than one-third of the urban population (some 17 million persons in 1970) in the non-Russian ethnoterritories as a cadre. In fact, the favored position of the Russians in the ethnic hierarchy has allowed them to establish themselves in non-Russian areas, to secure a disproportionately large share of the better urban industrial jobs, and to transplant their language and culture to these areas (especially in the cities).

One of the most startling features of Soviet society today is the extraordinary variation among ethnic groups in terms of population growth rates. Differences in the rate of population growth result from contrasting levels of fertility because mortality (the death rate) is uniformly low, and, of course, population growth (natural increase) is determined by the balance between births and deaths (Clem 1977).

Broadly speaking, the nationalities of the European USSR (the Baltic peoples, Belorussians, Ukrainians, and − importantly − the Russians) are characterized by low to very low fertility, whereas the ethnic groups of Central Asia (Uzbeks, Tadzhiks, Kirgiz, Turkmen, and Kazakhs) and certain ethnic groups of the Caucasus region (Azeri, Chechens, Ingush, and the peoples of Dagestan) are increasing in number at a phenomenal rate. Most of the smaller nationalities of the Volga and Ural regions (such as the Komi, Udmurts, Chuvash, Mordvinians, Tatars, and Bashkirs), plus two of the largest Caucasian groups (Armenians and Georgians), are intermediate in this regard. In fact, natural increase among the Central Asians and a few other groups is equivalent to that found in developing countries; the population growth rates in the European part of the USSR are about the same as those in developed countries.

Obviously, these natural increase differentials are causing a shift in the numerical balance among the various ethnic groups of the USSR, with the rapidly growing Central Asian and Caucasian nationalities gaining ground on the generally larger, but slowly growing, European groups. Many observers have attached particular importance to the erosion of the numerical majority status of the Russians. Although population projections are inherently risky, it seems safe to forecast that by the year 2000 the nationalities of the Caucasus and Central Asia will account for about one-quarter of the total Soviet population (as recently as 1959 their share stood at just over 10 percent). The Russian share can be expected to decline further. In addition, because most Soviet nationalities remain concentrated geographically in their respective ethnoterritories, the spatial aspect of this situation involves a relative shift in the country's population toward the southern tier of republics. That is, the Caucasus and Central Asian regions are acquiring a steadily larger share of the total Soviet population (Clem 1980).

Fertility is probably one of the most difficult aspects of any society to explain. We can say with some confidence, however, that factors known to be associated in general with different levels of fertility are operating in the Soviet Union, and these factors go a long way toward explaining interethnic variations in the birth rate. It seems, for example, that higher levels of urbanization, the shift from agricultural to industrial and service occupations, higher education levels, and change in the status of women (particularly their employment outside the home and their attainment of schooling on a par with men) are elements associated with lower fertility. These factors are evidenced among the European ethnic groups to a far greater extent (as noted earlier) than among the Central Asians and some of the Caucasian nationalities. Hence, birth rates tend to be lower in the former and higher in the latter (Lewis, Rowland, and Clem 1976, ch. 7).

The ramifications of differential ethnic population growth are wide ranging. In the economic realm, the current variations in natural increase translate into future spatial disparities in the growth of the working-age population. It is projected that virtually all new increments to the labor force will be located in the Caucasus and Central Asia. Remembering that the Soviet economy is, by comparison with most Western countries, labor-intensive, economic planners must choose whether to locate new development projects in the southern tier, where workers will be available (but where other economic conditions are not so favorable), or in the European or Siberian parts of the country, where economic conditions are more favorable (but the labor force situation is highly disadvantageous).

The issue takes on a social dimension when the question of migration is raised. One way of solving the economic efficiency–labor force supply problem would be through migration from labor surplus regions (the Caucasus and Central Asia) to locations where development would be optimal in terms of other economic criteria. It would be an understatement to say that there is considerable disagreement among scholars, both in the West and in the Soviet Union, regarding the likelihood and efficacy of such a migration (Lewis, Rowland, and Clem 1976, 354–81). If appreciable migration from the South to the North and West does take place, the ethnic mixing that would result could lead to heightened tensions, as it has in most other settings. On the other hand, if there is no significant movement out of the labor surplus areas of Central Asia and the Caucasus, the government will be hard pressed to provide sufficient jobs in situ for the rapidly growing population, and discontent might arise because of perceived disadvantage. Also, the indigenous nationalities in either case will probably take an increasingly dim view of the large Russian presence in their ethnoterritories, a presence that has, to a large extent, foreclosed many opportunities for the local groups in their own homelands.

The political aspects of the changing ethnic balance are even more intangible, but clearly the regime will need to make some tough decisions in light of this phenomenon. Not only will the economic and social factors involved have to be weighed, but also the decision-making process will have to include the impact of differential growth rates among the nationalities on the military (where ethnic Russians almost exclusively man the critical armored, motorized infantry, strategic rocket forces, and aviation components) and on the Communist party itself (Azrael 1977). As the share of the total population accounted for by the non-European ethnic groups rises, the Soviet leadership will need to decide to what extent these nationalities should be integrated further into the power structure, a decision obviously fraught with serious implications.

The Ethnic Factor

This century has witnessed, in virtually every corner of the globe, the maturation of ethnicity as perhaps the most important force for political change. The increasing identification of individuals with their respective ethnic groups has led almost inexorably to demands for alterations in the political, social, and economic status quo in a long and varied list of situations. Thus, ethnic differences have been at the root of violent conflict in the Basque separatist movement in Spain, the Palestinian problem in the Middle East, the Eritrean secession struggle in Ethiopia, and the Nigerian civil war. There are also many countries in which such grievances are being dealt with in earnest politically and, at least for the time being, peacefully: the new constitution in Belgium, decentralization of authority in Yugoslavia, and the troubles of the federal order in Canada are pertinent examples.

It was once widely thought that ethnic identity was a vestigial and retrograde quality, a primordial attachment that could be expected to vanish, or at least be reduced to insignificance, as the individual was integrated into the larger, modernizing society (Connor 1972; Enloe 1973) and experienced acculturation and assimilation.

The fact is that total assimilation has turned out to be much the exception rather than the rule. Instead of a diminution of ethnic identification, we are witnessing a resurgence of ethnicity throughout the world, with a wide range of social and political consequences. Walker Connor (1972; 1973) convincingly demonstrated with a number of examples that modernization led in most cases to heightened ethnic consciousness and from there to ethnic conflict. In his words, ". . . the accompaniments of economic development – increased social mobilization and communication – appear to have increased ethnic tensions, and to be conducive to separatist demands" (1972, 332).

The Implications of Ethnicity in the USSR

Many people insist or imply that Soviet society and its ethnic dimension in particular are unique and hence cannot be understood by reference to other societies and concepts derived from them. Ironically, this insistence on uniqueness is agreed on both by those in the West, who are largely critical of the Soviet regime and its handling of ethnic group relations, and by those in the USSR, who attempt to make the case that in no other instance have ethnic groups flourished to the extent that they have since the advent of Soviet power. The apparent bases for this agreement are the belief (in the West) that the totalitarian model obviates the sort of social–ethnic processes character-istic of Western societies and the belief (in the USSR) that the dialectical shift to socialism places all aspects of society, including ethnicity, on a plane qualitatively different from countries still in the capitalist epoch. Here we stress similarities rather than distinctiveness, in the belief that there is no basis a priori for assuming that generalizations relating to ethnicity would not apply to the Soviet case.

Daniel Bell's (1975) essay points to several key aspects of ethnicity in the contemporary world that are particularly relevant to the USSR. First, the politicization of ethnicity, wherein the proliferation of the state's power forces people to rely on ethnic groups as a means of bringing pressure to bear on the system, is clearly relevant to the Soviet situation. The "revolution from above" made it clear to all where the center of power is, establishing the state as the focus for any demands to be made by ethnic groups. As Glazer and Moynihan (1975, 8) put it, in the Soviet Union the state is obviously "the direct arbiter of economic well-being." The overwhelming centrality of power in the USSR and the legitimating of ethnicity have crystallized Soviet society along ethnic lines, a crystallization that will no doubt continue so long as the leadership directly or indirectly sanctions ethnicity.

The ethnic group is the ideal vehicle for making demands on the state, as Bell (1975) noted, because it combines an interest group function with an affective tie. The Soviet state has done much to validate this approach, because it insists on labeling individuals ethnically and has in fact acted (perhaps not always consciously) to stimulate ethnic awareness. This is not to suggest that the Soviet regime actively espouses the notion that ethnic groups should function as interest groups. On the contrary, expressions of nationality self-interest are usually dealt with severely if those advocating the ethnic cause confront the system openly. Yet, one suspects that there is sufficient latitude in the system even today for subtle pressure and, of course, for political infighting. It would be a mistake, in my opinion, to view the Soviet political system as totally unresponsive to ethnic group desires, as long as those desires are expressed in terms considered to be within the limits of propriety and are not openly threatening to the regime.

Second, Bell pointed to the decline of ideology as contributing further to the salience of ethnicity. In fact, he singled out the Soviet Union as a country in which ideology has become largely a rhetorical exercise. At this writing, the Bolshevik Revolution is some seventy years in the past, and one suspects that the ideological fervor characteristic of the early decades of the Communist regime is difficult for today's average Soviet citizen to understand at best. Other attempts to divert attention away from socioeconomic reality, such as the massive campaign to perpetuate the memory of the Great Patriotic War (World War II), are probably not much more effective than are appeals to revolutionary zeal. Hence, it is unlikely that future ethnic group demands can be put off by appeals to a higher purpose.

Third, societies that attempt to alleviate ethnic inequalities through "affirmative action" programs, Bell stated, run the risk of polarizing the populace along ethnic lines, as people seek advantage or attempt to maintain it through their respective ethnic groups. Although not much is known about the details of affirmative action-type programs in the USSR, the Soviet government apparently undertook some form of ethnic quotas in higher education and political appointments in the 1960s. It is hypothesized here that at least some motivation for the rise of Jewish dissidence was a response to such policies; as an achiever group that had attained a relatively advantaged socioeconomic status in Soviet society, the Jews stood to lose the most from redistributive policies. Also, the recent rise in Russian ethnic consciousness, as manifested in the "neo-Slavophilism," appears to be in the category of a "mirror-image response" (Foltz 1974), that is a defensive reaction by a group threatened with loss of relative position.

In 1967, on the occasion of the fiftieth anniversary of the founding of the USSR, and for years thereafter, a host of pronouncements concerning the way the victory of socialism had provided the ideal solution to ethnic conflict emanated from the Soviet leadership. The tone of these remarks was self-congratulatory and explicitly contended that ethnic problems in the USSR had ceased to be a matter for serious concern. In fact, the Soviet Union is facing greater, not lesser, difficulties relating directly or indirectly to ethnicity. In this regard it is not unlike other multiethnic states, although its ethnic diversity may pose greater problems than is ordinarily the case. The lessons learned from the universal experience suggest strongly that ethnicity is an increasingly more contentious feature of the contemporary world, and Soviet leaders can ignore this only at their peril.

Notes

[1] There are many definitions of and great confusion over the term *ethnic group* and its quality, *ethnicity*. Not wanting to add to either the confusion or the number of definitions, this

essay uses the definition of *ethnic groups* put forth by William Foltz, with the understanding that there is no universally accepted usage and that this is simply one among many (but, we believe, a good one). Foltz suggested that properties of an ethnic group would include shared physical characteristics, a common culture, linguistic affinity, and unique social-structural organization. Importantly, Foltz also warned against using these properties in presence–absence fashion, but rather advocated a "clustering" approach and the avoidance of precisely defined inter-ethnic boundaries. See William J. Foltz, "Ethnicity, Status, and Conflict," in *Ethnicity and Nation-Building*, ed. Wendell Bell and Walter E. Freeman (Beverly Hills, Calif.: Sage, 1974), pp. 103–104. For a discussion of the problems of usage connected with such terms as *ethnicity*, *nationalism*, *nation-state*, *tribe*, and so on, see Walker Connor, "A Nation Is a Nation, Is a State, Is an Ethnic Group, is a . . . ," *Ethnic and Racial Studies* I, no. 4 (1978), pp. 377–400.

[2] The terminological chaos that reigns supreme in the field of ethnic studies (see footnote 1) is very evident in the Soviet academic literature on the subject. The Soviet census enumerated people according to the nationality (*natsional 'nost'*) that they provided to the census taker. In the simplest meaning of this word, it is probably a good operational definition of ethnic group, and the two terms are used interchangeably here. Also, enumeration of ethnic groups by self-identification, as is the practice of the Soviet census, is the preferred method of determining ethnic affiliation.

[3] Because of its large size and the fact that it includes many subordinate ethnic units, the ethnic Russian republic is termed officially the Russian Soviet Federated Socialist Republic.

References

Allworth, Edward, ed. 1967. *Central Asia: A Century of Russian Rule*. New York: Columbia University Press.

Arutiunian, Iu. V. 1972. "Izmenenie sotsial'noi struktury sovetskikh natsii." *Istoriia SSSR* 4 (July–August): 3–20.

Aspaturian, Vernon V. 1968. "The Non-Russian Nationalities." In *Prospects for Soviet Society*, edited by Allen Kassof, pp. 143–98. New York: Praeger.

Azrael, Jeremy. 1977. "Emergent Nationality Problems in the USSR." Rand Corporation Report R–2172–AF, September.

Bahry, Donna, and Carol Nechemias. 1981. "Half Full or Half Empty?: The Debate over Soviet Regional Equality." *Slavic Review* 40 (3): 366–83.

Bell, Daniel. 1975. "Ethnicity and Social Change." In *Ethnicity: Theory and Experience*, edited by Nathan Glazer and Daniel P. Moynihan, pp. 141–74. Cambridge: Harvard University Press.

Bilinsky, Yaroslav. 1962. "The Soviet Education Laws of 1958–59 and Soviet Nationality Policy." *Soviet Studies* 14 (2): 138–57.

Bloom, Solomon F. 1967. *The World of Nations: A Study of the National Implications in the Work of Karl Marx*. New York: AMS Press.

Chuiko, L. V. 1975. *Braki i razvody*. Moscow: Statistika.

Clem, Ralph S. 1973. "The Impact of Demographic and Socioeconomic Forces upon the Nationality Question in Central Asia." In *The Nationality Question in Soviet Central Asia*, edited by Edward Allworth, pp. 35–44. New York: Praeger.

———. 1975. "The Integration of Ukrainians into Modernized Society in the Ukrainian SSR." In *The Soviet West: Interplay between Nationality and Social Organization*, edited by Ralph S. Clem, pp. 60–70.

———. 1976. "The Changing Geography of Soviet Nationalities and its Socioeconomic Correlates: 1926–1970." Unpublished Ph.D. dissertation, Columbia University, New York.

———. 1977. "Recent Demographic Trends among Soviet Nationalities and Their Implications."

In *Nationalism in the USSR and Eastern Europe*, edited by George W. Simmonds, pp. 37–44. Detroit: University of Detroit Press.

———. 1980. "Regional Patterns of Population Change in the Soviet Union, 1959–1979." *Geographical Review* 70 (2): 137–56.

Connor, Walker. 1972. "Nation-Building or Nation-Destroying?" *World Politics* 24 (3): 319–55.

———. 1978. "A Nation Is a Nation, Is a State, Is an Ethnic Group." *Ethnic and Racial Studies* I (4): 377–400.

———. 1973. "The Politics of Ethnonationalism." *Journal of International Affairs* 27 (1): 1–21.

———. 1984. *The National Question in Marxist-Leninist Theory and Strategy*. Princeton, N.J.: Princeton University Press.

Conquest, Robert, ed. 1967. *Soviet Nationalities Policy in Practice.* New York: Praeger.

Dienes, Leslie. 1972. "Investment Priorities in Soviet Regions." *Annals of the Association of American Geographers* 62 (3): 437–54.

Donnelly, Alton S. 1968. *The Russian Conquest of Bashkiria, 1552–1740*. New Haven: Yale University Press.

Dzyuba, Ivan. 1968. *Internationalism or Russification?*, 2d ed. London: Weidenfield and Nicholson.

Enloe, Cynthia H. 1973. *Ethnic Conflict and Political Development.* Boston: Little, Brown.

Fisher, Wesley A. 1977. "Ethnic Consciousness and Intermarriage: Correlates of Endogamy among the Major Soviet Nationalities." *Soviet Studies* 29 (3): 395–408.

Foltz, William J. 1974. "Ethnicity, Status, and Conflict." In *Ethnicity and Nation-Building*, edited by Wendell Bell and Walter E. Freeman, pp. 103–17. Beverly Hills, Calif.: Sage.

Glazer, Nathan, and Daniel P. Moynihan. 1975. "Introduction." In *Ethnicity: Theory and Experience*, edited by Nathan Glazer and Daniel P. Moynihan, pp. 1–26. Cambridge: Harvard University Press.

Goldhagen, Erich, ed. 1968. *Ethnic Minorities in the Soviet Union.* New York: Praeger.

Guthier, Steven L. 1977. "The Belorussians: National Identification and Assimilation, 1897–1970." *Soviet Studies* 29 (1 & 2): 37–61, 270–83.

Gwertzman, Bernard. 1972. "Protest on Soviet Laid to Latvians," *New York Times*, February 27, p. 11.

Hodnett, Grey. 1978. *Leadership in the Soviet National Republics.* Oakville, Ontario: Mosaic Press.

Holubnychy, Vsevolod. 1968. "Some Economic Aspects of Relations among Soviet Republics." In *Ethnic Minorities in the Soviet Union*, edited by Erich Goldhagen, pp. 50–120. New York: Praeger.

Jones, Ellen, and Fred W. Grupp. 1984. "Modernization and Ethnic Equalization in the USSR." *Soviet Studies* 36 (2): 159–84.

Katz, Zev, Rosemarie Rogers, and Frederick Harned, eds. 1975. *Handbook of Major Soviet Nationalities.* New York: Free Press.

Koropeckyj, I. S. 1965. *Location Problems in Soviet Industry Before World War II.* Chapel Hill: University of North Carolina Press.

———. 1972. "Equalization of Regional Development in Socialist Countries." *Economic Development and Cultural Change* 21 (1): 68–86.

Kozlov, V. I. 1969. *Dinamika chislennosti narodov: metodologiia, issledovaniia i osnovnye faktory.* Moscow: Nauka.

Lewis, Robert A., Richard H. Rowland, and Ralph S. Clem. 1976. *Nationality and Population Change in Russia and the USSR: An Evaluation of Census Data, 1897–1970.* New York: Praeger.

Low, Alfred D. 1958. *Lenin on the Question of Nationality.* New York: Bookman.

Lubin, Nancy. 1984. *Labour and Nationality in Soviet Central Asia.* Princeton, N.J.: Princeton University Press.

Matthews, W. K. 1951. *Languages of the USSR.* New York: Russell and Russell.

Miller, John H. 1977. "Cadres Policy in Nationality Areas." *Soviet Studies* 29 (1): 3–36.

New York Times. 1971. "Latvians Chided for Nationalism." *New York Times*, March 21, p. 17.

———. 1978. "Soviet Georgians Win in Language." *New York Times*, April 18, p. 12.

Perevedentsev, V. I. 1965. "O vliianii etnicheskikh faktorov na territorial'noe pereraspredelenie naseleniia." *Izvestiia Akademii nauk SSSR*, Seriia Geograficheskaia, 4: 31–9.

Pipes, Richard. 1968. *The Formation of the Soviet Union*, rev. ed. New York: Atheneum.

———. 1975. "Reflections on the Nationality Problems in the Soviet Union." In *Ethnicity: Theory and Experience*, edited by Nathan Glazer and Daniel P. Moynihan, pp. 453–65. Cambridge: Harvard University Press.

Pokshishevskii, V. V. 1969. "Etnicheskie protsessy v gorodakh SSSR i nekotorye problemy ikh izucheniia." *Sovetskaia etnografiia* 5: 3–30.

Raeff, Marc. 1971. "Patterns of Russian Imperial Policy Toward the Nationalities." In *Soviet Nationality Problems*, edited by Edward Allworth, pp. 22–42. New York: Columbia University Press.

Rakowska-Harmstone, Teresa. 1970. *Russia and Nationalism in Central Asia: The Case of Tadzhikistan.* Baltimore: Johns Hopkins Press.

———. 1974. "The Dialectics of Nationalism in the USSR." *Problems of Communism* 23(3): 1–22.

Rodgers, Allan. 1974. "The Locational Dynamics of Soviet Industry." *Annals of the Association of American Geographers* 64 (2): 226–40.

Rutgaizer, V. 1968. "Torzhestvo Leninskoi natsional'noi politiki v ekonomicheskom stroitel'-stve." *Kommunist* 18: 24–35.

Schroeder, Gertrude E. 1973. "Regional Differences in Incomes and Levels of Living in the USSR." In *The Soviet Economy in Regional Perspective*, edited by V. N. Bandera and Z. L. Melnyk, pp. 167–95. New York: Praeger.

Seton-Watson, Hugh M. 1967. *The Russian Empire, 1801–1917.* Oxford: Oxford University Press.

Silver, Brian D. 1972. "Ethnic Identity Change among Soviet Nationalities: A Statistical Analysis." Unpublished Ph.D. dissertation, University of Wisconsin, Madison.

———. 1974. "Levels of Socio-Cultural Development among Soviet Nationalities: A Partial Test of the Equalization Hypothesis." *American Political Science Review* 68 (4): 1618–37.

———. 1975. "Language Policy and the Linguistic Russification of Soviet Nationalities." Paper presented at the Conference on Population Change and the Soviet Nationality Question, Columbia University, December 5–6, 1975.

———. 1978. "Ethnic Intermarriage and Ethnic Consciousness among Soviet Nationalities." *Soviet Studies* 30 (1): 107–16.

———. 1986. "The Ethnic and Language Dimensions in Russian and Soviet Censuses." In *Research Guide to the Russian and Soviet Censuses*, edited by Ralph S. Clem. Ithaca, N.Y.: Cornell University Press.

Szporluk, Roman. 1979. "West Ukraine and West Belorussia: Historical Tradition, Social Communication, and Linguistic Assimilation." *Soviet Studies* 31 (1): 76–98.

Van Dyke, Vernon. 1977. "The Individual, the State, and Ethnic Communities in Political Theory." *World Politics* 29 (3): 343–67.

Whitney, Craig R. 1978. "Soviet Georgians Take to Streets to Save Their Language." *New York Times*, April 15, p. 3.

Wixman, Ronald. 1984. *The Peoples of Russia and the USSR: An Ethnographic Handbook.* Armonk, N.Y.: M. E. Sharpe.

Zwick, Peter. 1976. "Intrasystem Inequality and the Symmetry of Socioeconomic Development in the USSR." *Comparative Politics* 8 (4): 501–24.

2
The Soviet Working Class: Change and its Political Impact

Walter D. Connor

The internal political agenda of the new Gorbachev regime focuses heavily on economic concerns. One of the most critical of these concerns is dealing with the human factor in the Soviet economy. Whether – as it seems – the line to be taken is a technocratic one, demanding greater quantity and quality of work effort while maintaining a highly centralized system of virtually total state ownership (outside agriculture), or a more market form of organization, which could include the attractiveness and risks of private sector work for more of the labor force, the attitudes and reactions of the Soviet working class will be important in determining the results.

The working class is in a process of constant, if marginal, internal change. Cumulatively, however, it currently reflects critical transformations from its predecessor under Stalin and Khrushchev, or even during the early Brezhnev period. This chapter examines three aspects of that transformation: (1) the *hereditization* of the working class, that is, the process whereby yesterday's ex-peasant class has given way to one recruited from the offspring of workers; (2) the confrontation of a working class growing in years of general education completed with a job structure less prone to rapid change; and (3) the developing potential tensions in the area of perceived social justice, as understood by this new working class and as it may be affected by policies to be adopted.

Hereditization: The Process

Critical to an understanding of the impact of hereditization on the working class is an appreciation of how (relatively) late in Soviet history it occurred. Soviet statistics, and treatments of the topic, tend to be fragmentary – indeed, there is no reason to assume that data characterizing the picture for the whole USSR labor force exist.

In the main, hereditization has meant a shift away from a working class heavily weighted in the direction of ex-peasants: either males (and females) who spent part of their adult working life in agriculture, or who were born in rural–farm households and spent the period through adolescence in that environment. G. Bliakhman (1979, 62–9), reporting a long-term (1965–79) study of workers born since 1950 in various enterprises in the Russian, Ukrainian, Byelorussian, Moldavian, Latvian, Tadzhik, and Georgian republics, noted the rapid decline of the "peasant" element over the years. By 1979, in old industrial cities (presumably ones with a large recruiting pool of workers' children) no more than 15 percent of the factory work force born in 1950 and after were of peasant origin; only in newer cities did the share rise to 40 percent. More than half of Bliakhman's respondents were second, or third generation workers (1979, 63).

The situation Bliakhman outlined, based on sampling a broad range of geographical areas, took a long time for the Soviet economy and society to achieve. The great social transformations of the post-1928 period of the first two Five Year Plans – indeed, the whole period up to World War II – lie outside the scope of this chapter, so it need only be noted that in this period, as the USSR moved from an economy with 80 percent to less than 60 percent of the labor force in agriculture, the growth of the working class occurred virtually totally through the addition of recruits from the countryside, to the point that in most branches a solid ex-peasant majority characterized the makeup of the working "class."

Wartime losses and the still huge rural reserves meant that, well into the postwar and post-Stalin periods, significant inflows of peasants, upwardly mobile from village and *kolkhoz*, continued to dilute whatever hereditary elements were developing the working class. As one 1977 source put it, from the 1920s until "well after" World War II, the peasantry remained the large source of working-class recruitment (AN SSSR 1977).

Large-scale gross movement of nonhereditary workers continued well into the post-Khrushchev period, as Soviet economic growth rates still created demand sufficient to drive the process of upward mobility from peasant to worker. Large absolute numbers meant, of course, problems of absorption, adaptation to urban–industrial life, demands on housing and services, and so forth. But, as the receiving base of the industrial work force grew year by year, these impressive numbers grew more moderate as proportional additions to the working class. Writing at the beginning of the 1980s, three scholars observed that the contribution of migrants from rural to urban areas, and from agriculture to industry (roughly the same people), to industrial labor resources amounted to about 17 percent of the total growth in 1961–65, about 12 percent from 1967–70, and only about 9 percent in the 1970s (Babushkina, Dunin, and Zenkevich 1981, 44). At the same time, the proportional contribution of "school leavers and those discharged from the armed forces" grew from 30 percent (1961–65) to 57 percent (1966–70) to 92 percent approximately in the 1970s – though these categories do not exclude peasant–rural origin people.[1]

Thus, over the years, and in a natural way, the forces promoting the *self-reproduction* of the working class gained, for the first time, the upper hand. That change reflected (1) a gradual slowing of the economic processes that generated a demand for more and more new additions to the industrial labor force, (2) the maturation of a larger industrial labor force such that its numbers began to produce children who could contribute to the working class by entering that same world of work – a first generation of mobiles from the peasantry creating a second generation that was nonmobile but inherited worker status; and (3) the relative and absolute decline of the peasant recruiting pool in Soviet labor demographics. This happened at no precise, specifiable time, but it is history. It may be that a Soviet writer in 1964, asserting that the "internal reserves and the urban population have become the preponderant source of working-class replenishment" (Kim 1964, 6–7), made the claim early. But the structural change he specified has come, and with it a different profile of the industrial labor force.

Today's working class, then, is more a product of self-reproduction than ever before. Individual studies of the origins, sources, and composition of the work force in various areas, industries, or enterprise complexes cannot be summed into a comprehensive nationwide picture, but nonetheless they offer full confirmation of the phenomenon – especially when they present age-specific data reflecting the very different social–class origin pattern of younger versus older worker cadres. The data, however they vary between rather high to quite low shares of hereditary workers among the older groups, show that the tendency to hereditization is stronger as one reaches the young worker groups – those that have the great bulk of their career as workers ahead of them, and who are distinct in many other ways from their older counterparts.

A summary picture of the degree of hereditization is in a technical sense impossible, but the data arrayed in Table 2.1 (as comprehensive a list of hereditary origin as the author was able to assemble from a myriad of Soviet studies and references to studies) may provide some broad indications of the

Table 2.1
Workers of Working-Class Origin in Various Locales, as Percentage of
All Workers in Those Locales by Year

Location	Year	Percentage
Ufa-Orenburg	1966	38.0
Ufa-Orenburg	1970	44.6
Kazan	1967	49.0
Sverdlovsk (wood industry)	1967	54.0
Leningrad (machine building)	1970	54.7
Bashkir ASSR	early 1970s	55.8
Moscow oblast'	1973	55.8
Cheliabinsk	1973–74	56.2
Elista (Kalmyk ASSR)	1975–76	69.4
Magnitogorsk	late 1970s	70.3
Naberezhnye Chelni	late 1970s	69.1
Sterlitamak	late 1970s	51.8

Source: Various Soviet studies, available on request from author.

still dim general picture, as well as an indication of variations over time and place, in the USSR from the mid-1960s to the present.

Against these figures, it is perhaps useful to note the hereditization figure for the sample surveyed in the post–World War II Harvard Project on the Soviet Social System: 46.1 percent of the workers reported worker fathers, in what was regarded as a group rather successful by Soviet standards (Inkeles and Bauer 1961). This was probably a high figure. Barber's work on the early "plan era" shows the force of the peasant draft at its beginnings (see Barber 1978). In 1929, a figure of 52.2 percent is given for the hereditary share among workers in all branches of industry. This figure certainly fell, and fell rapidly. For example, of those who started work in 1926–27 in Leningrad's engineering and metalworking industry, 55.6 percent were from worker families – the percent fell to 38.8 percent for 1930 entrants. Figures for the same industry in the Ukrainian republic were 60.1 percent and 47.0 percent, respectively. In the metallurgy industry in the Urals area, the 1926–27 draft was 43.7 percent hereditary workers; this share fell to only 29.0 percent in 1930, as the first Five Year Plan hit its stride (Barber 1978, 15). The process of *peasantization* as the working class grew was under way. It would be decades before the trends of industrial maturation and slowing social change would once again create a mainly hereditary stratum of industrial workers.

The documents of the April 1923 (twelfth) party congress, when the young USSR was in the process of drawing its mainly hereditary proletariat back to the factories after the civil war disruptions, include the following words:

> . . . in the last analysis, the working class can preserve and strengthen its leading position not through the state apparatus, not through the army, but through industry, which reproduces (*vosproizvodit'*) the proletariat itself. (Lebedeva and Khabibulina 1972, 74)

The factual status of the working-class "leading position" is best left without comment for now – prospects for the formation of the Soviet system we know today were not so clear in 1923. It was, indeed, through industry and its growth that a large blue-collar work force was produced. Whether the process should have been called *reproduction*, since the growth constantly diluted the hereditary element of the working class, is questionable. It would be, as noted earlier, some time before the situation would justify the words of a 1967 Soviet study that the "working class, having become the largest class in society, began to replenish itself mainly in its own account" (Somova 1967, 112). Having arrived at that point, the Soviet working class presented to the analyst of social change, and to the person primarily interested in the political implications of such change, some important questions.

Hereditization: Context and Impact

Although all the questions are not yet answerable, they do turn on large-scale developments in the history of Soviet economy and society that either underlie the hereditization process just summarized or derive from that process, especially in the area of changes in aspirations, expectations, and frameworks for evaluating the performance of the regime.

From the launching of the initial Five Year Plan, first the USSR embarked on a process counter to hereditization that filled a growing proletariat with first generation workers. The success of this formation process, however, naturally provided the base for a second stage. Economic growth – in the sense of a concentration of the rapid, labor- and capital-intensive development of industry – created a demand for new workers. Pressures on the rural sector, such as collectivization in the early post-1928 years, low living standards, and the social–cultural stigmata of village life well into the post-Stalin years, provided a push to complement industry's pull. The slowing of growth later applied a brake to structural change in the overall labor force, and thus to the mobility processes evoked by that change.

Second, the now larger working class became more and more a self-recruiting segment of society, its educated sons (especially) retained in the category of their fathers. In structural terms, three elements in this transition are worth noting.

1. Past a certain point, the peasantry could no longer be treated as a recruiting pool, a labor reserve. As it grew smaller, there was less surplus to feed industry; as a relatively inefficient agricultural economy, the USSR needed a fairly large peasantry and could not afford to let all who wished to escape the countryside do so. Thus, the significance of the upwardly mobile peasant son input to the working class declined. The agriculture-to-industry transition could not be endless. In fact, it has fallen far short of the point reached by the United States or the developed capitalist West.

2. The intelligentsia has continued to grow, proportionally more rapidly than the working class, but it still remains small. Its base size and growth rate are insufficient to generate "demand" sufficiently large (over the inheritance of intelligentsia status by intelligentsia offspring) to take many aspirants out of the working-class's younger ranges. In general, the broadly defined service sector, weighted heavily toward white-collar work, has suffered severely arrested growth in the Soviet economy and has not provided alternate opportunities for large numbers of young offspring of workers.

3. The working class itself is growing, although quite slowly. The production bias of Soviet economic calculation, the relatively low per capita productivity in most branches, and the relatively high percentage of non- or minimally machine-assisted hand labor are indicators that the working class is likely to remain large. Hence, it needs its internal recruits.

Third, other state policies in the area of education have also tended to lock working-class youth into their origin categories, thus promoting further the hereditization of this class (as well as of the intelligentsia situated above it). The state put no obstacles directly in the way of working-class aspirations to complete secondary education (indeed the opposite), but it has not expanded the supply of spaces in higher education (nor does it intend to) to meet the demand generated by completion of secondary education by the overwhelming majority – rather than a small minority – of Soviet seventeen year olds. This is a policy response to a potential problem successive leaders have wished to avoid: a mix of levels of education and specialties out of synchronization with the projected needs of the national economy (i.e., the job structure as foreseen or projected by planners at a future time). Unacknowledged is the decision that Soviet leaders will not face the difficulty of dealing with an overly' large, underemployed intelligentsia, its appetite whetted for social, economic, and influence or power rewards the system cannot deliver.

Thus, the universalization of secondary education in the 1970s has placed a diverse mix of seventeen year olds at the transition bottleneck to higher education; they are, as the statistics on access to daytime higher education show, quite diverse in their success rates. Worker offspring pass the bottleneck at a less impressive rate than do the intelligentsia children, whose quest is to reproduce their parents' occupational status.[2]

All this moves us to consider the potential political consequences of hereditization. At a general level, a more hereditized working class presents the regime with questions of context and consciousness of a new sort, which may prove troublesome in the rest of the century.

In question is the evaluative context: the bases of comparison the worker may use to judge the performance of Soviet life in providing, however relevant, both a (broadly defined) living standard and the opportunity to improve it. It is generally accepted that the comparison standards of Soviet citizens are overwhelmingly temporal, rather than international: that, lacking the exposure to superior Western living standards possessed by so many East Europeans, they compare their todays with their own yesterdays. For the most part, such a comparison shows (at least until recently) the Soviet system and the regime in a good light. Older citizens, especially, who remember vividly the pre-1953 period, have reason to be impressed with their progress. Such people, whose base line lies in a period of severe food shortages and rationing, an exceedingly poor selection of consumer durables, and the urban world of crowded communal apartments, have seen cumulative change (especially perhaps in the area of housing) that increases their ability to absorb a certain amount of stagnation in current living standards, or even fallbacks in certain areas (such as that of food).

But for young workers – the self-recruits from working-class families – the context is not so favorable to the regime. First, the share of the population whose context includes the years of Stalin and depressed consumption is declining. We are dealing, overall, with a Soviet population heavily tilted toward people raised in a peaceful period, one wherein living standards have increased. But in the younger ranges of this group are those to whom even the Khrushchev period is a blank (people born in the month Brezhnev took power turned twenty-one in October 1985), and whose conscious experience coincides with years of slowing economic growth and moderate, if even perceptible, rises in the living standard. Young workers, then, must share in some sense a general *cohort effect* that arguably has elevated (1) the context of evaluation of living standards, (2) expectations about what the system must and should deliver as normal aspects of the Soviet welfare package, and (3) the definition of what can be regarded as notable improvements. Not the same as a revolution of rising expectations, this is, nonetheless, a potential problem for a regime that has failed notably in producing growth in per capita GNP sufficient to undergird continuing significant increases in welfare.

Beyond this, however, young workers may share another grievance: in the context of expectations fed by the past performance of the rapidly growing economy and a labor force rapidly changing shape, the opportunities afforded them for upward mobility, for exit from the class of their fathers, have not been impressive. The slowing of structural change, the deficit of places in higher education versus the increased output of secondary school graduates, and the disadvantages working-class youth face in competing with intelligentsia offspring for those places have reduced the available opportunities to move up into the intelligentsia.

The implications of these grievances, in the social context of a hereditized working class, for class-based perceptions of social justice are discussed later (as are counter-forces militating against a more demanding, combative working-class politics). Another set of issues deserves attention now. These issues flow from the fact that the statistical appearance of large numbers of working-class origin youth as unsuccessful candidates for entrance to higher education reflects something else as well – the completion of academic secondary education by unprecedented numbers of entrants to the working class. The impact has been complex.

Work Commitment: Education, Problems, Reform

With a good deal of warrant, Soviet commentators can take pride in the increase over time in average educational levels, as well as the increased output of persons with higher education. This, as much as the building of a large, predominantly industrial economy, is progress, another indication of the historical parting-of-company with the agrarian, marginally literate Russia of the past.

Yet, as ten-year complete secondary education has become more and more the norm, the qualitative and quantitative returns have been less than unambiguously positive. Indeed, an element of paradox exists in an emerging situation wherein the increased educational levels of young recruits to the working class complicate, rather than ease, their fit into the world of blue-collar work. From the past, where young entrants to the factory possessed only marginal general education and found the unfamiliar rhythms and skill requirements difficult to master, Soviet society has come to a present in which both objective and subjective indicators point to a lack of fit between heightened levels of general education and an occupational structure less upscale than the schooling and pretensions or expectations of those who must staff it now and in the future.

Soviet society remains industrial rather than postindustrial. "At present almost 76 percent of all workers are occupied in the sphere of material production, and in the future no essential changes are foreseen" (Panteleev 1983, 31). Within this industrial sphere, the share of simple, unmechanized, repetitive, and often dirty and arduous labor is comparatively quite large. The economic and organizational forces that have contributed to this situation are obviously not subject to rapid reversal. Hence, the words of three Soviet authors who, while affirming that the Soviet economy needed workers of high skills and quality, allowed that it also required "workers of average and even low skills" (Babushkina, Dunin, and Zenkevich 1981, 46). To be sure, Soviet figures show progress in reducing the share of purely manual (*ruchnyi*) labor, but they also indicate how large that share remains: from 1965–79, the share fell from 40.4 to 32.8 percent in industry and from 60 to 49 percent in construction (Foteeva 1984, 93–4). Considering the pace of technological innovation and reshaping of employment patterns in the industrial West in this period, it is the "backwardness" of the Soviet mix that impresses here.

This structure of blue-collar work opportunities is clearly out of line with the aspirations and expectations of those entering the labor force; nor is the tension completely resolvable by upscaling economic rewards in compensation.

> In a socialist society, a fully normal general dissatisfaction is developing with those job positions where the work has little content, is heavy and unprestigious. Growth of general education normally strengthens this phenomenon. Raising the pay for heavy, manual, low skill and low prestige work only compensates to a small degree for its social inferiority, its unattractiveness. (Kozlova and Fainburg 1982, 29)

Education, then, and its increase among youth who are fated to enter the manual workforce (whether they aspired to higher education or not), represents a property that renders adjustment to the nature and quality of much of the available work more difficult. The average job no longer presents challenges, interests, or conditions adequate for the average person with (an increasing) average education. As the then director of the USSR Academy of Sciences' Institute of Sociological Research put it in 1980, the "structure of work places, where there is a high proportion of unskilled work, today does not objectively correspond to the more developed skill structure of the workers themselves, holds back and limits their development" (Riabushkin 1980, 21). In fact, the rise in supply of unskilled jobs through the 1960s may indeed have continued, even if at a moderated rate, to the present time. From 1959 to 1969, according to one set of calculations, the number of workers in industry increased by 39 percent; among them, those who engaged in monitoring automated machines increased by 142 percent, those using "helping mechanisms and machines" by 72 percent, "and those engaged in (almost exclusive) manual work in auxiliary shops, etc." by 18 percent (Aitov and Eliseev 1985, 136). Keeping in mind the Soviet economy in 1959, and the tiny number then monitoring automated equipment, 18 percent is no small number of additional hand workers. Such trends are unlikely to provide a supply of jobs young workers consider attractive. In a study of more than ten thousand workers at the lower Kama industrial complex, researchers found that in 1982 two-thirds of the younger (evidently under age forty) workers "felt that their educational level was higher than that required by their work. Among workers older than forty, the picture was the reverse; two-thirds felt that their education was lower than that required by production" (Rybakov and Siniuk 1983, 106–07). As early as 1975, labor economist Iu. P. Sosin (1975) estimated in the authoritative Novosibirsk journal *EKO* that "industry is able to provide only 30 to 35 percent of young workers with work on a par with knowledge."

Two matters, actually, are involved here and are especially important in the case of the young entrants to the working class who, in the absence of any substantial downward mobility into it, are contributing so heavily to its hereditization: academic education per se and training in work skills. General Soviet demographic statistics indicate that the first certainly has risen. The more partial summaries and citations in Soviet writings on various labor force problems show the aspects of most interest to those concerned with these problems. A large study on Gorky oblast' traced changes between 1965 and 1979, showing that in 1965 the industrial work force in the area was, in its vast majority (86.8 percent) "short" of complete secondary education (fully 48.1 percent had only seven or eight years). By 1979, only 52 percent lacked secondary education, and of workers up to thirty years of age, only 20 percent were in this category (Riabushkin 1980, 23). In the Sverdlovsk area, in 1969, only 23.2 percent of those starting work had a ten-year education; by 1975, almost 80 percent of those beginning had education to this level (Ponomarev 1978, 30–1). Figures from the ZIL automotive plant in Moscow contrast two levels of education (primary only and complete secondary), over three time periods, for the plant's labor force as a whole and (in parenthesis) the portion under thirty years of age in the given year (Babushkina, Dunin, and Zenkevich 1981, 47).

	Primary	*Complete Secondary*
1959	53.3 (43.6)	8.4 (11.3)
1970	31.4 (10.0)	23.1 (38.7)
1979	15.2 (00.1)	50.7 (77.8)

Obviously, both the rise in educational level with declining age and the replacement of older, poorly schooled age cohorts by younger workers are changing the face of the factory labor force — faster, from the foregoing comments, than the occupational structure is changing. Industry and the working class have, in fact, come to the end of the time when new recruits can be found in large numbers among the really poorly educated or rural and undemanding. In the prewar and early postwar years the working class was fed by the redistribution of people from agriculture to industry, from rural to urban areas; by 1961–65, such shifts accounted for only 17 percent of the growth in labor resources, and this figure fell to 12 percent in 1967–70 and to 9 percent through the 1970s. Meanwhile, the share of growth attributed to school leavers and those discharged from the armed forces increased across the three periods from 30 to 57 to 92 percent (Babushkina, Dunin, and Zenkevich 1981, 44). As one author wrote in 1984, "Practically the single mass source of replenishing cadres has become youth with a high, as a rule, educational and cultural level" (Foteeva 1984, 94).

In all this, and without getting into calculations of what amount of general education (less than ten years) should be optimal for short-term adjustment to work of average attraction and requirements, arises the specter of an overeducated, blue-collar work force. Over the longer run, the diagnosis of the utility of ten years of schooling on the factory floor may change somewhat, interacting with problems and patterns of skill acquisition and advancement and with problems of labor mobility and job changing (a phenomenon especially marked among young workers). But in the shorter run, the confrontation of an industrial structure, through the first industrial revolution but hardly into the second or third, with a young labor force educated beyond it will remain a major problem.

Education consists of mathematics, science, language, history, and, in the Soviet variant, a heavy dose of various ideological topics. It does not include work skills, and despite the rhetorical emphasis through so much of the past on the *polytechnic* in Soviet education, the results of universalized secondary education have not reflected any major acquisition of skills on the part of the seventeen and eighteen year olds who go, in increasing numbers, from the classroom to the factory. As a study in the RSFSR in 1975–76 concluded:

> Over 44 percent of all young industrial workers are secondary-school graduates. . . . These educated youth are more demanding with regard to the nature of their job, and working conditions and the pay they receive. *But 80 percent of them have had no vocational training, and they are often used in unskilled jobs or those calling for heavy labor.* (Kotliar and Talalai 1977, emphasis added)

The phenomenon of producing educated seventeen year olds without job skills and matching them with the economy's presumed needs is a complex one, developed over time. In January 1977, the USSR Minister of Education, M. Prokofiev, noted that about 14 million people would complete secondary education in the 1976–80 period. Of these, 6.5 million would continue their education either in higher education, the specialized secondary track (*tekhnikum*), or in lower-level trade schools (*tekhuchilishche*). But 7.5 million would go to work.[3] In June of the same year, Prokofiev's deputy for labor training and vocational guidance cited the same figures and wrote optimistically about the "interschool production training combines" (*mezhshkol'nye uchebnoproizvodstvennye kombinaty*), organizations that evidently serviced academic secondary schools with vocational training. These organizations had grown from 250 nationwide in 1975 to about 500 in 1976–77, each serving an average of ten schools and offering instruction in "tens" of specialites. Summer work training was growing as well; in 1974, about 7 million ninth and tenth graders had participated, in 1976, 10 million (Averichev 1977, 130–32).

Some few years down the line, the optimism seemed misplaced. A 1977–79 study under Komsomol auspices (Belkin 1981, 106) found that vocational training in secondary schools (presumably of the MUPK variety) was generally useless. More than 3,000 students questioned reported such work as classroom cleaning, light repairs to school equipment (81.7 percent), picking up scrap metal (65.0 percent), and the like. Only 27 percent had had work training in the summer. (See also Kostin 1978.)

Research among tenth graders in Moscow secondary schools asked about their career plans in 1981 and recontacted in 1982 to see how these plans had worked out, provided a further grim appraisal of the relevance and effect of vocational training in academic secondary schools. The certificates of training issued by the MUPKs "had no force" in factories and plants, where it was generally necessary to retrain the newly hired in the same specialties ostensibly acquired in schools. Of the tenth graders questioned as to whether they wanted to work rather than study further the vocation they were learning via the MUPK, only 14.2 percent had answered yes; 50.9 percent answered no, and 34.9 percent had no response. In the 1982 assessment of actual outcomes (presumably among the percentage of all graduates who had entered the labor force), 23.9 percent were working in the area of their training, 13.1 percent partly so, the fully 63 percent reported no relation between their jobs and the UPK training (Zaslavskii, Kuz'min, and Ostrovskaia 1983, 132).

Thus, in the early 1980s, the arrangements to equip secondary school graduates (destined to enter the workforce in large numbers, in the same year they earned their diplomas) with useful skills hardly resembled a well-oiled machine. M. N. Rutkevich explained, in a *Sovetskaia Rossiia* article in 1983,[4] something of how the problem had occurred.

By the middle to late 1950s, higher educational institutions (VUZy) could not absorb all the graduates (then 40 percent of the seventeen year olds) of ten-year secondary schools. Khrushchev's 1958 educational reform attempted to correct the problem of the "misplaced" (in the sense that complete secondary education was preparation for higher education, pure and simple) by tracking the fifteen-year-old finishers of eighth grade (incomplete secondary education) to vocational–technical trade schools (*proftekhuchilishche*). But the latter, poorly developed and of low quality, could not do the job. Many fifteen year olds thus went to work unskilled and of little use to the economy. In 1965, about 42 percent of all eighth graders left school to join the work force; 40 percent went into ninth grade, and only about 17 to 18 percent went to some kind of trade school or *tekhnikum* training. As the drift into complete secondary education continued, the realization that relatively fewer members of this increasing population of high school graduates could find places in higher education prompted a recognition that more labor training was needed,in grades nine and ten. But such training obviously was not developed and organized to the necessary degree. Hence, by 1980, although virtually no eighth-grade graduates were going directly to work, 60 percent were continuing into the ninth grade and nearly 40 percent (some improvement) were directing their steps toward some kind of vocational–technical training.

However, whereas in 1965 only 16.2 percent of tenth-grade graduates had gone to work without further training, by 1980, 41.2 percent of the larger-by-then graduate population were doing so, while only 16.3 percent were continuing in full-time VUZy (vs. 41.4 percent in 1965). Of the remainder, 26.9 percent of the tenth-grade graduates were in vocational–technical training, and 15.6 percent were in *tekhnikums* of the "secondary specialized" variety. Both of these latter categories (as well as the 41.2 percent already working) represented, presumably, wasted effort in the ninth and tenth grades; vocational tracks could have been entered after the eighth grade to provide better preparation for the working life that awaited these young people after graduation.

Observations like these underlie to a large degree the agenda of the current Soviet educational reform – indeed, by 1983 some of these were part of the process of discussion and justification. With respect to the formation of the working class of the future, the centerpiece of the 1984 educational reform is the secondary vocational–technical school (*srednaia prof-tekhushilishche*, or SPTU). In the words of the draft reform document, the number of young people sent to these schools doubled from current levels.[5] What does this goal imply?

A major implication is the continued growth of a species of combined education and skill training that derived originally from many of the problems discussed earlier in this work. The secondary PTU (SPTU) was essentially a creation of the late 1960s, made by adding divisions or departments of general education to PTUs in order to allow them to confer the diploma indicating a ten-year academic education. This process of building up from the low-prestige PTU base accelerated, at least formally, in the 1970s. In the 1979–80 academic year, Soviet ninth and tenth graders were distributed, roughly, as follows: in the general academic secondary schools, 5.5 million; in SPTUs, 2.07 million; and in general PTUs, 1.87 million (O'Dell 1983, 127–28). (Some in this 16 to 18 year age group were already at work and do not appear in these figures.) A decade earlier (1970–71) there had been only 180,000 students in the SPTU track, indicating an increase of more than 1,000 percent during the 1970s, with a 555 percent increase (from 615 to 4,026) in the number of SPTUs themselves.

The network continued to grow in the early 1980s and, along the way, gave some indication that the SPTU had worked to reduce the share of age-eligible youth in the academic track, and hence the demand for entry to higher education. As one Western observer put it in 1981:

> Measures taken to redirect the educational and career orientations of Soviet school children proved surprisingly successful. The prestige of the PTU (*professional'no-tekhnicheskoe uchilishche* – trade school) and the *tekhnikum* (technical college) was raised by enriching their vocational programmes with a much larger element of general education, and by powerful campaigns of vocational guidance in the media. Some local authorities transformed many of their PTUs into "secondary PTUs," which provide a full secondary general education as well as trade training, and set quotas for the number of eighth-grade leavers who would have to enter them. This, combined with a greater realism amongst pupils about the prospects of obtaining a VUZ place led to a sweeping change in their educational aspirations. Pupils completing the eighth and tenth grades were attracted to the new secondary PTUs and post-secondary courses in tekhnikums. After decades in which it had enjoyed unrivalled prestige among Soviet youth higher education began to lose some of its attraction. (Avis 1983, 203)

If this seems a relatively benign assessment of a form of social engineering, the same author's noting that the redirection of so many young people (especially males [see O'Dell 1983]) into the SPTU track meant that some higher educational institutions, especially those in the applied technology area, faced a student "deficit," led him to go further, and more critically, into the process.

> It might indeed be claimed that Soviet boys have been "cooled out" to excess. Once they have taken up PTU or tekhnikum courses they seem to abandon higher education ambitions, even though the new general-education component of the curricula supposedly keeps open the chance of eventual VUZ entry. Perhaps this is not so surprising, as several Soviet commentators have pointed out, when skilled manual workers are as much in demand as graduate engineers and can command wages as high as, or even higher than, the latter. Moreover, the standard of teaching and attainment in the general-education part of PTU programmes is acknowledged to be much inferior to that in regular secondary

schools and hardly constitutes an adequate preparation for entry to higher education. Because of these considerations, not to mention the obligation on PTU and tekhnikum graduates to complete a compulsory work assignment after training or to be subject to military call-up, the vocational track effectively rules out or considerably reduces the chances of acquiring higher education after it. (Avis 1983, 207)

This is indeed a formidable account of what the SPTU does and how it serves some of the needs of the economy discussed previously.

Whatever the impact of the new, reform-linked SPTU in adding skills or in socializing the adolescent for entry into worker status, it will surely add an element of selection affecting the class destinations of large numbers of the young – and in a manner far from random. Directing more students toward the SPTU and away from "pure" academic secondary education is not meant to multiply the career options of adolescents by providing academic diplomas to those who would not otherwise earn them, but to point them toward entry into the working class. Who will escape this? Presumably people whose academic qualifications, tutoring, and other assets, as manifested in the eighth (soon to be ninth) grade, allow them to pass through the narrow gate into the acdemic track for the final two years (now grades nine and ten, under the reform eventually ten and eleven) of secondary education. These students are likely to be, disproportionately, those already favored by social origin based on the educational and occupational levels of their parents, the per capita income within the household, and the readiness to spend on supplementary training to encourage academic effort, and even use influence.

In this competitive context, the children of workers will be just as disadvantaged as they are now. This will remain especially true of sons, young males who, as we have seen, are more likely than females to choose the PTU/SPTU route. This process should intensify, creating an even *more* hereditized working class than otherwise.

Though the picture is not altogether clear, it seems unlikely that the social processes of the last fifteen years have moderated expectations among working-class youth to the point at which frustration with failure to cross the line between working class and intelligentsia is no longer widespread nor important. In this context, the hereditization already produced by forces discussed, and the likely impact of the new selection process under the educational reform, may well exacerbate these frustrations.[6]

Class Consciousness and Social Justice

It is in this connection that the question of consciousness – *class* consciousness, in a broad sense – arises. *First*, a class whose human content is rapidly changing and whose components are diverse is not likely to develop a common view of the world around it. The early Soviet working class – that of the plan era – grew rapidly from the bottom with the massive inflow of the peasantry, while losing members from the top through a combination of educational and political promotion into professional–managerial strata. The newcomers from the countryside became the majority in many sectors and branches, swamping the small core proletariat of the pre-1929 period. Meanwhile, whether one considers it an obvious economic consequence of growth or a conscious regime attempt to co-opt the young, ambitious, and talented of proletarian origin, and thus deprive a working class of its potential natural leaders (probably both), the upward mobility of some workers and working-class youth subtracted from the core proletarian element. The mix that resulted was, in a sense, not a class at all; it was too diverse to share any common perspective, even though built over time in the same socio-economic space (the mark of a class).

Second, as long as economic growth was sustained at a high rate, and given the structural change in the labor force, working and peasant youth could anticipate opportunities to solve, via upward mobility, whatever problems they encountered in their present status (typically also the status of their parents). Birth into the working class or peasantry was not, evidently, a life sentence. Some were content to follow in the previous generation's footsteps. Working-class youth who were not could anticipate mobility via education to the intelligentsia, providing they qualified mentally and combined the discipline and ambition necessary; peasant youth could also rise, via the demand for new hands, to a growing industrial sector.

There is a paradox here. Regime propagandists and leaders, from Lenin on, saw a guarantee of the stability of the socialist order in the creation of a conscious working class – a large phalanx of blue-collar supporters of a regime come to power before such a proletariat existed in Russia, and thus in a sense prematurely. However, in Stalin's and Khrushchev's time, and in the early Brezhnev period as well, the regime was arguably a beneficiary of something quite different – a social dynamism, a flow between social strata that helped prevent class formation. The opportunity to advance, to solve one's problems of living standard and status by individual mobility in a growing Soviet economy, was surely one key to the survival of the Soviet social order. Mobility opportunities are, in a sense, desolidifying. All people in a category whose status and rewards are limited – the peasantry, the manual workers – are not in the same boat if the most discontented see a way of leaving the boat. Soviet leaders from the 1930s through the 1960s could, and perhaps did, understand that this phenomenon made their tasks of social control easier, and lessened, in any period, the necessity to use coercive measures to ensure support or stifle opposition.

Third, the USSR has finally created a working class, one possessing many properties considered necessary for the formation of class consciousness, and one with the potential for becoming a political factor to be reckoned with more than in the past. The hereditized working class of today is not tapped, either at bottom or top, to the degree of previous times: neither inflow from the peasantry below nor outflow toward the intelligentsia above radically alters its composition. It is self-recruiting, and within the limits its internal diversity imposes, it is more homogeneous than in the past.[7] It is not growing rapidly but it is the largest category by far in the labor force. Slowing growth in an economic system still institutionally quite similar to what Stalin wrought guarantees, over the medium term, that the working class will remain large, will not be reduced by a large-scale shift to an expanded service sector, and will have to find its fate in an economy whose total output will not increase rapidly. The pie is not growing noticeably larger.

Such a working class – large, hereditized, relatively homogeneous – is one in which a common consciousness of common interests may develop, along with a conclusion that workers must pursue their goals as workers, via collective action. This, if not the whole, is a critical component of class consciousness; more critical, perhaps, than workers viewing their class interests as directly opposed to those of other groups (classes) in Soviet society. In any case, they constitute the largest class by far – the effective majority of Soviet society.

None of this argument, of course, equates the future political potential of Soviet workers with their Polish counterparts. Though an argument can be made[8] that similar hereditization in East European working classes, and similar advances in workers' educational levels, contributed to militancy, discontent, and near revolution (in the Polish case), the Soviet context is different in four important respects.

1. A political docility on the part of Soviet workers toward a strong, entrenched political order, influenced by a political culture that contains few, if any, Western elements
2. Patriotic attitudes widely diffused among the Soviet working class, signaling a general acceptance of the system as legitimate and domestically rooted (in contrast to the flawed legitimacy of externally imposed socialist political order in, for example, Poland, Czechoslovakia, and Hungary)
3. The perception and reality of the Soviet state (versus the Polish regime) as decisive, confident, ready to apply the coercion needed to resist or crush "illegitimate" demands from semiorganized or organized social forces
4. The lack, thus far, of an obviously impending, broad-scale economic

crisis in the USSR that immediately threatens the living standards to which workers have grown accustomed

Thus, the impact of the processes discussed here is not likely to manifest itself tomorrow or in a manner similar to the political and economic decomposition of Gierek's Poland and the rise of Solidarity in 1980. But the tension-producing effects are not necessarily relegated to the far future. If one takes Gorbachev's rhetoric seriously, the general thrust of his objectives is likely to confront working-class desires, preferences, and habits in four areas.

1. *Work discipline*. The heavy reliance on the rhetoric of discipline in Gorbachev's statements, the emphasis on achieving so much of the twelfth Five Year Plan's goals via increased labor productivity, promise a pressure on workers beyond that felt in recent times and lacking the prior "carrot" in the form of a perceptible increase in the rate of improvement in living standards.
2. *Labor mobility and unemployment*. Though Gorbachev's plans do not threaten structural unemployment, the expressed need to concentrate resources on efficient industries and take a harder line toward the inefficient may imply involuntary reallocation of blue-collar workers, and a break with the job-tenure-in-place pattern to which they have become accustomed. (The chapter by Lane in this volume considers this issue further.)
3. *Wage inequality*. The increase in wage inequality that must come if rewards are tied more tightly to some measure of the quality and quantity of work's results will create more self-described losers than winners. Whether this inequality is seen as truly linked to the individual's work or to the fortunes of the enterprise, it will generate elements of tension and feelings of violated expectations.
4. *Price increases.* Seemingly more decisive than his predecessors, Gorbachev may impose price increases. Although economically justified, price increases for goods (or possibly services, such as some medical care[9]), in the absence of better supply and higher quality, would again be an antipopulist policy, exacerbating for many the effects of greater wage–income differentials.

All these policy developments would be consistent with Gorbachev's plans, outlined only roughly thus far, for a technocratic refurbishment of the economy. Should he move, against the odds, toward a more decentralized, market, private enterprise reform, the social tensions of rising prices and perceived economic inequality will be all the greater in a more unfamiliar environment, wherein the favored workers in heavy industry may find themselves at an unaccustomed disadvantage (as did their Hungarian counterparts in the early days of the NEM).

However badly the Soviet economy works, Soviet citizens – among them the majority working class – have learned to "work" it. This working class is not as easily manipulated, for reasons of greater educational attainment and the sophistication attendant on hereditization, as its predecessors, a fact the Novosibirsk sociologist Tatiana Zaslavskaia recognized in her leaked "Novosibirsk document." Its potential to react in ways that are undermining and disruptive, if not militant, to an economic package it finds unpleasant and, by its standards, unfair, is significant.[10] Nor does it seem likely that the demagogic side of Andropov's (and his successor's) declaration of war against "shirkers, idlers, drifters" will galvanize worker morale against a putative minority and satisfy some long-felt thirst for discipline and justice. This working class is likely to realize that many of the practices they engage in, in the majority, are the targets of such rhetoric.

Thus, the years to come will test, in the context of a new economic program, the link between regime and working class that has been forged out of political culture, patriotism, and economic–welfare policies. Although hardly making workers the leading class, these policies have paid attention to their maintenance. Should Gorbachev's program prove little more than paper – as did the "Kosygin reform" of 1965 – then Soviet workers will confront the consequences of life in an economy less changed in style and rhetoric, but whose ever-slowing growth will impose on them problems perhaps no less severe; this at a time when the USSR can no longer afford to maintain its modest welfare safety net, without modification, under the largest component of its population. Internal and external historical examples – from the Novocherkassk riots of 1962 to the Polish worker unrest of the 1970s – and the direction of current trends suggest that careful attention to the working-class response to Soviet domestic policies over the years to come is amply warranted.

Notes

[1] Babushkina, Dunin, and Zenkevich (1981, 44). Indeed, for our own purposes, it is worth noting that rising levels of rural education during these years meant that an [eighth or tenth grade] school "leaver," rather than one with less education, became more typical of the countryside; moreover, the peasantry has always provided a larger number (share) of armed service personnel, whose discharge has been the occasion for them to go to the city and join the workers in industry or, often, in construction. Thus, the earlier figures on rural–farm contribution might be construed as reflecting a heavy intragenerational mobility of persons already working in agriculture; the latter reflecting more the intergenerational movement of younger people.

[2] There is, of course, much literature on class-based inequalities in access to higher education in the USSR, which contains ample evidence of the processes that, inter alia, contribute to the retention of working-class youth in that class. See, especially, Dobson 1980, and sources cited therein.

[3] *Izvestiia*, January 29, 1977, p. 5. (CDSP, February 23, 1977, p. 31.)

[4] *Sovetskaia Rossiia*, September 21, 1983, p. 3. (CDSP, November 2, 1983, pp. 1–4.)

[5] *Pravda* and *Izvestiia*, January 4, 1984. (CDSP, February 15, 1984, pp. 1–9, contains the whole reform document.)

[6] The degree of administrative rather than voluntary process in their entry to SPTUs is underlined in Voronitsyn (1985).

[7] This does not overlook the skill or economic diversity within the working class, but simply makes the point that, in terms of (often overlooked) origin, it is more of a class than in the past. For a view of diversity, see Pravda (1982).

[8] The current author made these arguments in two pieces in *Problems of Communism*. (See Connor 1977, 1980.)

[9] On the possibility of "*khozraschet* medicine" and its implications, see Dyker (1985, pp. 4–5).

[10] This, it seems to me, remains true under a quite different reading of the relevant attributes of the contemporary working class, suggested by several colleagues: that the main trend, rather than a hardening into a conscious class, is toward a *lumpenization* of the workers, a process marked by alcohol abuse, health problems, increasing corruption and indiscipline, for example. From this viewpoint, the new working class, while lacking political potential, represents a large population segment capable, under pressure, of creating massive economic and social problems in an unorganized reaction to unaccustomed pressure from above.

References

Aitov, N. A., and S. F. Eliseev. 1975. "NTR i izmeneniia v sotsial'noi structure rabochego klassa v razvitom sotsialisticheskom obshchestve." *Rabochii klass i sovremennyi mir* 1: 132–141.

AN SSSR, IMRD. 1977. *Sotsial'noe razvitie rabochego klassa SSSR*. Moscow: Nauka.

Averichev, Iu. 1977. "Proforientatsiia molodezhi i prestizh rabochei professii." *Sotsialisticheskii trud* 6: 130–32.

Avis, George. 1983. "Access to Higher Education in the Soviet Union." In *Soviet Education in the 1980's*, edited by J. J. Tomiak, pp. 199–239. London/New York: Croom Helm/St. Martin's Press.

Babushkina, T. A., V. S. Dunin, and E. A. Zenkevich. 1981. "Sotsial'nye problemy formirovaniia novykh popolnenii rabochego klassa." *Rabochii klass i sovremennyi mir* 3: 44–55.

Barber, J. D. 1978. "The Composition of the Soviet Working Class, 1928–41." University of Birmingham, Soviet Industrialization Project Series, No. 16.

Belkin, E. V. 1981. "Professional'no-tekhnicheskoe obrazovanie v zhiznennykh planakh molodezhi." *Sotsiologicheskie issledovaniia* 2: 105–109.

Bliakhman, G. 1979. "Sotsial'nyi portret sovremennogo molodogo rabochego," *Sotsialisticheskii trud* 10: 61–69.

Connor, Walter D. 1977. "Social Change and Stability in Eastern Europe." *Problems of Communism* (Nov.–Dec.): 16–32.

———. 1980. "Dissent in Eastern Europe: A New Coalition?" *Problems of Communism* (Jan.–Feb.): 1–17.

Dobson, Richard B. 1980. "Education and Opportunity." In *Contemporary Soviet Society*, edited by Jerry G. Pankhurst and Michael Paul Sacks, pp. 115–37. New York: Praeger.

Dyker, David. 1985. "The Complex Program for Consumer Goods Production." Radio Liberty Research, RL 351/85 (October 25).

Foteeva, E. V. 1984. *Kachestvennye kharakteristiki naseleniia SSSR.* Moscow: Finansy i statistika.

Inkeles, Alex, and Raymond A. Bauer. 1961. *The Soviet Citizen: Daily Life in a Totalitarian Society.* Cambridge: Harvard University Press.

Kim, M. P. 1964. "O nekotorykh osobennostiakh sovremennogo razvitiia rabochego klassa SSSR." In *Sovetskii rabochii klass na sovremennom etape* by AON pri TsK KPSS, pp. 6–7. Moscow: Mysl'.

Kostin, L. 1978. "Upravlenie trudovymi resursami strany." *Planovoe khoziaistvo* 12: 16–27. (CDSP, February 21, 1979.)

Kotliar, A. E., and M. I. Talalai. 1977. "Kak zakrepit' molodye kadry." *EKO* 4: 26–43. (CDSP, September 21, 1977, pp. 1–3.)

Kozlova, G. P., and Z. I. Fainburg. 1982. "Rabochii klass i obrazovanie." *Rabochii klass i sovremennyi mir* 4: 27–35.

Lebedeva, N. B., and R. Ia. Khabibulina. 1972. *Sovetskii rabochii klass: traditsii i preemstvennost' pokolenii.* Moscow: Mysl'.

O'Dell, Felicity. 1983. "Vocational Education in the USSR." In *Soviet Education in the 1980's*, edited by J. J. Tomiak, pp. 106–142. London/New York: Croom Helm/St. Martin's Press.

Panteleev, N. 1983. "Razvitie ekonomiki i podgotovka molodezhi k trudu." *Sotsialisticheskii trud* 9: 31.

Ponomarev, L. 1978. "Shkola – trudovoe vospitanie – vysokaia effektivnost' proizvodstva." *Sotsialisticheskii trud* 1: 30–31.

Pravda, Alex. 1982. "Is There a Soviet Working Class?" *Problems of Communism* (Nov.–Dec.): 1–24.

Riabushkin, T. V. 1980. "Pokazateli sotsial'nogo razvitiia rabochego klassa." *Sotsiologicheskie issledovaniia* 4: 19–24.

Rybakov, A. I., and A. I. Siniuk. 1983. "Vozrastnye razlichiia v tekuchesti rabochikh kadrov." *Sotsiologicheskie issledovaniia* 4: 106–108.

Somova, E. V. 1967. "Ob istochnikakh popolneniia rabochego klassa i inzhenerno-tekhnicheskoi intelligentisii." In *Protsessy izmeneniia sotsial'noi struktury v sovetskom obshchestve.* Sverdlovsk.

Sosin, Iu. P. 1975. "Faktory ukrepleniia trudovoi distsipliny." *EKO* 5. (CDSP, February 18, 1976, pp. 8–9.)

Voronitsyn, Sergei. 1985. "The Second Year of the Soviet School Reform Begins." Radio Liberty Research, RL 337/85 (October 8).

Zaslavskii, I. E., V. A. Kuz'min, and R. T. Ostrovskaia. 1983. "Sotsial'nye i professional'nye ustanovki moskovskikh shkolnikov." *Sotsiologicheskie issledovaniia* 3: 132–134.

3

Rural Society in the Soviet Union

Caroline Humphrey

During the late 1920s at least 80 percent of the Soviet population lived in the countryside. The USSR was an overwhelmingly peasant society: "The proletariat were still a minority who, when faced with calamity, war or famine, could easily take root once more in the place from which they had sprung, in other words the village" (Lewin 1968, 21). In the decades that followed population concentration shifted out of rural areas and into cities at a rate perhaps unparalleled anywhere else in the world. Two-thirds of the population was rural in 1940, and by 1985 this proportion had fallen to only about one-third.

There are, however, very significant regional differences in the pace of rural exodus. The consequences of this are further enhanced by the fact that rural birth rates tend to be highest precisely in areas in which there is the least out-migration. Thus, in 1984, 27 percent of the population of the Russian Republic lived in rural areas as compared with 42 percent in the Transcaucasian republics and 59 percent in the Central Asian Republics (Ts.S.U. 1975, 9–11; 1985, 5). There is a lack of rural labor in the Baltic region, the Northern and Central parts of Russia, and in Siberia, whereas the Transcaucasus and Central Asia have an excess.

The recency of Soviet industrial development and urban growth has meant that the examination of rural life is critical to understanding the society as a whole. This is clearly much more the case than in the already developed nations of the West. This chapter provides a broad overview of the culture, institutions, and directions of change in the Soviet countryside with particular attention to regional diversity.

The Countryside and Soviet Policy

Before looking closely at the characteristics of rural society, it is important to consider the major thrust of government policy. The aim of Soviet planning has always been to "liquidate the differences in material conditions between the town and the countryside" (Zoriktuyev 1982, 15). Explanations for low agricultural productivity, wage differentials between town and countryside, and farmers' dislike of certain jobs have focused on the backward conditions of everyday life and work, stressing particularly the low mechanization of productive work in rural areas. The Soviet government has therefore consistently pursued a policy that amounts to the urbanization of rural life. Gradually, this policy has deeply affected many spheres of the enormously varied rural societies of the USSR, making technology, standards of living, and settlement patterns even more homogeneous. More homogeneous and thereby more equal is the idea. The preservation of different ethnic cultures has regularly fallen victim to the greater urgency of equalizing conditions, opportunities, and services of the city and the village.

Only recently, and then prompted by literature and the arts in Russian culture, has there come to be an appreciation that there may be something special and valuable in traditional rural life in itself. From the standpoint of the Moscow intelligentsia, the Russian village may now seem a fragile and treasured link with a vanished past. But there are at least two reasons the Russian village cannot be preserved. First, conditions are in fact still far from equal, and rural people themselves migrate not only to the cities, but also to other country areas all over the Soviet Union where things seem to be better. Second, rural people of the European nationalities seem to prefer the values of modernity to those of tradition. Neither of these factors apply to the same extent to the indigenous ethnic groups of Central Asia and the Transcaucasus. Modernization may to some degree have been imposed on them. But the effect for the USSR in general is clear: the urbanization of the countryside has promoted a gradual, but irreversible, modernization of rural life in line with urban ideals.

However, the Soviet government's retention of collective and state farms as the major institutions of the agricultural economy has had some contrary effects. In structure, the ensemble of agricultural institutions has hardly changed since the early 1930s when it was first introduced. One effect, particularly with the regulations before 1975 making it difficult to leave farms, has been the isolation of the rural population. On the farm young people are specifically trained to assume positions within the rural work force. But the young are especially prone to migrate, leaving behind the older population. This encourages a localization of cultures and social structures that is at odds with the policy of homogeneous urbanization.

Economic development policy, however, has brought convulsive change to some rural areas while leaving others untouched. Dramatic shifts in population have occurred as a consequence of the opening up of virgin lands for agriculture, the construction of dams and railroads, the exploitation of mineral resources or timber, the industrialization of such regions as Kazakhstan, and the building of new cities. In the developing areas the occupational structure is different from the agricultural backwaters. In the Far East, for example, with its mining, shipping, and industry, only 20 percent of the rural population is engaged in agriculture, but Moldavia is still a "peasant" region with 70 percent of people working on farms (Staroverov 1978, 306).

In sum, three major forces are in tension with one another in Soviet rural society: (1) the policy of equalizing conditions in town and countryside, in effect a gradual and generalized process of urbanization; (2) the ongoing preservation of the structures of the state and collective farms, which have had the contrary effects of making rigid and separating off rural life; and (3) the effects of centrally planned economic directives, which have dynamized some regions but not others. All three forces link rural people inextricably with Soviet society as a whole. The link is not just economic, but also political and cultural. If we compare Soviet farmers with those, for example, of North America or Europe, an essential difference is that in the Soviet case economic institutions (e.g., state farms) are at the same time political structures, branches of the State, and instruments of cultural policy (it is part of Soviet culture to value material equality so highly).

Rural Institutions

The majority of the Soviet rural population is attached to either a collective or state farm (*kolkhoz* and *sovkhoz*). The families of registered workers on the farms are also members, and before the changes in the farm statutes in 1969 and passport laws in 1975, it was difficult to change this status. Other rural dwellers work in state institutions and enterprises (industry, health, education, administration, transport, forestry, etc.) and in ancillary farms or workshops attached to industrial or construction enterprises.

Collective and state farms are actually not very different. Both are subject to regional plans for their product, which they must sell to the State at set prices. All farm workers in production are given annual plans for their production, with similar minimal wage rates for achievement of the plan. On both types of farms each household is allocated restricted areas of land (around two hectares) for private production. The main difference lies in the fact that collective farmers jointly own their product, buildings, and machinery, whereas in the state farms all of these belong to the State. In a collective farm there is thus more room for maneuvre: within limits, the members can choose to use their income for saving, buying more machinery, allotting themselves higher bonuses, and so on. The chairman/chairwoman and other officers of a collective farm are elected, in a state farm they are appointed from above. Such matters in collective farms are decided at general meetings of the members, but in practice important decisions – especially in regard to "elections" – are taken by the Party, almost invariably at higher levels than that of the farm itself (Humphrey 1983).

The linking of the peasant to the State through farm institutions is not unique to the Soviet Union. Nor is the role of the local leader as political broker. Cooperatives have played a similar, though far more limited, role in Western Europe (Boissevain and Friedl 1975). The unfamiliar organization and vocabulary of the Soviet rural economy should not blind us to common processes affecting farming communities in modern nation states. However, the role of the Party in Soviet rural society is unique.

The Party provides a parallel institution in every farm, with sub-branches in each of the brigades – work collectives of usually one hundred or more individuals. Approximately one in ten workers is a Party member, with a higher proportion of young people being members of the Komsomol. The affairs of the Party are run by an Executive Committee, led by a Secretary, which normally overlaps in its membership with the Management Committee of the farm. The members of the Party have to obey directives from higher levels, that is, district, regional, and republic levels, and their duty is to guide the activities of the farm in the interests of Soviet society as a whole as they are defined by the Party. This means that there may be conflicts of interest between local farm concerns and Party policy.

The local soviet or *selsovet* has jurisdiction over an administrative area comprised of farms and other rural institutions. A typical *selsovet* contains one large farm, schools, a hospital, shops, and perhaps a small workshop, factory, or forestry station. The *selsovet*, run by a committee chosen from elected deputies from the population, has few resources at its disposal: a small budget from soviets at higher levels and a certain levy (not always paid) from the enterprises under it. The *selsovet* is responsible for such matters as registration of births, deaths, and marriages and in theory for discipline and the provision of village services. In practice, road maintenance, lighting, water, and housing are often controlled by the farm.

A collective farm has the structure shown in Figure 3.1. In a state farm the Chairman is replaced by a director and the General Meeting of Members does not have an overriding management function.

If we compare this structure with that of socialized farms in other countries, it is clear that the Soviet model has been widely copied. The Czech agricultural cooperative is almost identical (Salzmann and Scheufler 1974, 52), and those of East Germany, Bulgaria, Rumania, and Vietnam are very similar. The Mongolian *negdel* (cooperative) has the same structure, with the difference that the boundary of the farm coincides with the lowest administrative unit (Humphrey 1978); as used to be the case with the Chinese commune. In Poland, collective and state farms have an insignificant role in a predominantly individual, restricted, and poverty-striken agriculture (Lewis 1973; Hann 1985). In Yugoslavia, as in Poland, the great majority of farmers are individual owners, many of whom make ends meet by commuting to towns. However, the Yugoslavian cooperative has a genuinely greater degree of self-management than its Soviet counterpart (Mydall 1984). In Hungary the encouragement since the mid-1960s of "private" production within the framework of the collective, and the far greater role of state purchase directly from producing members of farms (very small-scale in the USSR), has resulted in greater prosperity than in the average Soviet farm (Hann 1980).

The Soviet form has been retained in the USSR mainly for purposes of control over the enormously varied resources and opportunities of this vast land. Some parts of the Soviet Union have great natural advantages over others, and wide disparities in wealth between farming communities exist even in the same region. There is the constant fear that if economic controls were relaxed, not only might key products fail to be produced, but also

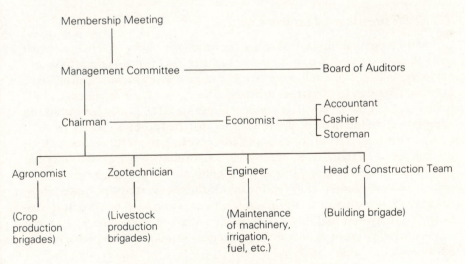

Figure 3.1. Structure of a Collective Farm

ungovernable differentials would result. From a Marxist viewpoint economic differentiation implies unpredictable, but certainly non-socialist, political results. However, as in all societies, there persists a wide variety of voluntary and spontaneous forms of economic activity that are often illegal and defy control.[1]

There are substantial regional differences among farms. In Estonia, where rural labor is scarce, the average farmer is at work for 300 days in the year, but in Tadjikistan, Moldavia, and Turkmenia for less than 180. Moldavia and the Transcaucasus and Central Asian republics have large rural populations, but they differ in other ways: in Moldavia most of the population is of working age, there are few dependents, and even 20 to 30 percent of pensioners work. In the Transcaucasus and Central Asia on the other hand, there are large numbers of dependents, mostly children. The rural exodus affects mainly people of working age, and the proportion of pensioners in the population is highest in regions with high out-migration: the Russian Republic, Belorussia, the Ukraine, and the Baltic republics (Staroverov 1978, 270–73).

Where rural settlements are large, as in Moldavia, there comes to be a relative lack of service intelligentsia (doctors, teachers, administrators) per head of population, because such people are stationed by village (Staroverov 1978, 293). Other research shows that remoteness of a farm from towns is associated with a higher than average proportion of low-paid, hard-worked, elderly and poorly educated workers (Ryvkina 1979, 250, 297, 322).

Settlements and Living Conditions

Settlement planning is one sphere in which the policy of "creating equal conditions between town and countryside" has had the most effect. It has not made the village like a mini-city (except in rare cases in which farms have been rich enough to construct apartment blocks for their members), but it has created central farm villages of ever larger size. The policy has meant the complete abandonment of many villages that had formerly been parts of farms. In the Buryat ASSR, for example, there were 2,483 settlements in 1959; this number was reduced to 785 by 1975 (Zoriktuyev 1982, 18). Over the years since collectivization in 1929–31, collective farms have been amalgamated into ever larger units, and many of them coverted into state farms. Since 1955 the policy of amalgamating farms has been most marked. It seems, however, that some stability has now been attained, and contrary to some suppositions, we may expect collective farms to continue to play a part in Soviet rural life (Miller 1976).

An average farm now has a central village, with some 1,500 to 2,000 inhabitants, together with some outlying hamlets, formerly the centres of collective farms and now the brigades or subdivisions of the main *kolkhoz* or *sovkhoz*. In these often half-abandoned settlements it is still possible to find the higgledy-piggledy streets with houses of various types separated in the midst of their private plots. But virtually all of the main villages have now been rebuilt according to strict rules. Streets are wide and straight; perpendicular to the street are the houses, each a regulation distance from its neighbors, surrounded by fences. In most parts of the Russian Republic, houses are built of wood, whereas administrative and other communal buildings are of brick or concrete. Houses are situated close together and most of the private land is in allotments outside the village. Cultural differences, at least in the Russian Republic, are ignored: it would be difficult from external appearances to tell a Russian from a Yakut, Buryat, or Tuvinian village.

The aim of such consolidation is the provision of services of an urban type. All farm center villages are electrified and have schools, a small hospital, a club, library, several shops, a hotel, post office, communal baths, a dining room, and workshops (garage, dairy, road maintenance station, etc.). In addition to the farm administration building, the office of the *selsovet* is often located here. There may be a local radio station, a sports stadium, and a garden with a memorial to the fallen in World War II. In the more remote areas few houses even in the farm centers have running water or bathrooms. Water is obtained from wells or taps down the village street. Latrines in the yard are the only toilets. It is rare to find central heating in rural settlements. Houses are heated by wood-burning stoves that have to be lit every morning.

When they are near towns, farm centers often have a variety of industrial enterprises situated in them. The Lenin Kolkhoz at Tokhoi in the Buryat ASSR, for example, has an agricultural machinery repair workshop, a gasoline station, an irrigation works, an automobile workshop, and a railway repair shop. From Tokhoi there is a regular bus service to a nearby town, and many inhabitants travel there to work. Tokhoi (population 3,500) has a mixed population of Buryats, Russians, Ukrainians, Tatars, and Armenians, and the way of life is more like that of a small town than a city (Zoriktuyev 1982, 20–21).

Compare this with the conditions in outlying hamlets of the more remote farms. Here there may be, at worst, temporary electricity, no schools, mobile shops only, and no regular transport to the center. Mainly livestock workers and general laborers live in these places. Pastoralists, hunters, and fishers have seasonal camps with even rougher conditions. In the last ten years great efforts have been made to ameliorate living conditions in permanent hamlets: almost all of them are now electrified, connected to radio and television networks, and have a medical center, a cinema, shop, and school. The houses may be as well built as those in the center. Increasingly, the main features differentiating distant hamlets from small towns are the distribution of consumer goods and personal transport. The choice of goods, even food and clothing, in rural shops is still very poor. Transport between towns, by bus or plane, is crowded but possible. But outlying settlements may be ten to fifteen kilometers from the farm center, let alone the nearest town. In vast tracts of the Russian Republic people have to make do with a horse and makeshift buggy, a boat, or walking. There are great differences between the regions of the USSR: the Baltic republics have relatively good transport facilities, but mountainous, forested, and swampy areas may be cut off for weeks to all except air service, especially in spring and autumn. For further discussion on wages and incomes in different regions of the USSR, see MacAuley (1979).

Occupational Structure, Income, and Way of Life

There is an association between occupation and type of settlement. People in the administrative and skilled jobs tend to live in the largest centers, closest to the town. Collective farmers tend to live in a more remote location. Nine-tenths of the workers in Soviet collective farms in 1975 were doing physical, as opposed to mental, work (Simushin 1976, 71).

In a study conducted between 1972 and 1975, Ryvkina (1979, 117–18) selected 2 district towns, 34 selsovet centers, and 142 village settlements in Western Siberia (Novosibirsk Oblast) as genuinely typical of the rural Soviet Union. The percentage of persons in each occupation is shown in Table 3.1.

Table 3.1
Occupational Distribution in Selected Collective Farms

Managers and chief specialists	1.9
Managers of middle and lower rank	5.4
Specialists with higher education	5.6
Technicians with middle education	2.4
Non-specialist employees	3.8
Mechanics	14.2
Milkers	8.1
Livestock and field workers	12.3
Workers in industry, building, transport, trade, and supply	27.9
Unskilled laborers	18.2
Total	99.8%

Source: R. V. Ryvkina, *Obraz zhizni sel'skogo naseleniya* (Novosibirsk: Nauka, 1979), p. 250.

The substantial differences in income among occupations is suggested by the percentage distribution of yearly incomes shown in Table 3.2. This was income from both public work and the sale of produce from private gardens. Wädekin (1975, 11) has estimated that by 1975 the income of collective farm families rose to the same level as families in state farms, though in both cases incomes were less than those of industrial workers. In 1984 the average monthly income of workers on state farms was 174 rubles, while workers in industry earned 205 rubles, those in building earned 238 rubles, and transportation workers received 215 rubles (Ts.S.U. 1985, 417).

Of course these income figures are only crude averages. Each collective farm can set its own wages and bonuses for overplan production. Some jobs have much greater possibilities than others for making extra money: shepherds can rear more than one hundred lambs from one hundred ewes, milkers can squeeze out hundreds of litres, drivers can generally make something on the side by fetching and carrying unofficial goods. But the manual laborers are stuck with the odd jobs, and many of these workers are unemployed for much of the winter when farming is slack. These people, not surprisingly, devote a great deal of time to the private plot.

The importance of the private plot is shown by the rural families in the study by Ryvkina (1979, 179). In 1977, 98.2 percent of the rural families grew potatoes, 68.6 percent produced meat of some kind, 96.9 percent planted vegetables, 57.6 percent produced eggs, 59.9 percent produced milk, and 33.3 percent made butter. People emphasized that private farming of this kind, even on a tiny scale, was much cheaper than buying the equivalent food, and that one advantage of living in the countryside was the private plot. Asked what made a family well off, 17.4 percent of people replied "A well-managed private plot" (1979, 179). Women with children but no husband frequently obtain their fundamental income from the plot, as do "families with no workers." This last category shows that people do exist in

Table 3.2
Distribution of Yearly Income in Selected Collective Farms
(Figures in percentages)

Up to 399 rubles per year	3.6
400– 599 rubles	16.6
600– 799 rubles	28.2
800–1099 rubles	31.0
1100–1599 rubles	15.8
Over 1600 rubles	4.8
Total	100.0%

Source: R. V. Ryvkina, *Obraz zhizni sel'skogo naseleniya* (Novosibirsk: Nauka, 1979), p. 250.

the Soviet Union who maintain themselves outside the official system. In some areas the proportion is quite high. Arutyunyan (1973, 10) notes that 14.7 percent of the population of the Aga Buryat National Okrug in 1970 supported themselves entirely from their private plots.

The private plot is still a marker of rural culture. Few town dwellers have a private plot (10 percent) and of those who do, more than 60 percent say they keep it primarily for recreation. In the villages the private plot is a source not just of important subsistence, but also of pride and prestige. People who buy milk and do not keep a cow are criticized. Farmers told Ryvkina in the 1970s that the plot would only disappear when products were freely and cheaply available and when rural people changed their values and began to prefer to spend their free time in cultural pursuits (1979, 182). Despite a very low level of mechanization, the private plots deliver 28 percent of agricultural products in the USSR with only 9 percent of the productive funds (181). As the villagers say, "Without a plot you can't get anything, but with one you have no rest."

Generally speaking, the plot is too heavily restricted and dependent on manual labor to provide much wealth. All it can do is just about even up the incomes of rural and urban workers. With informal links, agricultural produce can be exchanged for town goods. Only in parts of the USSR where it is possible to produce something exceptional, for example, fresh flowers in the South or furs in Siberia, is it worthwhile trying to overcome transport difficulties to set up regular sales in such big cities as Moscow. Except when sales are organized in the very bureaucratized collective farm markets, they border on illegality and are therefore risky.

Occupation strongly influences the time spent on the plot, the length of work day, the seasonality of labor, and the amount of leisure time. In considering these variables, Ryvkina (1979, 288–308) divided the rural community into four categories, each associated with a distinct way of life, as shown in Table 3.3. Type 4 is contradictory in terms of Soviet values. Here are responsible and experienced workers who nevertheless work disproportionately long hours, have the lowest level of formal education, and have the least income; 43 percent of them have no free days at all, and 63 percent never take the holidays to which they are entitled. Almost 50 percent earn between 31 and 50 rubles a month, and only 5.5 percent more than one hundred rubles. Even the unskilled workers (Type 3) do better in income, mainly because they are not so encumbered with public work and can devote more time to their private plots. If we compare the rural skilled workers (Type 4) with skilled people living in urbanized villages (Type 1), the majority of whom do not work in agriculture, the latter are younger, have better access to training courses, earn more, and work shorter hours; 80 percent of them take their allotted holidays. Nearly a third of them do not work in the private plot – not for lack of time, but rather because they can afford not to. This group has the highest average income, and more than 28 percent of them earn more than one hundred rubles a month (Ryvkina 1979, 298).

Table 3.3
Four Types of Collective Farmers

	No Work in Private Plot	8-hour Work Day or Less	2 Free Days Per Week
Type 1 (29.6% of total)			
Skilled manual workers in urbanized villages	29.3%	79.9%	68.3%
Type 2 (28.2%)			
Rural intelligentsia	19.6%	75.6%	9.6%
Type 3 (23.2%)			
Unskilled manual workers in rural villages	1.8%	70.2%	31.1%
Type 4 (19%)			
Skilled manual workers in rural villages	25.0%	33.0%	7.1%

Source: R. V. Ryvkina, *Obraz zhizni sel'skogo naseleniya* (Novosibirsk: Nauka, 1979), p. 288–308.

It is significant, too, that the rural intelligentsia (Type 2) has a lower average income than the skilled workers of urbanized villages. Despite the fact that 86 percent of the rural intelligentsia are specialists who completed high school and 7 percent are managers and specialists with higher education, only 11 percent of them earn more than one hundred rubles a month.

In Soviet conditions, however, income is only one factor in assessing general well-being. Another significant dimension is use of services provided by the state: polyclinics, hospitals, pharmacies, post offices, communal baths, hairdressers, dining rooms, clothing and footwear repair shops, clubs and "houses of culture." All of these are considered traditional in rural areas. New services, that is, services not yet present everywhere, are sports stadiums, telephone, savings bank, repairs for domestic appliances, dry cleaners, laundry, and library. Skilled workers in urbanized villages on average use three or four services, around 9 percent of them use all the services available (in most places around six services), and only 3.7 pecent use no services at all. Of Types 3 and 4, on the other hand, a massive 66.6 percent and 75 percent respectively, use only one service or none (Ryvkina 1979, 237, 294).

Two other factors are important in people's sense of satisfaction with their lives: the extent to which they can obtain further education/training, and the degree to which they can participate in management. Whereas more than a quarter of the rural intelligentsia work in some managerial capacity, this it true of less than 10 percent of the other groups. Not surprisingly, the rural intelligentsia and workers in urbanized villages have more opportunity for study that do the other workers in rural villages (Ryvkina 1979, 305).

There are significant differences in the status of men and women in rural areas (see the chapter by Sacks in this volume). Men comprise nine of every ten mechanics and four of every five rural industrial workers, whereas 97 percent of milkers and 91 percent of workers in trade and supply are women. Three-quarters of unskilled workers are women as are 70 percent of lower rank specialists and office workers. Men comprise 83.9 percent of the managers and leading specialists (Ryvkina 1979, 286–87). Women clearly predominate in Types 2 and 3 according to their way of life (1979, 297). Women earn the same as men when they do exactly the same work, but because women are concentrated in low paid occupations, their earnings average much less than those of men. (See, for example, Arutyunyan 1973, 189).

Ryvkina's study is complex, but we can certainly draw the conclusion that conditions and opportunities in Soviet rural society vary greatly. The rural intelligentsia, in many respects, does less well than skilled, mainly non-farm workers of urbanized settlements. Here we see the influence of development projects, which have introduced industrial conditions in rural localities. Ryvkina also shows that trained, experienced rural workers are in some respects less well off than the untrained. This is mainly due to the structure of collective and state farms, which places huge burdens of work and responsibility on some types of workers while leaving others underemployed (see Humphrey 1983, ch. 5). Furthermore, many farms are not sufficiently mechanized to provide suitable jobs for people with training. Many people are working in jobs below their capacities (Humphrey 1983, 311).

Ryvkina notes (1979, 307) that if people live in a remote rural settlement and are engaged in agriculture, these facts will affect their way of life no matter what job they have. Nevertheless, the job one is able to get is very important, at it affects where one can live and what services are available. Unlike workers in Western countries, the majority of Soviet people have their jobs allocated to them by the farm management, by schools and colleges, and by the Party and the Selsovet. Ryvkina (1979, 176) found 57.3 percent of her surveyed population to be working in jobs they had not chosen. Even migration may be to order (Humphrey 1983, 46). This does not necessarily mean that such jobs are not desired, but on the farm there is great competition for preferred occupations. Good relations with the management are all-important. For its part, the management needs the workers to perform well in order to fulfill its own production plans. The result is a complex "political" bargaining in which the workers, though not able to strike, can certainly work slowly (See Humphrey 1983.)

Geographical Mobility

Is the village a self-enclosed community? One indicator is the extent to which people go out to visit the town. There is a contrast here with Western rural society. Soviet sociologists have found that people visit the regional town center (*oblastnoi tsentr*) very rarely (around 56 percent go less than once a year or never), though they visit the district town (*raitsentr*) twice as often. The great majority go to town for shopping, with lesser numbers going on official matters, to visit relatives, or to the theatre or cinema. Only 6 percent of the population goes to town to sell products and 3 percent to study. In Ryvkina's survey (1979, 176, 227) a surprisingly small number (6 percent) went to towns to work, most of them general laborers. The picture is one of a remarkably immobile population. However, Ryvkina is probably out of date here, as ever increasing numbers of cars are sold to people in rural areas (Zoriktuyev 1982, 105). The condition of the roads is probably still a limiting factor.

The number of people who live in the countryside but go to towns to work or study has been rising rapidly in the USSR as a whole (from 2.5 million in 1965 to 5.5 million in 1975). But there are large differences between regions. In Siberia the proportion is small, but in Estonia it reaches 10 percent of the rural population in some places (Likhoded 1977, 8).

There is greater movement from farm to farm within the countryside. In one Buryat state farm in Western Siberia, for example, out of 710 registered workers in 1970, 119 either came or went during the year, that is, 16 percent of the work force was on the move (Belikov 1974, 148). At certain periods there have also been population flows from the towns to the country, when regional governments have "sent" skilled workers from the cities to invigorate agriculture (Humphrey 1983, 450). There are also mobile teams of builders and craftsmen (*shabashniki*) that tour the countryside looking for contracts with farms. Their help is much needed, especially in the scarce labor regions, but because of its uncontrolled and unsocialist nature it is little discussed in Soviet sociology, and we do not know the number of people involved.

Arutyunyan (1973, 98–99) found that many rural workers wished to move to the town. This was particularly true among the middle and higher specialists (39 percent wanted to live in the town). Managers were much more likely to want to stay (18 percent). This reflects the fact that a managerial position is likely to be the culmination of a career, whereas specialists are still in the process of upward mobility. Laborers and seasonal workers were least interested in a move to the city (9 to 16 percent).

There is evidence that ethnic minorities, particularly those with a Muslim heritage, are more content with their work and available services and less likely to want to move than are their Russian counterparts. In predominantly Tatar villages a massive 41 percent of Russian inhabitants wanted to move as compared with 19 percent of the Tatars. However, in mainly Russian villages the picture was reversed: 24 percent of Tatars and only 21 percent of Russians hoped to leave (Arutyunyan 1973, 61). This points to the fact that migration is only partly explained by ethnic group and occupation. The attitudes of rural people to their own community must also be considered in order to understand population movement.

The Village as Community

In Russian literature we see, for example, the sadness of the elderly collective farmers whose village is due to be inundated to make way for a hydroelectric scheme, or the loving description of the incorruptible values of the old peasant woman who is rejected in different ways by each of her children (Rasputin 1974, 1976; discussed in Hosking 1980). The attachment to rural life seems to be founded on ancestral ties to place (it is the graves that the villagers in Rasputin's story are so concerned to preserve), on the texture of village life and neighborliness. Sociological analyses do not convey these subtleties, but nevertheless they do provide us with some gross information. Ryvkina (1979, 334) discovered, for example, that her Russian West Siberians placed love of nature as the main reason for liking village life, followed by the possibility of having a private plot, and peace and quiet. Crowding was the main reason for not liking the city. Reasons for preferring urban life were work conditions, leisure facilities, and better supply of goods; it was the lack of these, together with the lack of transport and necessity for having a private plot, that inclined some people against the village. Arutyunyan (1971, 222) found that older people loved the old, small villages and hamlets for their quiet and tradition, but the young generation wanted the greater range of work, the clubs, and schools of the large village.

Certain social groups have more tenuous ties to the village. The teachers, doctors, cultural workers, and educated specialists are often sent in from outside. These people spend their leisure hours together, tend to intermarry, and then move on.

Villages in the European part of the Russian Republic and in the Ukraine are comprised largely of only one ethnic group, but elsewhere in the USSR villages are ethnically heterogeneous – a result of the spread of the Russian peasantry, the "sending in" of cadres, and the dispersal of such ethnic groups as Tatars, Ossetians, and Germans after World War II (see the chapter by Clem in this volume). The different ethnic groups may live separately on the farm, but they work together in common teams. The great majority (around 70 percent in Arutyunyan's sample) say that ethnic differences should not influence friendship, work contacts, or marriage choice. There is in fact little evidence of ethnic discord in Soviet rural society, though this may be less true in the cities. No separate ethnic organizations exist, and public institutions, such as the Soviets and Party, have ethnic quotas at the local level in order to promote participation by all ethnic groups.

Family and Society

If the village is the focus for Russian attachment to rural life, it seems that among the Asian minorities this is replaced by the family and kinship. Arutyunyan (1973, pp 198, 223) found that Tatars tend to have larger families, live closer to kin and extended kin, and be happier with family life than Russians. Official statistics tend to present Soviet rural families as more similar in structure and more nucleated than they really are. This stems from the advantages in formally splitting the family early, as soon as children come of age, in order to qualify for private plots. Terent'yeva (1984, 150) showed that for Latvian peasantry, the prewar (i.e., pre-Soviet) pattern of high dowry and late inheritance and marriage, not unlike the case of Irish peasantry, led to the emergence of a high proportion of single, unmarried people. This tendency was exacerbated by the "artificial" splitting of the family in the postwar Soviet period. Statistics hide many cases in which individuals are actually part of families. For example, children of working age employed outside the farm may keep a common budget and economy with their old single parents who live on a pension, but the pensioners might claim a private plot from the kolkhoz for themselves. They accomplish this by registering this group as two or three families. Such "abuses," attributed to "consumerist attitudes," are now being stamped out in Latvia (Terent'yeva 1984, 152), though they appear to be tolerated in the Buryat ASSR in Siberia (Basayeva et al. 1984, 85).

Despite sometimes misleading statistics, it is clear that Asians (e.g., Uzbeks, Kazakhs, or Buryats) consistently have larger families than do Russians. But it is not clear how far into the future these differences will continue. Buryats are already having fewer children than they did in the 1950s and 1960s, and many factors promote the nuclearization of the family all over the Soviet Union: increasing desire for economic independence by the younger generation, their greater mobility, and differences in cultural values between them and the older generation (Basayeva et al. 1984, 83, 88).

Basayeva (1984, 94) found that Russians and Buryats hold many attitudes in common regarding the family. For example, the "head of the family" – a status encouraged by Soviet officialdom's insistence that there should be such a person – is nearly always the man, even if the wife has higher qualifications and earns more. There is a clear sexual division of labor, although women are expected to be capable of almost all kinds of work including heavy physical labor, which women showed they could do during the war. Men consider domestic tasks beneath them (cleaning the house, cooking, washing clothes, etc.). In such families the man is the center of the family. The Russian wife refers to her husband as "himself" (*sam*), as in "himself is not at home," "himself will decide." In younger families such attitudes are becoming rare, but Buryats in particular retain a respectful, tactful, and loving attitude to their older relatives.

What differentiates Buryats and other Asian minorities from Russians are the unquestioned loyalty given to the family and the spread of wider kin who are recognized as family. Buryats maintain relations with second, third, and even fourth cousins, not just inviting them to weddings and funerals, but also preserving close contacts and giving help. It is common to find country cousins making presents of produce from the plots, while town cousins give difficult-to-obtain urban goods and visit the countryside to help with the harvest. Such exchanges are considered obligatory, and neglect of them gives rise to general criticism (Basayeva et al. 1984, 96; Humphrey 1983, 382–401).

Conclusion

The direction of change in the countryside in the future appears clear. We see it in the attenuation of ethnic differences among young people. The processes creating a common Soviet culture are very strong: rising educational standards, a commom curriculum all over the country, the domination of centralized culture (most books and newspapers in ethnic languages are translations from Russian), the prevalence of bilingualism and the Russianization of small minority languages, and the increasing number of common "Soviet rituals" (at marriage, induction into the army, first day at work, etc.) all tend to eradicate cultural differences (see the chapter by Field in this volume). In general, for young people, Soviet culture is not only what is inculcated at school, but also to what they aspire in their working lives.

The policy of urbanization of the countryside only intensifies this process. In recent years the USSR has begun to see a slowing down in the rural exodus. Soviet writers attribute this to success in improving rural standards of living (Zaslavskaya and Korel 1984). It may be due also to decreasing job opportunities in cities or to increased efficiency in enforcing the registration system for city dwellers.[2] But it is clear that the countryside is becoming ever more Soviet in culture, despite differences in conditions. Even if the organization of collective and state farms promotes localization of attitudes and interests, this is counterbalanced by the multiethnic make-up of most farms and relatively high rate of migration between them. The great economic developments that take place in rural areas – the building of the BAM railway through East Siberia and the Far East, for example, to which young people in the 1970s flocked with some enthusiasm for the transformation of their country – are not oriented to rural values. Rather, they serve as yet another mechanism for the broadening of aspirations, for the lifting of sights from the family, the village, and the farm to the sometimes inspiring vision of the Soviet Union as a whole.

Notes

[1] Katsenlinboigen (1977) has described the various "colored markets" (black, brown, grey, etc.), which involve their own types of exchange and social relations. The "second economy" (Grossman 1977) is embedded in the informal ties of kin, workmates, neighbours and patrons and seems unlikely to disappear in any of the socialist economies (Sampson 1983).

[2] Residence permits, *propiski*, are required for stays of longer than one and a half months, and they are particularly difficult to obtain for large cities. The applicant must show evidence of having a job and housing, and yet these are not normally given to people who do not have a propiska. There are numerous subterfuges to get round this vicious circle, including marriages of convenience, which are quite common between rural girls and city men.

References

Arutyunyan, Yu. V. 1971. *Sotsial'naya struktura sel'skogo naseleniya.* Moscow: Nauka.

———. 1973. *Sotsial'noye i natsional'noye.* Moscow: Nauka.

Basayeva, K. D. et al. 1984. "Sem'ya i semeinyi byt." In *Sovremennyi byt i etnokul'turnyye protsessy v buryatii*, edited by P. T. Khaptayev, pp. 61–104. Novosibirsk: Nauka.

Belikov, V. V. 1974. "Sotsial'no-professional'nyi sostav rabotnikov sovkhoza 'Kizhinginskii'." *Etnograficheskii Sbornik* 6, Ulan-Ude.

Boissevain, Jeremy, and John Friedl. 1975. *Beyond the Community: Social Process in Europe.* The Hague, Netherlands: University of Amsterdam.

Dunn, Stephen P, and Ethel Dunn. 1967. *The Peasants of Central Russia.* New York: Holt, Rinehart and Winston.

Grossman, Gregory. 1977. "The Second Economy of the USSR." *Problems of Communism*, 26 (5):25–40.

Hann, C. M. 1980. *Tazlar: A Village in Hungary.* Cambridge, England: Cambridge University Press.

———. 1985. *A Village without Solidarity: Polish Peasants in Years of Crisis.* New Haven, Conn.: Yale University Press.

Hosking, Geoffrey. 1980. *Beyond Socialist Realism: Soviet Fiction since Ivan Denisovich.* London: Granada Publishing and Paul Elek.

Humphrey, Caroline. 1978. "The Role of Herdsmens' Cooperatives in the National Economy of Mongolia." *Development and Change* 9:133–60.

———. 1983. *Karl Marx Collective: Economy, Society and Religion in a Siberian Collective Farm.* Cambridge, England: Cambridge University Press.

Katsenlinboigen, Aron. 1977. "Coloured markets in the Soviet Union," *Soviet Studies* 29 (1): 62–85.

Khaptayev, P. T. 1984. *Sovremennyi byt i etnokul'turnyye protsessy v buryatii.* Novosibirsk: Nauka.

Lewin, Moshe. 1968. *Russian Peasants and Soviet Power: A Study of Collectivization.* New York: W. W. Norton and Company.

Lewis, Paul G. 1973. "The Peasantry." In *Social Groups in Polish Society*, edited by David Lane and George Kolankiewicz, pp. 29–87. New York: Columbia University Press.

Likhoded, V. N. 1977. "The Development of Commuter Migration of the Rural Population in the USSR." Unpublished doctoral dissertation, Moscow.

McAuley, Alastair. 1979. *Economic Welfare in the Soviet Union: Poverty, Living Standards and Inequality.* Madison: University of Wisconsin Press.

Millar, J. R. 1971. *The Soviet Rural Community.* Urbana: University of Illinois Press.

Miller, Robert F. 1976. "The Future of the Soviet Kolkhoz." *Problems of Communism* 25 (2):34–50.

Mydall, H. 1984. *Yugoslav Socialism in Theory and Practice.* Oxford, England: Oxford University Press.

Pimenov, V. V. 1977. *Udmurty, opyt komponentnogo analiza etnosa.* Leningrad: Nauka.

Rasputin, V. G. 1974. *Zhivi i pomni.* Moscow: Sovremennik.

———. 1976. *Povesti.* Moscow: Molodaya Gvardiya.

Ryvkina, R. V. 1979. *Obraz zhizni sel'skogo naseleniya.* Novosibirsk: Nauka.

Salzmann, Zdenek, and Vladimir Scheufler. 1974. *Komarov: a Czech Farming Village.* New York: Holt, Rinehart and Winston.

Sampson, Steven L. 1983. "Rich Families and Poor Collectives: An Anthropoligical Approach to Romania's 'Second Economy'." Contributions to Soviet and East Europe Research, vol. 1. Sweden: Russian Center for Soviet and East European Studies, Uppsala University.

Simushin, P. I. 1976. *Sotsial'nyi portret sovetskogo krest'yanina.* Moscow: Politizdat.

Staroverov, V. I. 1978. *Sotsial'naya struktura sel'skogo naseleniya SSSR na etape razvitogo sotsializma.* Moscow: Nauka.

Tepicht, J. 1973. *Marxisme et Agriculture: le Paysan Polonais.* Colin, Paris: Armand.

Terent'yeva, L. N. 1984. "The Latvian Peasant Family." In *Kinship and Marriage in the Soviet Union: Field Studies*, edited by Tamara Dragadze, pp. 130–168. London: Routledge and Kegan Paul.

TsSu SSSR. 1975. *Narodnoye Khozyaistro SSSR v 1974 godu: Statisticheskii Yezhegodnik.* Moscow: Statistika.

———. 1985. *Narodnoye Khozyaistro SSSR v 1984 godu: Statisticheskii Yezhegodnik.* Moscow: Statistika.

Wädekin, K. E. 1975. "Income Distribution in Soviet Agriculture." *Soviet Studies* 27 (1): 3–26.

Zaslavskaya, T. I. and L. V. Korel. 1984. "Rural-Urban Migration in the USSR: Problems and Prospects." *Sociologia Ruralis* 24 (2):229–41.

Zoriktuyev, B. R. 1982. *Sovremennyi byt buryatskogo sela.* Novosibirsk: Nauka.

4

Women, Work and Family in the Soviet Union

Michael Paul Sacks

In all societies there are differences between the work women and men tend to do. This division of labor reflects and is often used to legitimate beliefs about the basic characteristics associated with gender. Yet, as Margaret Mead's (1935) classic study and abundant subsequent research by others have shown, male and female behavior varies considerably from one society to the next. What males or females are capable of doing must clearly not be judged solely by gender differences prevalent in any single society.

In the United States widely accepted views of the behavior deemed appropriate or even possible for men and women are changing as a consequence of the women's movement and the changes in women's work force participation. Early in the twentieth century a relatively small proportion of women worked for wages (about 20 percent), and they did so almost exclusively at a young age before marriage and childbearing. Today, with more than half of all married women bringing home a paycheck, the presence of even very young children does not prevent women from combining employment with domestic responsibilities: more than one-third of women with children under age three are working (Oppenheimer 1970, 3–8; Hayghe 1978, 53).

There are important differences in the pattern of twentieth-century change for women in the United States and those in the Soviet Union, where except in urban areas during the 1920s and early 1930s, the working-age woman engaged solely in housework was a rarity. Today nine out of ten women, aged twenty to forty-nine, are employed — a figure higher than any other industrialized nation (Sacks 1977b, 199). In the United States 30 percent of women workers are employed part time, whereas this is true of only 0.5 percent of Soviet women (Moskoff 1984, 30).

This chapter examines the factors that contributed to the very high rates of female work in the Soviet Union and how this work has been influenced by the woman's role within the family. The chapter concludes with a look at some of the variation in female and male employment between regions and ethnic groups. To stress the broader significance of studying the Soviet case, however, it is important first to review key theoretical questions.

Theoretical Perspectives

William J. Goode (1963) contends industrialization is associated with a change toward egalitarian values and fosters female employment outside the home. The importance of gender declines as employers come increasingly to evaluate job applicants on the basis of their ability to perform work tasks. Goode argues that egalitarianism is also manifested in the family. Rights and responsibilities previously allocated according to sex and age increasingly become based on "the uniqueness of each individual . . . the 'human' qualities of warmth, emotionality, character and so on" (1963, 21).

Marxist writings also stress the close association between female employment and progress toward sexual equality. The change in the work activity of women, however, is the critical factor, and the diffusion of altered values is viewed as a result rather than a cause of employment. In *The Development of Capitalism in Russia*, Lenin (1964, 545–46) states that large-scale industry draws women into the work force and out of the stifling isolation of their patriarchal households. It "stimulates their development and increases their independence" despite the harsh work conditions that prevail under capitalism.

A third position, one this author argues is best supported by evidence pertaining to Soviet women, is that of Louise A. Tilly and Joan W. Scott (1975, 1978). They contend that historical developments in England and France refute both Goode and the Marxists. The early employment of women neither resulted immediately in women's liberation nor derived from what Goode called the "gradual, logical, philosophical extension to women of originally Protestant notions about the rights and responsibilities of the individual" (Goode 1963, 56). To the contrary, women's early employment in factories involved work that was directly related to their traditional domestic activities and was at least initially marked by continuity in women's status. Women's work was "less the product of new ideas than of the effects of old ideas operating in new or changing contexts" (Tilly and Scott 1975, 42).

The survival of the household depended on economic contributions from every member, and the demand for female labor in industry made it possible for women to fulfill traditional obligations in a novel work setting. This was merely an extension of the common pattern in which mothers combined bearing and raising children with production for family consumption or for exchange, while both daughters and sons made an economic contribution from a very early age and, depending on the family's needs, would later either work at home or "be sent off to seek jobs as servants and apprentices" (Tilly and Scott 1978, 34). The fact that the immediate impact of new employment opportunities associated with economic development may not liberate women and may even worsen their status is supported by a wide range of research on women in currently underdeveloped nations (Bossen 1984, Fernandez-Kelly 1983, Boserup 1970; Stacey 1983).

Tilly and Scott (1978, 230–31) concede that values did change, but only gradually, and this change appears to be associated with developments that reduced women's productive activities. By separating the household from the place of work, industrialization increased the difficulty of combining motherhood and wage labor. Married women's employment declined further as a consequence of a sex-based division of labor, which limited the types of work available to women; the rise in male wages, which reduced the necessity for women to work; and the "new emphasis on the needs of children" (Tilly and Scott 1978, 231), which increased women's domestic responsibilities.

To an important extent, the distinct employment pattern of Soviet women can be explained by difference in the timing and presence of these factors. The values that emerged, however, appear to be surprisingly similar to those of other industrialized nations. Tracing the change in the supply of and demand for female labor in the nonagrarian sector reveals the unique aspects of Soviet development.

The Case of the Russian Republic

Comprising three-quarters of the territory and more than half the population of the USSR, the Russian Republic is by far the largest of the fifteen republics and contains the most important centers of political and economic activity (see the chapter by Clem in this volume). This present chapter focuses initially on this area, for it is here that one would expect the most direct impact of the Communist ideology, the drive for industrialization, and the devastation and rapid recovery from World War II. (In some cases, however, the absence of data for the Russian Republic has necessitated substituting figures for the USSR as a whole. This does not appreciably distort the general picture.)

Employment in Tsarist Russia

The overwhelmingly peasant society of nineteenth- and early-twentieth-century Russia had a strong tradition of both female subordination and arduous labor for women.

> The most desirable wife was one who even as a girl demonstrated her capacity for work. Work, paid and unpaid, was the focal point of existence for peasant women as well as men. The specific niche occupied by peasant women, assigned them by tradition and modified by the exigencies of an industrializing economy, thus provided them with a legacy of expectations quite favorable to the move from farm to factory. To work hard, to contribute to their own survival and that of their families, was in no way a transformation of their destiny. (Glickman 1984, 57)

Women had worked in tsarist factories since at least the eighteenth century, though they primarily earned wages as agrarian laborers, servants, and charwomen (Kharchev 1964, 18). The 1897 census revealed that in European Russia nearly 40 percent of adult female industrial workers were married (Troinitskii 1906, Table 2, 2–6). They constituted about a fifth of all workers in industry but were heavily concentrated in textile and clothing manufacturing. Because women were less active in politics and accepted lower wages than men, it was not surprising that they were hired in growing numbers in the 1890s and became even more desirable employees after the Revolution of 1905 (Bonnell 1983; Glickman 1984). The substantial increase in the demand for women workers during World War I resulted in their representation in nearly every type of industry. By 1917 women constituted about 40 percent of factory workers (Sacks 1976, 25–26).

Thus, the Soviet era began with a well-established heritage of female employment in the nonagrarian sector. As discussed below, the rise in male wages and the restrictive sex typing of occupations – factors that reduced the proportion of women combining work and family responsibilities in Western Europe – were either lacking or very different in nature in the Soviet Union. The type of work done by Soviet women changed substantially, but the proportion of women working showed only a slight and temporary decline in the course of economic development. The prospects are that this will change little in the foreseeable future.

Female Labor: Supply and Demand

The shift of women from agriculture to employment in the urban industrial economy can best be appreciated in terms of a supply-and-demand model. This directly parallels the analysis of the U.S. labor force initially elaborated by Oppenheimer (1970), and the contrast with her findings is enlightening. The sharp rise in female employment in the United States between 1940 amd 1960 was the result of a surge in the demand for workers in the clerical and service sector, and much of this work was labeled as appropriate only for females. Unable to substitute male labor and facing a declining pool of young women (due to a lower age at marriage and a longer period of schooling), employers were forced to hire older and married women in growing numbers.

On the supply side, more women have been seeking employment. In recent decades, as a result of the rise of the divorce rate and the later age at marriage, more American women are unmarried, and these women are more likely to pursue employment. Kingsley Davis (1984) sees the high probability of divorce (today reaching more than half for first marriages in the United States) as eventually altering the work of married women as well.

> [t]he exploding divorce rate struck at the heart of the nineteenth century sex role system. If a young wife could not count on her husband's remaining married to her, she could not count on his economic support either. Divorce thus broke the central bargain of marriage by which a woman traded her services as wife and mother for the financial support of the husband. Her best hedge against the disaster of divorce was to earn her own money, by outside employment. (1984, 411)

In 1980, 56 percent of women workers were married. Another factor that contributed to married women seeking work was the decline in births since the mid-1960s (although work rates have risen most sharply among mothers). They were also encouraged by the changing attitudes of employers noted above and by the more attractive job opportunities that resulted from their increased educational attainment. Finally, economic necessity compelled married women to work. "In the 1970s, even better-off married women have been compelled to work because of inflation and recessions that have hit hardest in manufacturing industries that traditionally employ mostly men" (Waite 1981, 5–6).

The demand for labor in the Soviet Union was much more extreme and more general. Thus, it contributed to the employment of women in a much broader range of occupations. Furthermore, some of the same dire conditions that fostered this demand also produced a massive supply of women seeking work in the nonagrarian sector. Except perhaps temporarily during the Depression or World War II and among impoverished groups (Kessler-Harris 1982), factors influencing the supply of American women were never as powerful.

In 1910 the population within the territory of what is now the Russian Republic approximately equalled that of the United States, but in the next half-century the two had dramatically different patterns of mortality. By 1970 the United States contained 205 million people, compared with only 130 million in the Russian Republic. According to estimates for the USSR as a whole, the population declined by 2.8 million each year during the Revolution and the Civil War (1917–21). During the forced collectivization of agriculture (1929–35), about 5.5 million perished. Political purges and widespread famine in these decades also took a heavy toll, but even these tragedies were dwarfed by the population loss of 20 to 25 million during World War II (Dodge 1966, 20; Matthews 1972, ch. 1).

During the early 1920s the heavy migration to cities and the disruption of the economy resulted in widespread unemployment. Fears were expressed that women especially would suffer under the planned stress on heavy industry, where traditionally few females were employed. Norton Dodge (1966, 175–76) argues that during this period "agitation for an increase in the employment of women was motivated by a desire to relieve unemployment and to secure the economic independence of women rather than to mobilize unused manpower reserves" for production purposes. However, the rapid industrial growth of the late 1920s and early 1930s created a major labor shortage. Housewives in the city, unlike migrant families from rural areas, constituted a source of workers that would not further aggravate the problems of providing food and housing. Thus, it is surely the fit between the ideology relating women's work to their liberation and the needs of the economy that fostered even greater efforts to provide occupational opportunities for women.

Between 1932 and 1937 industry expanded by more than 4 million workers; 82 percent were women. In the decades that followed, the priority placed on rapid economic development, plus the population decimation of World War II, assured that the demand for female labor would never again slacken. Moreover, the use of female labor would itself fuel industrial growth, for it made possible the heavy allocation of production to investment rather than consumption. Not only were there more workers per urban family, but employed women also served their nation doubly by providing household services that, if supplied by the market, might have diverted considerable investment from other sectors of the economy (compare Ofer 1973, ch. 9).

The heavy investment in education greatly benefitted women and assured that they would be qualified for the emerging positions in the economy. In 1897, 85 percent of the women were illiterate, compared to 56 percent of the men. By 1939 in the Russian Republic, the literacy gap between males and females in the employed population was already small: 13.5 percent of the males and 10.9 percent of the females had at least some secondary education. The latest census (1979) showed that the comparable figures were 80.6 percent for women and 80.0 percent for men, and even the percentage of employed women who completed higher education (10.2) slightly exceeded that of men (10.0) (Ts.S.U. RSFSR 1981, 15). The increased attendance at school and the expanding readership of the press also must have provided the state with improved channels for influencing women's employment.

The supply of females was most strongly influenced by the very demographic conditions that had resulted in the labor shortage, for the fatalities of war and political conflicts were much greater among males than among females. Enormous numbers of women were left to support their families. There were several decades during which countless other women lived with the prospect that such a situation could easily befall them. In the Russian Republic as early as 1926, the sex ratio (the number of males per one hundred females) was ninety-one. In 1959 this ratio was ten points lower, and in the age group of thirty-five to fifty-nine there were only six men to every ten women (Ts.S.U. 1930, Table 1, 3; 1972a, 5).

But even if a male wage earner were present in the household, economic necessity required women to work outside the home. A husband's salary was simply insufficient to support a family, and this remains the norm today. When questioned about their motives for working, Soviet women are quick to note their financial need (Mikhailyuk 1979, 4; Kharchev and Golod 1969, 448; Slesarev and Yankova 1969, 421).

With a pace of urbanization that "has probably been the most rapid in the history of mankind" (Lewis and Rowland 1979, 158), females increasingly had to pursue wage labor outside of agriculture. The forced collectivization launched in 1928–29 provoked substantial out-migration from rural areas; the perception of growing employment opportunities in cities was a persisting attraction. Between 1926 and 1939 the urban population of the Russian Republic more than doubled, and it nearly doubled again by 1959. The proportion of the population that was urbanized burgeoned from 18 to 52 percent in just over three decades. In 1985 nearly three-quarters of the population lived in an urban area (Ts.S.U. 1963, 11; Ts.S.U. SSSR 1985, 14). Furthermore, the urban population became more concentrated in large cities, where work in agriculture was surely very limited. Thus, in the Russian Republic the number of workers in agriculture (excluding those engaged in work on private plots of land) dropped from 46 million in 1926 to 20 million in 1939 and to only 14 million by 1959 (Ts.S.U. 1963; 39, 280, 290; 1972, 77).

Child care and domestic responsibilities make employment especially difficult for women unless other family members are available to share these chores or unless they can be reduced through a network of service institutions. In 1919, Lenin wrote:

> Notwithstanding all the liberating laws that have been passed, woman continues to be a *domestic slave*, because *petty housework* crushes, strangles, stultifies and degrades her, chains her to the kitchen and to the nursery, wastes her labor on barbarously unproductive, petty, nerve-racking, stultifying and crushing

> drudgery. The *real emancipation of women* ... will begin only when ... this
> petty domestic economy ... is transformed on a mass scale into large-scale
> socialist economy. (The Woman Question 1951, 6; emphasis in the original)

Except perhaps, since about the mid-1960s, it is clear that such change did
not occur. The increase in the supply of women seeking nonagrarian
employment cannot be attributed to a decline in housework. Severely
overcrowded urban apartments have lacked hot water, and as late as 1956
only one-third had any form of plumbing. Modern appliances have been in
short supply and of poor quality. There are endless complaints about
cafeterias and the whole range of service institutions. In 1970 it was reported
that laundries had handled only 3 percent of the nation's requirements and
that the combination of all the service institutions reduced the time spent on
housework by a mere 5 percent. Child-care facilities have not met the
demand; in 1960 only 13 percent of children aged one through six could be
accommodated in preschool institutions (Sacks 1976, 43–53).

Soviet men, like their counterparts the world over, devote little time to
housework. A comparison of studies of time use from the 1920s and the
1960s shows no change in this highly unequal division of domestic labor
(Sacks 1977a). Furthermore, although there is evidence that the extended
family has been uncommon among workers during the entire Soviet period, it
is clear that in recent decades married women have received very little help
from their mothers. Young couples prefer to live apart from their parents, and
this is probably also the preference of most parents (Sacks 1976, 41;
Shlapentokh 1984, 193–95).

The number of children that women bear has declined, but this has been
accompanied by a sharp reduction in infant deaths. Until relatively recently,
the consequence has been an insubstantial change in the number of children
who survived in each family (Mazur 1967). But with childbearing concentrated over a much briefer period, the presence of a child old enough to care
for young siblings has been much less likely. Furthermore, the urban nuclear
family is relatively isolated, making it difficult to share child care with other
women or to combine such tasks with productive labor, as mothers might do
in a rural setting (although child-care facilities are much less adequate in the
countryside as compared with urban areas; Gordon, Solov'ev, and Breev
1985).

In sum, women have had to combine arduous family responsibilities
with nonagrarian employment. There was a change in the type of work
women did, not in the fact that they were engaged in productive labor. Using
women in industry and even substituting them for men in a wide variety of
occupations when there was a labor shortage was not a cultural innovation of
the Soviet era. It was, therefore, predictable that with the difficult financial

conditions – a product of low male income levels and broken or vulnerable households – plus the acute demand for all types of workers, women would respond by seeking to take advantage of expanding occupational opportunities. The national investment in education enhanced their employment prospects and facilitated the spread of an ideology supportive of women working outside the family. Work was portrayed not only as a means of contributing to national strength, but also as a source of personal development and even as a prerequisite for a woman to be an appropriate role model for her children (Danilova 1968, 38–40). A Soviet commentator remarked, "In families in which women do not work, the youngsters are inculcated with a scornful attitude toward women and their work" (Labzin 1965, 102).

This work ideology fit well not only with women's traditional obligations to contribute to the household, but also with the new demands on the family and the leadership's goal of rapid economic development. As such, the ideology has come to be widely accepted. However, it is not possible to determine the extent to which adherence to such beliefs influenced women to seek employment independent of the other factors compelling them to alter their behavior.

The 1926 census shows that among those aged sixteen to fifty-four, nearly 90 percent of women were working, but in cities this fell off to only 40 percent (Gruzdeva 1978). Work rates of these urban women appear to have risen steadily with the onset of the First Five Year Plan in 1928 (Dodge 1966, 33). Subsequently, the only decline in employment occurred among those aged fourteen to nineteen – a result of increased school attendance – and among women in their fifties due to retirement.

The birth rate dropped quite steadily during the Soviet period, with no appreciable baby boom following World War II. This meant that the surge of labor force entrants in the 1960s and early 1970s seen in the United States and Western Europe was absent in the USSR. Consequently, there were increased efforts to recruit the remaining pool of young women, who were engaged solely in homemaking and tending private gardens, and to raise the work rates of older women. Qualification for increased pensions provided the incentive for older women to return to work. Since this reserve of labor consisted of many women with low education and limited work skills who would receive low wages, the rise in the minimum wage also proved an effective incentive. Day-care centers expanded and could accommodate a fifth of all preschoolers by 1965 and nearly a third by the early 1970s (Sacks 1976, 43). The number of children in the centers has continued to grow from 11.5 million in 1975 to 15.8 million in 1984 (Ts.S.U. SSSR 1985, 463). It was reported that in 1979, in a typical large city of the Russian Republic, child-care facilities were sufficient to accommodate all but about one-fifth of children aged one to eight (Gordon, Solov'ev, and Breev 1985, 40).

A full two-thirds of the women recruited to the Soviet work force between 1961 and 1970 were formerly housewives or engaged only in private agriculture. Work rates reached such a high level that future entrants could come only from among the youth (Litvyakov 1969, 106–07, 192–93). In the 1970s such conditions promoted experiments with part-time work and even cottage industry in an effort to maintain the high work-force participation of women and also to increase the birth rate. However, this type of work has remained very limited (Feshbach and Rapawy 1973, 494; Radko 1979; Moskoff 1984, 26–33). Small birth cohorts in the past assure little slackening in the demand for female labor.

The Consequences of Nonagrarian Employment

Just before World War II, nearly two-thirds of the female workers in the Russian Republic were engaged in agriculture (including the private sector). By 1959 this had fallen to 40 percent, and by 1970 it was only 17 percent (Ts.S.U. 1963, 156, 286; 1973a, 165; 1973b, 171). How did the combination of high labor-force participation rates and a rapid shift out of agriculture influence the relative status of men and women, both at work and in the family?

The double burden of the working woman has already been mentioned: full-time employment is combined with many hours of housework and child care, and this appears unaltered over the Soviet era. (Such continuity in the face of technological advancement is consistent with an extensive cross-national study conducted in 1965 [Robinson, Converse, and Szalai 1973] and time–budget data for the United States during the period from the 1930s to the 1960s [Vanek 1973]). A working woman's career is deeply affected by the heavy demands of her domestic obligations. She has less time to devote to study and other activities that could promote her occupational advancement. Indeed, her total work burden adversely affects the general quality of her life · by reducing recreation and even sleep, relative to a man. In urban areas a Soviet man has about as much free time as a woman has housework (Sacks 1977a). A Soviet woman laments, "modern life has narrowed the domestic concerns of the male urbanite to a minimum, while the duties of a wife and mother remain the same – endless" (quoted in Novikova 1984, 5). A man benefits directly from this domestic division of labor.

> By freeing males from the performance of routine household maintenance and child care, which would otherwise divert time and energy from educational and professional activities, Soviet women in effect advance the professional mobility of males at the sacrifice of their own. (Lapidus 1978, 278)

A second indicator of sexual inequality is the disparity of the paychecks of men and women. This disparity results in part from the fact that women are concentrated in sectors of the labor force in which wages are low. But in a sophisticated secondary analysis of Soviet data from the capital city of the Armenian Republic, Michael Swafford (1978) concludes that even if there were no differences between men and women in their educational backgrounds, their levels of skill, and the industries in which they were employed, women would still earn only about 72 percent as much as men. Although there are problems with this analysis and with generalizing the results to the USSR as a whole, the finding is consistent with a number of studies indicating that female earnings are between two-thirds and three-quarters those of men (Chapman 1977; Lapidus 1978, 192–94; McAuley 1981, ch. 2). Again, the finding is hardly unique to the USSR: in the United States in 1984, women working full time year-round earned 62 percent as much as their male counterparts. "A woman with four years of college still earns less than a male high school dropout" (Hewlett 1986, 72; see also Suter and Miller 1973).

Differences in earnings reflect the vertical structure of occupations: the higher the prestige and authority of the position, the smaller the percentage of women among the personnel. This structure appears to be true in virtually every field. Textile manufacturing is a particularly vivid example, for it is an industry long dominated by women. In the Russian Republic in 1959, women constituted 85 percent of textile workers, but they accounted for a mere 15 percent of the assistant foremen. Although the category was omitted from the 1970 census publications, we can assume that time alone did not alter this inequity.

Female underrepresentation is particularly blatant in the professional occupations, for which there is greater detail in the published census categories (Sacks 1981). Women constitute 90 percent of persons in the field of medicine; this falls to about 60 percent of chief doctors and heads of hospitals. Although women predominate in education, they account for only a quarter of the directors of secondary schools. Fewer than one in ten enterprise directors are female (Dodge 1977). At the upper levels of state and party, women are even more scarce (Moses 1978, 15; Lapidus 1978, ch. 6).

The bottom of the status hierarchy also reveals important sex differences. A study of machine–construction workers, aged twenty-five to twenty-nine, showed that the least skilled work categories contained 70 percent of the women, as compared with only 17 percent of the men (Kotlyar and Turchaninova 1975, 73; see also Steshenko 1984, 82–84). Other evidence reveals that in many industries women constitute the great majority of workers performing tedious and physically demanding unmechanized tasks (Mikhailyuk 1970, 66), and that a woman spends three times as long as a man in the lowest job categories before she receives a promotion (Shteiner and Karpukhin 1978, 8). In the Soviet census the number of women among manual workers lacking any specialized skill (*raznorabochie*) is conspicuously omitted (Sacks 1981).

It is possible to summarize the overall extent to which women are under- and overrepresented in a series of occupations by using a commonly applied measure of segregation. This measure can be interpreted as the proportion of men or women who would have to change occupations in order for women to have the same representation in all occupations. It is similar to measures of racial segregation that show the proportion of pupils who would have to be bussed to integrate a school system. (Because we are interested in comparisons over time and between regions, a standardized measure is used. This controls for variation in the structure of the total labor force. The procedure entails assuming simply that there is the same number of workers in each of the nearly one hundred nonagrarian occupational categories for which appropriate data were available in the Soviet census [Sacks 1976, 79–87]. Unfortunately, because of differing occupational classifications, the measure cannot be used to compare the Soviet Union with other nations.)

The finding for the Russian Republic over the period for which we have comparable data – 1939 through 1970 – is quite surprising. Despite the societal disruption engendered by World War II, the pace of industrialization, and women's gains in educational achievement, there was no change in the overall extent to which occupations were either male- or female-dominated. Neither the extreme demand for women nor their increasing skills had altered the sex labeling of occupations. Thus, for example, females continued to predominate among food, garment, postal, textile, and public dining workers, as well as among doctors, typists, telephone operators, secretaries, and teachers. Males remained well over the majority of those in the field of law, among composers, painters, radio-telegraphers, plumbers, wood-workers, and of those in transportation, machine construction, and metal-lurgy. The many small changes in female representation tended to cancel each other out.

Comparable research on the work force of the United States using a different and much more detailed occupational classification shows that although change was slow and even absent in some decades of the twentieth century, World War II appears definitely to have reduced occupational sex differences (Williams 1976). Sex segregation probably declined at a moderate rate in the 1970s, but the level remains quite high (Bianchi and Rytina 1986).

The meaning of this trend in overall sex differences must be interpreted with caution. Although different has often meant unequal, this is not always the case. The greater access of Soviet women to professional employment is an important example. Census data show that while the percentage of females in the total work force of the Russian Republic rose by five points (from 49 to 54) between 1939 and 1959, the percentage point increase among professional and semiprofessional personnel was four times as great (from 34 to 54). The number of women in these occupations grew by more than 3.5 million, while the number of men actually declined by 300,000. Women's rapidly rising educational attainment – a significant achievement in itself – was fundamentally important in opening opportunities to them. Between 1959 and 1970, despite the more balanced sex ratio, women continued to enter professional and semiprofessional occupations in disproportionate numbers: They constituted nearly three-quarters of the additional personnel (Sacks 1976). In 1970 women constituted a larger proportion of those in the semiprofessional categories, yet they still were more than half of all professionals (Dodge 1977, 208).

Although the number of women is relatively low in the higher professional ranks, they remain much better represented than their counterparts in Western Europe or the United States. Consider, for example, the fact that in the Russian Republic women account for about 40 percent of the engineers, more than 25 percent of both the judges and the neurosurgeons, more than 50 percent of the specialists working in research institutes, 45 percent of the teachers in schools of higher education, 43 percent of the principals of secondary schools, and 86 percent of all economists and planners (Ts.S.U. 1973b, 170–74; Dodge 1977; Ts.S.U. RSFSR 1981, 333).

The segregation of women from men in the work sphere may be positive for women if it results in interaction and broader awareness that, in turn, may promote women's organization and greater political effectiveness. Particularly relevant here are observations of Colette Shulman, based on her discussion with Russian women:

> If I had to select the one satisfaction most widely felt by the working woman at all levels of society, I would say that it is the work-collective as a source of community and communication and of mutual support in coping with daily problems of life. And here I mean not the official formal collectives, but the intangible organic ones that women themselves create, with their own leaders and norms of conduct and laws of friendship. (1977, 376)

The segregation of the young and highly educated professional women may have especially constructive ramifications. Women's isolation within the confines of the family appears to have been a significant obstacle to the recognition of common grievances and perception of their problems as rooted in the structure and priorities of the broader society.

There is also significant sex segregation within the educational system. In the Russian Republic women constitute about nine of every ten students in specialized secondary education programs in the fields of health, of economics and law, and of education, art and cinematography, and about two-thirds of the college-level students in these areas (Ts.S.U. RSFSR 1981, 351). Thus, associations and perspectives nurtured at work may build on the school experience of female professional and semiprofessional personnel.

Women have been able to lobby for the elimination of health and safety hazards through a special commission on women established in 1969. Women's councils have also proliferated as a part of the local Party committees in factories and on farms (Moses 1978, 21–22). Browning (1985) pursuasively argues, however, that women's councils lack autonomy from the Communist party. She sees them serving primarily to reinforce traditional images of women and being "unable to challenge the neglect of women in power politics" (233). From this perspective, male dominance of the power structure is the key problem: "So long as the majority of the top Soviet leaders are male, it seems that the woman question will remain subordinate to economic, demographic and patriarchal imperatives" (Buckley 1985, 50).

Women are nearly absent from the pinnacle of political power (only one woman has ever been a member of Politburo, and the percentage of females on the Central Committee peaked at 4.2). However, Jerry Hough (1977, 141–48) argues that women are afforded significant input as a result of their substantial representation at lower levels and their predominance among "professionals normally involved in policy advocacy and analysis as part of their vocation." To the extent that occupational segregation promotes awareness of their mutual interests, it may act to enhance the importance of these channels of influence for women.

Finally, the movement of women out of agriculture itself indicates improvement in their status. This peasant proverb is cited as a symbol of women's position within nineteenth-century rural Russia: "A hen is not a bird, a woman is not a person" (Glickman 1984, 29). Unquestionably, there has been change during the Soviet era. Collectivization gave peasant women greater control over their own earnings and thereby may have contributed to their allegiance to the Soviet state (Dodge 1966, 65–66). However, women's opportunities for advancement in agriculture remain exceedingly narrow; significant upward mobility necessitates migration to the cities. Remaining behind is clearly more costly to women than to men. Most females are engaged in difficult manual labor with very low remuneration and long hours (though significant mechanization of work with livestock must be bringing some improvement [Steshenko 1984, 82–83]). Tractor operators are almost exclusively male. Housework is more arduous because services and household amenities are fewer than in urban areas. It is, thus, a positive sign that whereas men initially were more readily able to take advantage of urban opportunities, in recent decades in the Russian Republic women have ceased to be overrepresented among agricultural workers (excluding private agriculture) (Sacks 1976, ch. 6).

Change and Continuity in Beliefs about Women

Has the change in women's work roles been associated with the diffusion of an egalitarian ideology? Is there now less emphasis on sex differences as women have come to prove themselves capable of succeeding in such diverse work spheres?

In their study of Western Europe, Tilly and Scott argue that the growing middle class was associated both with a change in values and with a decline in married women's work. Rising prosperity – largely a product of high male income and reduced job instability – altered relations between both parents and children and men and women; it fostered an ideology supportive of women's confinement to the domestic sphere.

> Goode assumes that the idea of "woman's proper place" with its connotations of complete dependency and idealized femininity is a traditional value. In fact, it is a rather recently accepted middle-class value not at all inconsistent with notions of "rights and responsibilities of the individual." The division of labor within the family which assigned the husband the role of breadwinner and the wife the role of domestic manager and moral guardian emerged clearly only in the nineteenth century and was associated with the growth of the middle class and the diffusion of its value. (Tilly and Scott 1975, 41)

Unlike Western Europe, in the Russian Republic married women's employment outside the home did not decline. However, other conditions may have been conducive to the diffusion of similar values. Recent years have seen a rise in the standard of living; the deficit of males has been reduced, allowing for more normal nuclear family relations; and the population is far more concentrated in urban areas and has achieved substantial educational attainment. Although couples are having fewer children, the sharp decline in infant mortality, especially in the post–World War II period, has assured the survival of nearly all children to adulthood. The investment of love, attention, and material resources in children is further enhanced by the opportunities for social advancement via the educational system and job market. This, again, increases the possible rewards for such investment, as parents' aspirations for their children rise in response to such opportunities (Tilly and Scott 1978, ch. 8). The Soviet state's emphasis on the critical importance of caring for children has also had a positive impact on parents' sense of responsibility (Bronfenbrenner 1970; Liegle 1975). Finally, the population has had increasing exposure to the values of Western societies regarding women and children.

Vera Dunham (1976) has analyzed the themes in the fiction of the Stalinist period as an indicator of the changing values and role models the regime chose to extol. She convincingly demonstrates that the censors permitted stories to be published in which bourgeois ideals were viewed favorably. The state, Dunham concludes, gave legitimacy to these ideals in a deliberate attempt to broaden political support, especially in the critical years following World War II. Such support was deemed essential not only because of widespread popular discontent, but also because of the necessity to elicit further sacrifice to recover from the vast destruction. Coercion alone was inadequate; the demands could be met only by the "search for new and reliable allies in the population."

> The Soviet political leadership had chosen and nurtured certain allies in the past. It had relied in those earlier days on the workers. It had appealed too to the intelligentsia, but this time it looked for a new force, sturdy and pliable. And it was the middle class which offered itself as the best possible partner in the rebuilding of the country. The middle class had the great advantage of being "our own people": Totally Stalinist, born out of Stalin's push for the industrialization, reeducation, and bureaucratization of the country, flesh of the flesh of Stalin's revolution from above in the thirties, and ready to fill the vacuum created by Stalin's Great Purge and by the liquidation of the Leninist generation of activists. (Dunham 1976, 13)

Although it was unacceptable to advocate that women devote themselves solely to household tasks, the stories show that they still had primary responsibilities for creating "domestic bliss." The ideal wife would "comfort her shellshocked husband and ... support his aspirations." To demand equality at work and at home would surely have been viewed as a selfish act in the fiction of the period.

Rosenthal (1979) presents an intriguing alternative perspective. She argues that what is occurring in the USSR is quite different from the West. The traditional view of women as "sacrificers" for the sake of husband and children took an extreme form with the efforts to revolutionize Soviet society. "The injunction to sacrifice one's own needs for the good of society, built into socialism, renders women particularly vulnerable." To make matters worse, Rosenthal further argues, in contrast with nearly everywhere else in Europe, Russia "lacked any tradition of courtly love. Women of all classes placed their own needs last" (76).

Sexist values are widely evident. Letters to the press illustrate how extreme these values may be among men: "Free a woman from the kitchen and you give her freedom to be a silly hen. Who needs such a woman? A woman is supposed to adorn the family hearth, just as flowers adorn the meadows" (quoted in Kuznetsova 1967, 7). There are many professionals who stress women's natural propensity for raising children and the importance of making changes in employment to allow women to devote more time to this. A 1979 survey of a large city in the Russian Republic showed that the majority of parents felt that it was best for children under age three to be raised at home (Gordon, Solov'ev, and Breev 1985, 45). Legislation in 1981 appears to be a significant move in this direction: it increased the time women can take off from work to bear and care for their children and bolstered the economic incentive to have children. Recommendations were made to increase the amount of part-time work available for women as a way of easing the fulfillment of domestic responsibilities. The basic premise is that "work in the home is a female preserve" (Buckley 1985, 46–49).

There is evidence of a sharp clash between men and women over these issues. Shlapentokh (1984, 202) contends that "the major cause of the bellicosity of Soviet females lies in the deep contradiction between their occupational and social status on the one hand, and the necessity for them to carry on their old roles in the family, on the other." There are many female adherents to the "feminist" population policy position that opposes measures designed to encourage childbearing in a way that they see as directly competing with women's occupational advancement (Yanowitch 1977, 179–80). In recent years there has been increasing discussion of the importance of altering the early socialization of males and pressuring adult men to ensure that they assume a more equal share of housework (see, for example, Yankova 1975, 48–49).

Soviet researchers see the sharply rising divorce rate as due in large part to conflict regarding domestic roles (Matskovsky 1985, 5). In response to a letter by a man who decries the loss of male authority in the home, a Soviet woman asks:

> Do women really ask so much of men? Warmth, participation, compassion. The ability to be large-minded, to avoid nitpicking. To be magnanimous. But apparently this too is burdensome to the man. After marrying he thinks he has accomplished the greatest feat of his life, and he has no desire to expend any more energy. He would prefer to sit idle, but the woman presses him, and the cornered husband remembers that attack is the best means of defence. (Mamaladze 1985, 5)

However, these attitudes are not necessarily incompatible with the acceptance of inherent gender differences. Drawing on his conversations with leading women intellectuals in the Soviet Union, Jerry Hough observes:

> Several spoke of lower rates of political participation as the result of a natural and not particularly worrisome division of labor: both men and women have regular

jobs, and the man combines his with political activities (really duties) and the woman hers with household responsibilities.

Few Soviet women with whom I have spoken would have any quarrel with the female vice-president of the Academy of Pedagogical Sciences and a member of the Presidium of the Committee of Soviet Women who asserted in a published interview that "woman by her biological essence is a mother – a teacher trainer (*vospitatel'nitsa*)" and that she has "an inborn ability to deal with small children, an instinctive pedagogical approach." (1977, 150–51)

Without longitudinal data on public opinion, it is impossible to ascertain either the class origin or the time at which these views on sex differences emerged and spread. Even though Tilly and Scott's argument is plausible, it is also possible that contemporary values are a direct extension of traditional perspectives. In any case, the transformation of women's work roles outside the family is clearly compatible with views that stress the distinctions between males and females. To the extent that this bolstered the unequal division of labor in the home and attitudes that women are less capable in leadership positions, such distinctions have detracted from women's attainment of status and opportunity equal to that of men.

Occupational Sex Differences in Soviet Central Asia

The focus of this chapter so far has been on the situation of women in the Russian Republic. It is also important to recognize the significantly different conditions in other regions and how they have influenced female status. This section focuses particularly on Central Asian Republics.

Although there is considerable controversy over the exact ranking of socioeconomic development of the republics, those in Central Asia – Kirgizia, Tadzhikistan, Uzbekistan, and Turkmenistan – are all consistently placed at or bordering on the bottom (Silver 1974; Divilov 1976; Dellenbrant 1977; Wagener 1971). Russian peasant women lived in a highly patriarchal society, but the Muslim culture of the indigenous population of Central Asia restricted women's activities to an even greater extent. Massell's (1974) study of Soviet efforts to alter the subordinate status of these women before 1930 shows the fierce resistance to change. The absence of development meant that there was no class of industrial workers to foment the destruction of prerevolutionary power structure. Massell's interpretation is that there was a deliberate strategy to use women as a "surrogate proletariat" and to exacerbate sexual and generational tensions as a substitute for class struggle. The explosion of violent opposition actually resulted in an uncontrollable situation for Soviet authorities and necessitated a retreat from this direct attack on male privilege.

However, a number of characteristics of this setting actually might have been conducive to greater female entry into the male domain of the work force than occurred in the Russian Republic. The very strength of this traditional culture may have provided especially deficient guidelines for allocating male and female labor in the modern economy, which emerged rapidly and at a later stage than in the Russian Republic. World War II provided a substantial boost to this economic development. As a consequence of the Nazi invasion of June 1941, the Soviet government was compelled to relocate major enterprises and their personnel to Central Asia and other regions away from the anticipated war zone (Lewis, Rowland, and Clem 1976, 76).

Even though this sharp discontinuity with the traditional society may have enhanced the potential for innovation, there also existed a political apparatus and a communications and transportation network that probably made it much more possible to take advantage of this potential than was true in the Russian Republic in the 1920s. At this later stage the state may have had the resources necessary to direct change in the economically developing cities. But perhaps the most significant asset was that those recruited were likely to be receptive to change. As Ralph Clem discusses at length in chapter 1 in this volume, Russians predominated among the population taking advantage of opportunities in Central Asia. They had the requisite skills, education, and work discipline. Their migrant status meant they were likely to be young and relatively free of family responsibilities.

It seems likely, therefore, that as a consequence of changes associated with World War II there may have been reduced occupational sex differences in Central Asia. But one would also expect the rise in the proportion of indigenous ethnicity within the work force during the 1960s to halt such a decline in differences. The indigenous ethnic groups were likely to enter the labor force in growing numbers as a consequence of their rising level of educational attainment, the rapidly increasing numbers of young persons in the population, their greater presence in urban areas, and their increased access to the communications and transportation network. These factors promote "social mobilization": "The process in which major clusters of old social, economic and psychological commitments are eroded or broken and people become available for new patterns of socialization and behavior" (Karl Deutsch, as quoted in Dellenbrant 1977, 12).

Important here is the interrelated sex and ethnic hierarchy of mobilization: males before females and Russians before indigenous Muslim ethnic groups. The indigenous males are likely to be recruited at a time that overlaps with Russian females. It may have been only in the 1960s that large numbers of indigenous females entered the nonagrarian work force — and this, I argue, is the critical change. Compared with women of Slavic ethnicity within

Central Asia, Muslim women are at a distinct disadvantage in competing with men because of their larger family size, lower educational attainment, lesser work experience, and, possibly, their early socialization to be more submissive.

The paucity of Soviet data on the ethnic composition of the labor force makes it difficult to test the arguments sketched above. For example, there are no figures on the number of women working outside of agriculture by ethnicity. One is compelled to resort to occupational data available only for the population of the republics as a whole. The measure of occupational sex differences in the nonagrarian occupations shows that, indeed, in the Central Asian republics there was a decline between 1939 and 1959 in the extent to which females were either over- or underrepresented (Sacks 1982, ch. 5). It would appear that the years of war, rapid industrial growth, and an accompanying heavy influx of Russians reduced the measure in these republics from a level that was considerably above that of the Russian Republic to an equal or a lower level. As predicted, the occupational differences were relatively unchanged during the period between the two censuses of 1959 and 1970.

These aggregate changes may be deceptive, however. A close look at the relatively low occupational gender differences in Central Asia indicates that this is due primarily to male presence in occupations that elsewhere in the USSR are likely to show low male representation. It is not clear that there was a significant achievement for females.

Since the female nonagrarian labor force in Central Asia is so heavily dominated by Russian women, it is not surprising that the occupations of women in Central Asia are similar to those of women in the Russian Republic. But Muslim males have been drawn into the nonagrarian work force in large numbers and in sectors that are quite different from those of Russian men in Central Asia. Muslim males work particularly in the service sector of the economy. Their work appears to result in the overall lower occupational gender differences in central Asia, because they are employed in areas that elsewhere in the USSR are predominantly or exclusively female. These occupations include postal workers, food workers, sales personnel, dentists, teachers, and textile weavers. What is especially significant for the future is that these are occupations that in Central Asia have shown a growing female presence since at least 1939 and thus have increased the likelihood of male–female interaction in the job setting (this and the following related discussion are based on Sacks 1988).

In the past Muslim male workers outside of agriculture were segregated from female workers because of the severe restrictions on the work of Muslim women and because women workers of nonindigenous ethnicity worked in cities. Muslim men may have engaged in similar labor, but they did so in rural localities. In Soviet Central Asia in 1970, about 90 percent of all Russians, Ukrainians, and Belorussians lived in urban areas as compared with only about one-quarter of the indigneous ethnic groups (Sacks 1982, 58–59). Thus, the lower occupational gender differences in Central Asia may have been due to the work of men least likely to accept the idea of working side by side with women! This could occur because of the geographic segregation of male and female workers.

A number of trends are eroding this segregation. First, the Muslim population in cities is growing, and contact with Russians must be increasing. This is, in part, associated with the rising labor surplus in rural areas of Central Asia due to the mechanization of agriculture and continued population growth. Secondly, Muslim females are increasingly entering the nonagrarian work force and often work in male-dominated occupations. In many cases this may be occurring in occupations Muslim males are choosing to leave because of changes in the character of the work involved (for example, as a consequence of the elimination of handcrafts by industrial production, as in the case of textile weaving, or in teaching, as a result of the secularization of schools and entry of female students) and the fact that they no longer have the pay or prestige of the recent past. Finally, Muslim males are achieving higher levels of education and job experience outside of agriculture, which could increase the likelihood that they will aspire to jobs now dominated by Russian males (see Lubin 1984 for an opposing view on this last point).

Thus, overall decline in occupational sex differences in many republics between 1939 and 1959 may have been due not to women entering men's occupations, but to men of lower-status ethnic groups entering occupations the Russians label "women's work."

Conclusion

The Soviet case shows that some aspects of gender differences are remarkably resistant to change. Time use in the family and the pattern of over- and underrepresentation of women throughout the occupations are convincing evidence that neither the fact of women working outside the home nor the process of industrialization itself will eliminate the labels "women's work" and "men's work." The sharp disparity in the pay of males and females, the inordinate number of women among those in arduous unskilled labor, their underrepresentation at the upper end of the status hierarchy, and their having to assume most household chores even after a workday as long as that of their husbands, all point to the need for an effective Soviet women's movement. Such a movement cannot take the same form as that in the United States because of differences in permissible forms of manifesting discontent and differences in the available channels for shaping change. Future change will reveal the political significance of Soviet women's occupational segregation, of their high level of educational attainment, of their predominance in many professional occupations that afford them input into policy decisions, and of their growing activity in such groups as women's councils.

Inadequacies in socialist theory may be a significant source of the problem. Stacey (1983, 262–63) sees the goal of liberating women as undermined by the preoccupation of Marxism with class struggle and by its lack of a "conceptual framework for an analysis of a relatively autonomous sex-gender system." But as Lapidus (1978, 346) has noted, such a framework is receiving ever greater elaboration within the feminist movement of the West, and this is likely to influence events in the USSR.

Future change is likely to be rooted in the Soviet women's view that their sacrificing for collective goals is no longer legitimate or at least must be equally shared with men. Under Gorbachev there may be new opportunities for women's grievances to be expressed more effectively, for the real meaning of *glasnost'* appears to be the enhancement of channels for feedback from the society.

Finally, some form of change or accommodation in Central Asia is likely to deal with the decline in the geographic segregation of male and female labor markets and the problems this may have created for Muslim men.

References

Bianchi, Suzanne M., and Nancy Rytina. 1986. "The Decline in Occupational Sex Segregation during the 1970s: Census and CPS Comparisons." *Demography* 23 (1):79–86.

Bonnell, Victoria E. 1983. *Roots of Rebellion: Workers' Politics and Organizations in St. Petersburg and Moscow, 1900–1914.* Berkeley: University of California Press.

Boserup, Ester. 1970. *Women's Role in Economic Development.* London: Allen and Unwin.

Bossen, Laurel Harbenar. 1984. *The Redivision of Labor: Women and Economic Choice in Four Guatamalan Communities.* New York: University of the State of New York Press.

Bronfenbrenner, Urie. 1970. *Two Worlds of Childhood: U.S. and U.S.S.R.* New York: Russell Sage Foundation.

Browning, Genia. 1985. "Soviet Politics – Where Are the Women?" In *Soviet Sisterhood*, edited by Barbara Holland, pp. 207–36. Bloomington: Indiana University Press.

Buckley, Mary. 1985. "Some Interpretations of the Woman Question." In *Soviet Sisterhood*, edited by Barbara Holland, pp. 24–53. Bloomington: Indiana University Press.

Chapman, Janet G. 1977. "Equal Pay for Equal Work?" In *Women in Russia*, edited by Dorothy Atkinson, Alexander Dallin, and Gail W. Lapidus, pp. 225–39. Stanford: Stanford University Press.

Cooney, Rosemary Santana. 1975. "Female Professional Work Opportunities: A Cross-National Study." *Demography* 12:107–20.

Danilova, E. Z. 1968. *Sotsial'nye problemy truda zhenshchiny-rabotnitsy.* Moscow: Nauka.

Davis, Kingsley. 1984. "Wives and Work: The Sex Role Revolution and Its Consequences." *Population and Development Review* (10) 3:397–417.

Dellenbrant, Jan Ake. 1977. "Regional Differences in the Soviet Union: A Quantitative Inquiry into the Development of the Soviet Republics." *Bidrag til Ostatsforskningen*, vol. 5. Sweden: Research Center for Soviet and East European Studies, Uppsala University.

Divilov, S. I. 1976. *Chislennost' i struktura zanyatykh v narodnom khozyaistve: metodika perspektivnykh raschetov.* Moscow: Ekonomika.

Dodge, Norton T. 1966. *Women in the Soviet Economy.* Baltimore: Johns Hopkins University Press.

————. 1977. "Women in the Profession." In *Women in Russia*, edited by Dorothy Atkinson, Alexander Dallin, and Gail W. Lapidus, pp. 205–24. Stanford: Stanford University Press.

Dunham, Vera S. 1976. *In Stalin's Time: Middle Values in Soviet Fiction.* Cambridge, England: Cambridge University Press.

Fernandez-Kelly, Maria Patricia. 1983. *For We Are Sold, I and My People: Women and Industry in Mexico's Frontier.* Albany: State University of New York Press.

Feshbach, Murray, and Stephen Rapawy. 1973. "Labor Constraints in the Five Year Plan." In *Soviet Economic Prospects for the Seventies*, pp. 485–563. Washington, D.C.: U.S. Government Printing Office.

Glickman, Rose L. 1984. *Russian Factory Women: Work Place and Society, 1880–1914.* Berkeley: University of California Press.

Goode, William J. 1963. *World Revolution and Family Patterns.* New York: Free Press.

Gordon, L. A., Iu. P. Solov'ev, and B. D. Breev. 1985. *Netrudocposobnoe naselenie: Sotsial'no-demograficheskie aspekty.* Moscow: Nauka.

Gruzdeva, Ye. V. 1978. "Vocations and Qualifications: Statistics on Work Done by Women." *Ekonomika i organizatsia promyshlennovo proizvodstva* no. 3: 47–53, condensed in *Current Digest of the Soviet Press* 30, no. 31:9.

Hayghe, Howard. 1978. "Marital and Family Characteristics of Workers, March 1977." Special Labor Force Report no. 216. Washington, D.C.: U.S. Department of Labor, Bureau of Labor Statistics.

Hewlett, Sylvia Ann. 1986. *A Lesser Life: the Myth of Women's Liberation in America.* New York: William Morrow and Company.

Hough, Jerry F. 1977. *The Soviet Union and Social Science Theory.* Cambridge: Harvard University Press.

Kessler-Harris, Alice. 1982. *Out of Work: A History of Wage-Earning Women in the United States.* Oxford, England: Oxford University Press.

Kharchev, Anatoly G. 1964. *Brak i sem'ya v SSSR.* Moscow: Mysl'.

Kharchev, Anatoly G., and S. I. Golod. 1969. "Proizvodstvennaya rabota zhenshchin i sem'ya." In *Sotsial'nye problemy truda i proizvodstva*, edited by G. V. Osipov and Ya. Shchepan'sky, pp. 439–56. Moscow: Mysl'.

Kotlyar, A. E., and S. Ya. Turchaninova. 1975. *Zanyatost' zhenschchin v proizvodstve.* Moscow: Statistika.

Kuznetsova, Larisa. 1967. "Whose Job Is the Kitchen?" *Literaturnaya gazeta.* July 12, p. 12, translated in *Current Digest of the Soviet Press* 19, no. 33:7–8.

Labzin, A. L. 1965. "Stroitel'stvo kommunizma i ustranenie ostatkov neravenstva v polozhenii zhenshchiny." *Filosofskie nauki* no. 1:98–106.

Lapidus, W. 1978. *Women in Soviet Society: Equality, Development, and Social Change.* Berkeley: University of California Press.

Lenin, V. I. 1964. *The Development of Capitalism in Russia.* Moscow: Progress.

Lewis, Robert A., and Richard H. Rowland. 1979. *Population Redistribution in the USSR: Its Impact on Society, 1897–1977.* New York: Praeger.

Lewis, Robert A., Richard H. Rowland, and Ralph S. Clem. 1976. *Nationality and Population Change in Russia and the USSR: An Evaluation of Census Data, 1897–1970.* New York: Praeger.

Liegle, Ludwig. 1975. *The Family's Role in Soviet Education.* New York: Springer.

Litvyakov, P. P. 1969. *Demograficheskie problemy zanyatosti.* Moscow: Ekonomika.

Lubin, Nancy. 1984. *Labour and Nationality in Soviet Central Asia.* Princeton: Princeton University Press.

Mamaladze, Irma. 1985. "Polemical Notes: the Last Privilege – Once More Authoritarian Women, Unmanly Men and Children Who Are Left without Papas." *Literaturnaya Gazeta,* January 23, p. 11, translated in *Current Digest of the Soviet Press* 37 (5):4–5.

Massell, Gregory J. 1974. *The Surrogate Proletariat: Moslem Women and Revolutionary Strategies in Soviet Central Asia: 1919–1929.* Princeton: Princeton University Press.

Matskovsky, Mikhail. 1985. "The Young Family: Problems of Formation." *Molodoi Kommunist* (6): 51–57, translated in *Current Digest of the Soviet Press* 37 (5):5–6.

Matthews, Mervyn. 1972. *Class and Society in Soviet Russia.* New York: Walker.

Mazur, Peter D. 1967. "Reconstruction of Fertility Trends for the Female Population of the U.S.S.R." *Population Studies* 21, no. 1: 33–52.

McAuley, Alastaire. 1981. *Women's Work and Wages in the Soviet Union.* London: George Allen & Unwin.

Mead, Margaret. 1935. *Sex and Temperament in Three Primitive Societies.* New York: Morrow.

Mikhailyuk, V. B. 1970. *Ispol'zovanie zhenskovo truda v narodnom khozyaistve.* Moscow: Ekonomika.

Moses, Joel C. 1978. "The Politics of Female Labor in the Sovet Union." *Western Societies Program Occasional Paper* no. 10. Ithaca, N.Y.: Western Societies Program, Cornell University.

Moskoff, William. 1984. *Labour and Leisure in the Soviet Union: The Conflict between Public and Private Decision-Making in a Planned Economy.* New York: St. Martins Press.

Novikova, S. 1984. "Twofold burden. – A Specialist Comments on Mail about 'Family Affairs.' " *Pravda,* June 9, p. 3, as translated in *Current Digest of the Soviet Press* 36 (23):5, 24.

Ofer, Gur. 1973. *The Service Sector in Soviet Economic Growth: A Comparative Study.* Cambridge: Harvard University Press.

Oppenheimer, Valerie Kincade. 1970. *The Female Labor Force in the United States: Demographic and Economic Factors Governing Its Growth and Changing Composition.* Berkeley: Institute for International Studies, University of California.

Radko, N. 1979. "Mama Works at Home." *Literaturnaya gazeta,* May 16, p. 13, condensed in *Current Digest of the Soviet Press* 31(22):15.

Robinson, John P., Philip E. Converse, and Alexander Szalai. 1973. "Everyday Life in Twelve Countries." In *The Use of Time: Daily Activities of the Urban and Suburban Population in Twelve Countries,* edited by Alexander Szalai, pp. 17–86. New York: Russell Sage Foundation.

Rosenthal, Bernice Glatzer. 1979. "Women under Communism." *Society* 17 (1):73–7.

Sacks, Michael Paul. 1976. *Women's Work in Soviet Russia: Continuity in the Midst of Change.* New York: Praeger.

———. 1977a. "Unchanging Times: A Comparison of the Everyday Life of Soviet Working Men and Women between 1923 and 1966." *Journal of Marriage and the Family* 39 (Nov.): 793–805.

———. 1977b. "Women in the Industrial Labor Force." In *Women in Russia,* edited by Dorothy Atkinson, Alexander Dallin, and Gail W. Lapidus, pp. 189–204. Stanford: Stanford University Press.

———. 1981. "Missing Female Occupational Categories in the Soviet Censuses." *Slavic Review* 40 (2):251–62.

———. 1982. *Work and Equality in Soviet Society: The Division of Labor by Age, Gender, and Nationality.* New York: Praeger.

————. 1988. "Shifting Strata: Ethnicity, Gender and Work in Soviet Central Asia." In *Soviet Society and Culture: Essays in Honor of Vera S. Dunham*, edited by Richard Sheldon and Terry Thompson. Boulder, Colo.: Westview Press.

Shlapentokh, Vladimir. 1984. *Love, Marriage and Friendship in the Soviet Union: Ideals and Practices.* New York: Praeger.

Shteiner, A. B., and D. N. Karpukhin. 1978. "Women's Work and Work by Women." *Ekonomika i organizatsia promyshlennovo proizvodstva* no. 3:36–47, condensed in *Current Digest of the Soviet Press* 30(31):8–9.

Shulman, Colette. 1977. "The Individual and the Collective." In *Women in Russia*, edited by Dorothy Atkinson, Alexander Dallin, and Gail W. Lapidus, pp. 375–84. Stanford: Stanford University Press.

Silver, Brian. 1974. "Levels of Sociocultural Development among Soviet Nationalities: A Partial Test of the Equalization Hypothesis." *American Political Science Review* 68 (Dec.): 1618–37.

Slesarev, G. A., and W. A. Yankova. 1969. "Zhenshchina po promyshlennom predpriyatii i v sem'e." In *Sotsial'nye problemy truda i proizvodstva*, edited by G. V. Osipov and Ya. Shchepan'sky, pp. 416–38. Moscow: Mysl'.

Stacey, Judith. 1983. *Patriarchy and Socialist Revolution in China.* Berkeley: University of California Press.

Steshenko, V. S., ed. 1984. *Trudovaya aktivnost' zhenshchin.* Kiev: Naukova dumka.

Stinchcombe, Arthur L. 1965. "Social Structure and Organizations." In *Handbook of Organizations*, edited by James G. March, pp. 142–93. Chicago: Rand McNally.

Suter, Larry E., and Herman P. Miller. 1973. "Income Differences between Men and Career Women." *American Journal of Sociology* 78 (Jan.): 962–74.

Swafford, Michael. 1978. "Sex Differences in Soviet Earnings." *American Sociological Review* 43 (Oct.): 657–73.

Tilly, Louise A., and Joan W. Scott. 1975. "Women's Work and Family in Nineteenth Century Europe." *Comparative Studies in Society and History* 17 (Jan.):36–64.

————. 1978. *Women, Work and Family.* New York: Holt, Rinehart, and Winston.

Troinitskii, N. A., ed. 1906. *Chislennost' i sostav rabochikh v rossii na osnovanii dannykh vseobshchie perepisie Rossiiskoi Imperii 1897.* Moscow: Gosudarstvennii ministr vnutrennikh delenii.

Tsentral'noe statisticheskoe upravlenie pri sovete ministrov RSFSR (Ts.S.U. RSFSR). 1981. *Narodnoe khozyaistvo RSFSR v 1980: statisticheskii ezhegodnik.* Moscow: Statistika.

Tsentral'noe statisticheskoe upravlenie pri sovete ministrov SSSR (Ts.S.U.). 1930. *Vsesoyuznoi perepis' naseleniya 1926 goda.* Vol. 26: *Rossiiskaya Sotsialisticheskaya Federativnaya Sovetskaya Respublika, otdel 2: zanyatiya.* Moscow: Izdanie Ts.S.U. Souza SSSR.

————. 1963. *Itogi vsesoyuznoi perepisi naseleniya 1959 goda: RSFSR.* Moscow: Gosstatizdat.

————. 1972. *Itogi vsesoyuznoi perepisi naseleniya 1970 goda.* Vol. 2: *pol. vozrast i sostanyanie v brake naseleniya SSSR.* Moscow: Statistika.

————. 1972. *Itogi vsesoyuznoi perepisi naseleniya 1970 goda.* Vol. 16: *raspredelenie naseleniya SSSR po obshchestvennym gruppam.* Moscow: Statistika.

————. 1973. *Itogi vsesoyuznoi perepisi naseleniya 1970 goda.* Vol. 6: *raspredelenie naseleniya SSSR po zanyatiyam.* Moscow: Statistika.

Tsentral'noe statisticheskoe upravlenie SSSR (Ts.S.U. SSSR). 1985. *Narodnoe khozyaistvo SSSR v 1984 g.: statisticheskii ezhegodnik.* Moscow: Finansy i statistika.

Vanek, Joann. 1973. "Keeping Busy: Time Spent in Housework, United States, 1920–1970." Ph.D. dissertation, University of Michigan.

Wagener, Hans-Juergen. 1971. "Regional Output Levels in the Soviet Union." *Radio Liberty Research Paper* no. 41. New York: Radio Liberty Committee.

Waite, Linda J. 1981. "Women at Work," *Population Bulletin* 36 (3). Washington, D.C.: Population Reference Bureau.

Williams, Gregory. 1976. "Trends in Occupational Differentiation by Sex." *Sociology of Work and Occupations* 3 (Feb.):38–62.

The Woman Question: Selections from the Writings of Karl Marx, Frederick Engels, V. I. Lenin and Joseph Stalin. 1951. New York: International Publishers.

Yankova, Z. A. 1975. "Razvitie lichnosti zhenschiny v sovetskom obshchestve," *Sotsiologicheskie issledovaniya*, no. 4:42–51.

Yanowitch, Murray. 1977. *Social and Economic Inequality in the USSR: Six Studies.* New York: Sharpe.

The Universality of Demographic Processes in the USSR

Robert A. Lewis[1]

About two decades ago, I initiated a project on population change in Russia and the USSR that has continued to the present. The first and central question asked in this project was, How universal have demographic processes been in the USSR? Or stated another way, To what extent are the patterns of births, deaths, and migration consistent with those known to be common in regions of the world with very different political and economic systems? If these patterns are consistent, it is possible to apply existing general demographic and geographic theory to explain demographic processes in the USSR. This chapter reviews this issue after two decades of empirical research on the population of the USSR and makes some observations on demographic research on that country.[2]

Soviet Population Patterns and Government Policy

A growing body of research by academic demographers demonstrates the considerable universality of demographic processes in the USSR.[3] There are few demographic surprises in the USSR. The patterns of population change that have occurred are similar to those in all other developed modernized countries. The Soviet Union has largely gone through the population transition from high birth and death rates to low ones, and the less developed regions and groups in the country are the last to go through the transition. These less developed regions are, therefore, experiencing a very high rate of population growth due to a combination of high birth rates and low death rates – a situation common to less developed regions elsewhere in the world. A massive and fundamental redistribution of the Soviet population has occurred in this century, largely in response to changing economic conditions. This redistribution has involved unprecedented rates of urbanization and considerable rural depopulation. The conditions that produced this population change have largely been the conditions associated with such change in other developed countries.

Despite the authoritarian and centrally planned nature of the Soviet political system, the Soviet government has not formulated a comprehensive population policy and probably does not control demographic behavior any more than most other developed countries. In fact, a common complaint among Soviet demographers is the lack of such a policy; various party congresses in the USSR have also called for demographic policy. Population variables that are closely interrelated with the economy and society are difficult to control, because extensive social change is usually required to influence such variables as fertility, internal migration, urbanization, rural depopulation, and ethnic assimilation. In general, the Soviet government has been less successful in controlling these aspects of demographic behavior than in controlling mortality, which is not as closely related to the socioeconomic environment. For example, considerable migration occurs from labor deficit areas, and large cities continue to increase their share of the total and urban population, despite policies to the contrary. Thus, migration is not fulfilling its economic function. The overall effectiveness moreover, of the few policies directed at population control to date has not been great, although at times it is difficult to determine what would happen without a policy and to distinguish long-term and short-term effects. In short, Soviet demographic policy is neither comprehensive nor very effective, a pattern common to most countries.[4]

The research on Soviet population patterns cannot be examined in great detail in the short space of one chapter, although important aspects are considered in the chapters by Clem, Jones, Humphrey, and Sacks in this volume. Rather, the aim here is to demonstrate how this research and the fundamental tenets in the social sciences directly point to the importance of testing universal formulations with respect to demographic processes in the USSR.

Rationale for the Universal Approach

The essence of scholarly research is asking the right question. In the study of the population of the USSR – aside from the question of how does one know (epistemology) – the first and most logical question is, How universal are demographic processes in the USSR? The general tendency in the study of the USSR in the West, however, has been to treat the USSR as if it were a unique entity, although in the past two decades there has been much more concern for universals in the study of Soviet population, particularly among academic demographers. Knowledge progresses primarily by the formation and testing of theories or concepts, not primarily by the accumulation of descriptive facts or data.

Universal formulations, however, cannot completely or always explain population change in the USSR, because theory may be inadequately formulated – as it often is – and frequently data are insufficient or of dubious reliability, as they most certainly are in the USSR. Although long-term trends may be consistent with patterns common to all industrializing nations, certain aspects of population change in the USSR are clearly the immediate consequences of conditions specific to Soviet society, such as wars, famine, epidemics, and forced migrations.

A major constraint on the application of population theory in the Soviet context would be an effective government policy. Theory attempts to explain practice; policy attempts to control practice. A successful policy would control and explain practice, but the control of demographic behavior is generally very difficult. Moreover, as noted above, the Soviet government lacks a comprehensive population policy, and policies that do exist have not been successfully implemented.

Nevertheless, the most reasonable approach is first to test general demographic and geographic concepts in the USSR to determine if, or to what extent, they explain the processes under investigation, and second, where necessary, to examine conditions specific to the USSR in order to explain further these processes. As a matter of scientific policy, one should logically concede some peculiarity or uniqueness to the societal processes only in the face of compelling empirical evidence that cannot be explained by existing theory. Our chief working hypothesis is that people throughout the world tend to react the same way to socioeconomic forces that influence their demographic behavior – whether they live under "capitalism" or "communism" or anything in between.

The Advantages of Testing Universals

Explanatory Utility

There are a number of advantages of testing universals in the Soviet context. The most important one already discussed, is the utility of universals in explaining demographic processes and trends as opposed merely to describing them. As the universality of these processes is revealed, this demystifies Russia, its strange lands and strange people, its riddles wrapped up in enigmas, and so forth. It seems to highlight the fact that people are much the same the world over, especially with respect to demographic behavior.

The universal approach highlights the fact that one cannot understand demographic and other societal processes in the USSR solely by studying the USSR. If one is to understand the population growth in Soviet cities, for example, one should first understand urban processes in general. These processes are not unique in the USSR. This understanding, of course, requires much greater effort than just surveying the Soviet literature on demography; Soviet scholars tend to be conceptually weak in that their ideology denies a universality of demographic process, and thus they lack a comparative perspective. Furthermore, demographic methods are not as well developed in the USSR as in the West, probably because for a long period after the 1926 census demographic data were scant, and consequently the fields of demography and population geography waned. Moreover, scholarly standards in general are not as high in the USSR as in the West. All this is not to deny that in the past decade or so there has been a marked improvement in demographic scholarship in the USSR, and that there are a number of reputable Soviet demographers, despite the disabilities of undue secrecy and bureaucracy.

Verification

A second major advantage of testing demographic concepts in the USSR is that by testing these concepts, which have by chance been formulated in the West on an ever broader geographic and ideological basis, one can verify them further and broaden our understanding of these processes. Testing demographic formulations in the Soviet context is a form of comparative research, because the concepts being tested have largely been derived from the study of widely diverse regions, and one essentially is making comparisons of the USSR with the universal experience.

Comparative research also provides a necessary perspective for interpreting demographic developments in the USSR. For example, there is a very clear pattern of change in the causes of death as a country modernizes. Improvements in sanitation and nutrition and, of more recent significance, large-scale use of antibiotics, vaccination, and pesticides have resulted in a sharp fall in deaths due to communicable or infectious diseases (pneumonia, tuberculosis, diptheria, etc.). People become much more likely to die from degenerative diseases (heart disease, cancer, stroke, diabetes, etc.). This change is associated with an increase in the life expectancy and also with differences in the susceptibility of men and women to such diseases. Appreciating the stage of the Soviet Union in this development means that a rise in heart disease for middle-aged men in the USSR would not be a surprise that is blamed on the Soviet government. It is for the same reasons that middle-aged American men are losing weight, exercising more, reducing intake of animal fats, and quitting smoking. The comparative approach provides balance and insights to our interpretations, particularly if both temporal and spatial comparisons are made that provide historical and geographic perspectives.

Evaluation of Demographic Data

Another major advantage of the universal approach is that it facilitates the evaluation of demographic data. Movements and levels of data should be consistent with our conceptual knowledge. For example, Soviet measures indicated that in the Central Asian republic of Tadzhikistan in 1970 women on average could expect to bear two more children, as compared with slightly more than a decade earlier (Borisov 1976, 78). This increase in the statistics was not accompanied by changes in conditions that promote a rise in fertility, but rather by changes that normally reduce childbearing. These changes included increased urbanization, higher educational attainment, and a decline in early marriage. In addition, it is clear that the fertility rates for the earlier period (1958–59) were unexpectedly low, and there are reports of underregistration of births in Central Asia (Borisov, 68; Karakhanov 1970, 21, 334). This information strongly indicates that this is not a true rise in fertility, but largely the consequence of increased accuracy in birth recording. Statistical trends must make sense conceptually before they are accepted, and Soviet demographic data should be treated with considerable skepticism because of the dubious reliability of much of the demographic data. This lack of complete reliability can be expected in a statistical system that is improving with time. This is not to imply that all Soviet population data are seriously deficient, even though their quality varies over time, by region, and by variable, or that data collected in censuses are not reasonably reliable.

In the study of population, however, data skepticism is extremely important and the mark of scholarly maturity. The mindless acceptance of published data as being accurate or representative of the phenomena under investigation often results in erroneous interpretation, because virtually all population data contains errors resulting from deficiencies in collection and tabulation and inconsistencies in response to questions. These types of errors occur in censuses, even though census data are usually collected more systematically and the questions are more straighforward than most other kinds of socioeconomic data. Errors in the registration of births and deaths are even more common, because of the difficulty in defining some demographic events, regional variation in reporting facilities and the use of medical facilities, and other factors that affect reporting. Data for the USSR as a whole can be misleading due to regional variations in data quality, as well as the size and diversity of the USSR.

Because of these data problems, the questions asked should be appropriate to the accuracy of the data. Some questions can be answered with relatively bad data; others cannot. The most reasonable question to ask is not, Are the data accurate? Rather, How accurate are they and are they sufficiently representative of the subject under investigation?

There are, unfortunately, rather frequent examples in the study of Soviet population in the West, and the USSR of insufficient data skepticism, particularly with respect to recent trends in Soviet mortality. An excellent illustration of this is the widely publicized work by Feshbach, in which he asserts that infant deaths have risen sharply, a trend that "is unique in the history of developed countries" (Davis and Feshbach 1980; Feshbach 1982b). If one takes a more skeptical approach to the data and carefully examines regional figures rather than aggregated data for the USSR as a whole, the results are remarkably different and not quite as newsworthy.

There was a rise in the reported infant mortality rate (the number of deaths during the first year of life per thousand live births) from 22.9 (1970–71) to 27.9 (1973–74) or 5 points per thousand, in the USSR. But the Slavic and Baltic areas registered a rise of 2 points during this four-year period. This rise in infant deaths (0.05 percentage points per year) is very slight and consistent with a plateauing of infant mortality and a slight improvement in reporting, as has occurred in other developed countries. Although no data on infant mortality in the USSR were published for the latter half of the 1970s, data for the 1980s indicate a plateauing in the mid twenties, varying from twenty-five to twenty-seven per thousand (*Ekonomicheskaya Gazeta* 1986, 6).

To give a sense of proportion and historical perspective to the crisis, it is important to consider that an infant mortality rate of between twenty and thirty per thousand means that 97 to 98 percent of all children survive to age one, which is up from about 73 percent in 1913 for European Russia, although none of these figures is firm.

What has clearly pushed up the Soviet rate as a whole are the trends in the remainder of the USSR, where the rise was 11 points during the four-year period. The most significant area is Central Asia, precisely the region in which reporting has been a particular problem. Warren Eason (1981) has demonstrated how capriciously and irrationally the infant mortality data in these areas have moved and how unrealistically low they have been, until recently, relative to the Slavic areas. Moreover, Anderson and Silver (1986a) have made a strong argument that definitional changes have been an important factor in the rise in infant mortality in the USSR, as well as improvements in reporting.

After similar observations about the unreliability of the infant mortality data in the southern tier of the USSR, Fred Grupp and Ellen Jones (1983, 224) document the recentralization of health-care management. By the early 1970s this was manifested by national norms of medical service, a unified system of statistical record keeping and accounting within the health-care network, and computerized record keeping techniques. This improved medical record keeping resulted in a sharp rise in the number of infant deaths that were reported in the southern tier. This rise was accompanied by a series of programs to improve the care of pregnant women, to increase the number of births that were medically assisted, and to improve infant care. They also document a general improvement in infant and maternal health, including an increasing proportion of births in hospitals. Moreover, they cite a Soviet study that reports that, as late as 1969, in Uzbekistan 4.9 percent of the births and 9.3 percent of the deaths were not reported, and in one region in Uzbekistan the corresponding percentages reached 12.8 and 28.0

To repeat, trends in the data must make demographic sense. Clearly, the rise in reported infant mortality was due primarily to improved reporting and not to a real rise in mortality resulting from a deterioration in medical care or a rise in mothers' alchohol consumption or cigarette smoking. It is, however, worth noting that in the recent past infant mortality in Soviet Central Asia was remarkably high by Western standards.

Furthermore, a number of recent articles published in the United States discuss the rise in reported deaths of Soviet adults, particularly males, most of which occurred in the late 1960s and early 1970s and were related to a rise in heart disease. None of the authors, however, devoted sufficient attention to evaluating the data or displayed sufficient skepticism as to the data's accuracy.[5] By not questioning the accuracy of the data, apparently they considered the data accurate and the trends real.

Underregistration of deaths, however, is a problem the world over. For example, in the United States, which has a good system of vital reporting, the publications on mortality of the National Center for Health Statistics are replete with warnings about the quality of the U.S. mortality data, in particular, the deficiencies in the data as to cause of death, changing definitions, and rural–urban and racial differences in reporting.[6] That no such warning appears in the publications of the Central Statistical Administration of the USSR does not mean that the statistical system of the USSR is superior to that of the United States or that the data are accurate. That Soviet scholars rarely attempt to evaluate the data they work with also does not mean that the data are accurate, because criticizing the data could be construed as criticizing the government.

A survey of the studies of life expectancy in the cities of the USSR between 1958–59 and 1969–70 indicates that there was a rise in life expectancy at birth in the cities of western USSR, but a decline in the remote northeastern areas, primarily for males and in some instances for females (Bednyy 1979, 139). This is consistent with the universal tendency for improvements in reporting to be made last in remote, backward areas.

Furthermore, if one disaggregates the data and makes regional comparisons, there are numerous inconsistencies and questionable patterns and levels of mortality. For example, that the mortality rate over age seventy in Uzbekistan in 1966 was much less than half that of Sweden does not make demographic sense. As elsewhere, the cause-of-death data are probably seriously deficient, and there have been changes in definition over time (Bednyy 1979, 129). If one assumes errors to be random, however, it is difficult to account for the fact that the rise in adult mortality has been concentrated among males, and that there is a considerable differential by sex in mortality trends.

Nevertheless, definitive statements about mortality trends should not be made until the data have been subjected to more evaluation and more research, particularly comparative research, because the mortality patterns that the USSR is experiencing are similar to those that have occurred in other developed countries. The message of environmental medicine and medical geography is that mortality relates to the total environment and not just to medical care; therefore, causes are difficult to establish. But a conceptual reason for the reported increase in death rates must be established before it is accepted as a true rise and not just as an improvement in reporting. The cataloging of deficiencies in medical care does not demonstrate a deterioration in medical care, particularly when all objective indicators show an improvement in health care. Systemic factors cannot account for the large sex differential in mortality, unless it is assumed that medical care is being denied to males. Nor should the effect of alcohol consumption on health and mortality in the USSR be exaggerated, because per capita consumption is not high by European standards (Treml 1975, 297). Moreover, it has been observed that reported increases in male mortality are not consistent regionally with alcohol consumption (Anderson and Silver 1986b, 207).

It is also conceivable, if not likely, that mortality in the USSR has been much higher than reported and suspected, and that the improved data are highlighting persistent major health problems, particularly among less modernized nationalities, to which the government is currently reacting. Even if there were a rise in mortality, improvements in reporting would exaggerate that rise. Frankly, the assumption that life expectancy at birth in the year 2000 will be sixty-three years for men (accepted by the U.S. Bureau of the Census for future estimates of the Soviet population) must be based on the most dire evaluation of future conditions in the USSR (US Congress, 295).

Guarded Forecasts

Yet another advantage of testing universals is that if there is a considerable universality, one can make guarded forecasts regarding future trends based on the universal experience. For example, if we can assume that urbanization will continue apace in the USSR and we demonstrate that, as elsewhere, there is lower fertility in urban areas, we can forecast that there will be a further decline in fertility, all other factors being equal. One test of a theory, of course, is its power to predict future events. The term *guarded forecast* suggests that to predict demographic trends, one would also have to be able to predict social, economic, and political trends, which is beyond the capacity of social science theory. A "soft" probabilistic determinism is more appropriate to the social sciences than is the "hard" determinism of the physical sciences.

Methodological Approaches

Modernization

The conceptual framework that best systematizes and explains population change, and links it to social change in general, is the process of modernization. Although it is clear that not all aspects of population change can be directly attributed to modernization, this dramatic form of social change has had a profound impact on the population of any society that has modernized.[7]

Population change is one aspect of modernization, which also includes economic development, changes in social, family, and political structure, and changes in attitudes and values. Economic development, through the creation of job opportunities in nonagricultural sectors, is the major agent of population change. With modernization and economic development, dramatic changes occur among all elements of population change. A massive redistribution of the population occurs, with substantial migration from rural to urban places and from one region to another, because economic development normally takes place in a few areas and cities and ultimately results in high levels of urbanization. Mortality declines with improved agricultural technology, food distribution, and public health. Fertility declines as family size is controlled to facilitate the attainment of social and economic aspirations, or the economic utility of children decreases, as family structures realign, and as women enter the modern work force. Changes in fertility and mortality result in changing natural increase and age distribution. The elements of population change interact with the other aspects of modernization and with one another.

This, then, is a very broad outline of the conceptual framework that has received considerable confirmation the world over, although there are some important exceptions, particularly in the early stages of development, and some regional differences. However, the demographic changes associated with modernization appear to have been virtually universal, occurring in all countries that have been modernized.

Marxism

Another approach, whose adherents tend to be both ideological and dogmatic, is Marxism. Marxist thinking is based on the contention that each historical means of production has its own characteristic utilization of labor and thus its own law of population. Consequently, each historical system should be studied separately in regard to population theory. Thus, Marxists believe that, in the last analysis, national productive relations are the determining factors in demographic behavior, although they acknowledge the influence of historical, religious, moral, and legal factors in the superstructure of a society, as well as biological and environmental ones.

Soviet demographers have no problem defining the population laws of capitalism; Marx dealt with these in some detail in *Das Kapital*. They cannot, however, define with any precision the socialist law of population, which they normally characterize in broad economic terms as full employment and rational utilization of labour resources in socially useful work resulting from the planned economy. Some Soviet demographers add such factors as improvement in the condition of life and the total development of the people. That "communist" and "capitalist" population trends in developed countries are similar has caused some anxiety among Soviet demographers, but they normally maintain that these trends are the result of favorable conditions in the communist countries and unfavorable conditions in the capitalist countries. They do not acknowledge that the processes of modernization and population change are similar in these countries, independent of their political systems or ideological factors.

Suffice it to say, modernization and thus population change can occur under a variety of ideologies or political systems, and with respect to population change the results seem, on the basis of available evidence, to be very similar. Political systems are important insofar as they affect modernization and economic development. In any case, to restrict demographic generalizations a priori to historical systems without considerable verification is clearly unscientific, even though one chief claim of Marxism is that it is scientific.[8]

Uniqueness

A long-standing, antiscientific tradition in the social sciences and history maintains that societal phenomena are unique and thus not amenable to generalization, primarily because they are *culturally conditioned* and *historically determined*. Because the validity of this antiscientific tradition has been adequately refuted, it is not necessary to consider the argument in detail here (Grunbaum 1953, 766–77; Hempel 1965, 231–43; Nagel 1961, 447–502; Schaefer 1953). Uniqueness of phenomena is a conclusion that must be tested and verified, and we can extend our generalizations to the USSR, where there appear to be few demographic surprises.

However, the USSR frequently is viewed as a unique entity. Formerly, the argument for uniqueness of societal phenomena in the USSR was based on the "totalitarian" nature of Soviet society, but after this assertion was found wanting, the argument moved to one of cultural conditioning of the non-European peoples, in particular, the Turkic-Muslims. As to the contention that totalitarianism results in uniquely different demographic processes, this simply cannot be confirmed in the Soviet context, for the Soviet government has been no more effective than most other developed countries in controlling demographic behavior, and most population change has been related to the forces of modernization.

The outstanding characteristics of the past century have been modernization, economic development, social change, and the accompanying change in human behavior that has affected the lives of millions of people. The universal effect of these processes on human behavior has been widely confirmed and accepted. Indeed, it would be remarkable if there were a group of people whose culture totally shielded them from the powerful forces of modernization.

The general tendency in the West in the study of the Turkic-Muslims, however, is to treat them as if they were immune or nearly so to the forces of modernization, because of their strong adherence to the Turkic-Muslim culture. Carrère d'Encausse (1979, 249) makes this position explicit when, after acknowledging the usual effect of modernization in changing and standardizing human thought, she maintains that the "attempt to transform human thought has run into an almost impenetrable socio-cultural situation." Other researchers assume this position by repeatedly emphasizing the strength of the Turkic-Muslim culture and neglecting consideration of modernization, social change, or the general attributes of this group (for example, see Bennigsen and Broxup 1983, 124–152; Rywkin 1982). The uniqueness of the Turkic-Muslim response to modernization is assumed and not operationalized and tested. Frequently, the uniqueness approach is more a lack of a methodology than a studied position. It appears that the more obscure the group, the greater the enthusiasm for this claim.

Even if one acknowledges that the Muslim religion dominates the lives of its members to a greater degree than, say, the Christian religion, it is a jump of impressive dimensions from this position to the conclusion that the Muslim people will not migrate in response to economic inducements, as they actually have done on numerous occasions (Lewis and Rowland 1979, 417–24). Soviet attitudinal surveys and surrogate measures of social change, such as marriage age, fertility, and education, indicate that there has been considerable social and cultural change among the Turkic-Muslims (Jones and Grupp 1987).

With respect to population change, proponents of the unique approach conclude that the Turkic-Muslims of Central Asia will not migrate out of their homeland in response to conditions that would result elsewhere in migration to labor deficit areas of the USSR, largely because of their adherence to their culture, love of homeland, failure to acquire the values of the Russian ethnic group, and other idiosyncratic factors (see, for example, Feshbach 1979, 656–710; Rywkin 1979; Wimbush and Ponomareff 1979; Lubin 1984). Limited space precludes an explanation of this issue. Suffice it to say that because there has been considerable modernization in Central Asia, it is logical to extend the conceptual framework of modernization and population change to the Turkic-Muslims of Central Asia (see Lewis and Rowland 1979, 412–24; Lewis, Rowland, and Clem 1976, 354–81). Lewis and Rowland summarize this position as follows:

> Our argument is based conceptually and is essentially that, if current demographic and socioeconomic trends in Central Asia and other parts of the USSR persist, this will create a set of determining conditions that elsewhere in the world resulted in considerable out-migration; the same outcome can be expected in Central Asia, because the processes involved are largely universal and strong. The linchpin of this argument is that there will be deteriorating economic conditions in the region, but if for reasons of policy or the welfare nature of Soviet society, wages and employment are maintained in Central Asia, one reasonably cannot expect significant out-migration. (1979, 416–17)

Although the rapidly growing indigenous population of Central Asia has been to date relatively immobile, a recent Soviet study based on a survey explains this immobility in terms consistent with migration theory. In short, the population has been reacting to economic inducements. The study indicates that the living standard of rural residents and those in urban-type settlements was higher than that of the urban population, except for residents of republic capitals, because of income from auxiliary farming operations. Because of the widespread employment of children on the farm, the larger the family, the greater was the income (Zyuzkin 1983, 2). With respect to factors affecting interregional migration, the study concludes:

If all the basic factors determining a family's financial situation are taken into consideration, the aggregate average earnings of workers and office employees in Uzbekistan would, according to our study, be 34.4% higher than the earnings of those in Western Siberia; the average collective farm family's income in Uzbekistan is higher than it is in several other regions and is roughly equal to that of a collective farmer's family in Western Siberia. (Zyuzkin 1983, 4)

This, of course, explains the lack of out-migration. The general thrust of this study was that the dominant factors affecting demographic behavior in Central Asia were economic and not particularly cultural. Clearly, there is no reason to assume that the Turkic-Muslims of Central Asia are immune to the forces of modernization, or that these indigenous ethnic groups need to acquire a new value system before they will migrate.

The Danger of Demographic Determinism

Even though the previous sections have stressed the contribution of a conceptual knowledge of demography to understanding the USSR, this knowledge can also provide an appreciation of the problems and distortions that may arise from explaining aspects of society *solely* in terms of population characteristics. In other words, conceptual knowledge can correct a commonly encountered tendency to exaggerate the societal implications of demographic processes. Far from denying the importance of demographic factors, this section stresses the necessity of viewing them in proper perspective.

We are born, we age, we go to school, we work, we reproduce, we move, we die – all of these activities are primary concerns in the study of population. The most momentus and pivotal events in human history have been the dramatic declines in mortality and fertility and the rapid urbanization of society; they have affected virtually all aspects of society and our lives. In addition to economic, political, geographic, and social factors, demographic forces shape a society, and they must be studied if we are to understand society and make guarded forecasts as to future trends (this argument is elaborated in Lewis 1987).

But because demographic processes interrelate with a variety of societal factors, one must avoid what might be termed *demographic determinism* in appraising the effects of population change on a society. The fallacy of environmental and economic determinism was not the emphasis on determinism, but the gross exaggeration of the influence of one factor in the human milieu. That is, one must avoid exaggerating the influence of population change and realize that these processes are interrelated and very complex, and should not be oversimplified.

There has been a considerable exaggeration, however, of the impact of population change on Soviet society, and much of it has been featured in the press. As noted in the chapter by Clem in this volume, much attention has been given to the slow decline in the Russian share of the population to below 50 percent, from majority to plurality status, that will occur sometime around the turn of the century, and to the rise in the proportion of Turkic-Muslims, or the "yellowing" of the Soviet population and, in particular, of the Soviet army (Meyer 1978, 158; Feshbach 1982a; Carrère d'Encausse 1979, 47–121; Bennigsen and Broxup 1983, 124–42; also see the interview with Murray Feshbach in *US News and World Report* 1982). These studies generally feature an almost exclusive focus on the instability and other problems that will result.

However, a careful review of the change in status of the Russians from majority to plurality reveals that, in the late Tsarist period, the proportion of Russians was much lower than at present and that dominance does not relate just to brute numbers (Lewis, Rowland, and Clem 1976, 291–93). Despite claims to the contrary, Jones (1985, Ch. 7; see also the chapter by Jones in this volume) has convincingly demonstrated that neither ethnic rivalry nor language competence is a serious threat to combat capability in the Soviet armed forces. However, the rate of growth of the work force in the USSR will decline in the 1980s and be primarily concentrated among the non-European population; this should cause problems for the Soviet economy, which is characterized by full employment and relatively low labor productivity. Whether it is a crisis depends on one's definition and one's evaluation of the Soviet government's ability to solve such problems.

As to exaggerating the number involved, after briefly discussing fertility differentials by nationality, Bennigsen maintains that "If the trend continued, in the year 2000 the Soviet Union would probably have a Turkic and Muslim majority and a Russian and even a Slavic minority" (Bennigsen 1971, 174). A growth of the Turkic-Muslim population in about thirty years from about 15 percent to more than 50 percent of the Soviet population would exceed the reproductive capacity of any known group and be unreasonable (Lewis, Rowland, and Clem 1976, 291–93). Feshbach (1979, 658), using the growth between 1959 and 1970, estimated the Muslim population to be 29 percent in the year 2000 and rounded this percentage to "almost 1 of every 3 Soviet citizens." Because Turkic-Muslim fertility was declining in the 1970s, and mortality probably changed relatively less than fertility, it is unreasonable to assume a constant 1959–70 growth rate after 1970; and 29 percent is closer to one in four than to one in three. Moreover, the current most reasonable estimate is about one in five (see the chapter by Clem in this volume; Anderson and Silver 1981). However, with respect to ethnic problems, the redistribution of Turkic-Muslims is probably more important than their growth, depending, of course, on political and socioeconomic conditions.

In summary, the issue of population change and its impact on Soviet society is not totally resolved, but it is not as simple or dire as generally depicted. If by the turn of the century, the share that Turkic-Muslims comprise of the total population rises several points to about 20 percent and the Russian share declines to below 50 percent, it will not particularly disrupt Soviet society, especially if one does not assume a natural animosity between Russians and Turkic-Muslims or that all population change is detrimental to Soviet society. It is also worth noting that the exaggerated emphasis on crises is also directed toward other aspects of society, such as the economy and the medical care system (Goldman 1982; Eberstadt 1981). A common feature of these writings on population time bombs, demographic morasses, and crises of all kinds in the USSR are their tendencies to be conceptually weak and to overlook considerable contrary evidence.

Considering the state of nuclear weaponry and our relations with the USSR, a realistic view of the Soviet Union, in general, and its demographic situation, in particular, is imperative. We cannot afford a groupthink on such an important issue (Janis 1983, 349). As George F. Kennan has so cogently written:

> But all this being said, I must go on and say that I find the view of the Soviet Union that prevails today in large portions of our government and journalistic establishments so extreme, so subjective, so far removed from what any sober scrutiny of external reality would reveal, that it is not only ineffectual but dangerous as a guide to political action. (1982, 2)

Conclusions

At this juncture in our history, for obvious reasons, there is probably no more important knowledge than an understanding of the Soviet Union. Yet, ideology, dogmatism, and the desire for press coverage can, and often do, hinder the search for truth with respect to societal processes in the USSR. For example, writing in the *Washington Post*, Suplee (1983) observed: "Better Red than dead? By the time you're through listening to Murray Feshbach in the *Atlantic* you'll wonder: What's the difference?" What follows is a "portrait of the USSR as a vast Orcus of decay." Eberstadt reports in the *Washington Inquirer*:

> In some sense, these prospects for the Soviet peoples are even worse than for the Bengalis. No modern nation would be unable to maintain its national health unless its society were in the midst of a *fundamental* breakdown. From what I can make out, the USSR is indeed in the midst of a social and spiritual collapse and the likes of which we in the West have never seen, and in fact can scarcely imagine. (1983, 7)

What we should ask is, How do current social conditions in the USSR compare with the past and with other developed countries? A reasonable interpretation would be that compared to the turn of the century, there have been great economic and social advances in the USSR; that politically it is more stable than at any other time in Soviet history; and that like other developed countries, the Soviet Union has social and economic problems, but they are not crucial and there is more stability than is generally thought. Instead of all the writing about economic, demographic, medical and ethnic crises, more attention should be given to the elements of stability in Soviet society, if we are to understand it. Crisis mongering and predictions of the collapse of the Soviet Union have been put forth in the West regularly since the founding of the state. From current Western literature one derives the impression that here is a country characterized mainly by weaknesses and few strengths, and yet the country appears to be quite stable. Such interpretations, as illustrated by the previous quotations, reveal more about the authors than about the Soviet Union and involve considerable wishful thinking.

Because of the importance of understanding the USSR, it is necessary to reaffirm periodically our dedication to the pursuit of truth, in response to the stark ideological differences between our society and Soviet society and the attendant superpower rivalries. The best way to achieve a more objective, realistic view of the USSR is to analyze it in terms of existing socioeconomic theories and concepts and from a comparative perspective. Testing the universality of demographic processes in the USSR provides a balanced interpretation, because it provides a comparative and historical perspective, a skepticism about data, and a fuller appreciation of the appropriate ways of assessing the significance of valid findings.

Notes

[1] The work leading to this report was supported in whole or in part by funds provided by the National Council for Soviet and East European Research.

[2] For a discussion of our general approach and the importance of testing demographic and geographic theory in the Soviet context, see Lewis, Rowland, and Clem (1976, xix–xxxiii).

[3] For example, with respect to ethnicity and population change, see the chapter by Clem in this volume and Silver (1974). With respect to migration, see Fuchs and Demko (1978); Demko and Ball (1978); Grandstaff (1980); Rowland (1982); and Anderson (1979). With respect to fertility, family, and gender see Mazur (1973); Jones and Grupp (forthcoming); and the chapter by Sacks in this volume.

[4] For a detailed discussion of Soviet demographic policy, see Lewis (forthcoming).

[5] For example, see the articles devoted to demographic patterns in the USSR in US Congress (1982).

[6] For example, see US Department of Health and Human Services (1981) and Kitagawa and Hauser (1973).

[7] For a more detailed discussion of modernization and population change, see Lewis, Rowland, and Clem (1976); Goldscheider (1971); United Nations (1973).

[8] For appropriate documentation of this discussion, see Lewis, Rowland, and Clem (1976, 21–33).

References

Anderson, Barbara. 1979. *Internal Migration during Modernization in Late Nineteenth Century Russia*. Princeton, N.J.: Princeton University Press.

Anderson, Barbara, and Brian D. Silver. 1981. "Estimating Russification of Ethnic Identity among Non-Russians in the USSR." Paper presented at the Annual Meeting of the Population Association of America, Washington, D.C.

———. 1986a. "Infant Mortality in the Soviet Union: Regional Differences and Measurement Issues." *Population and Development Review* 12 (December): 705–38.

———. 1986b. "Sex Differentials in Mortality in the Soviet Union: Regional Differences in Length of Working Life in Comparative Perspective." *Population Studies* 40 (2):191–214.

Bednyy, M. S. 1979. *Mediko-demograficheskoye izucheniye narodonaseleniya*. Moscow: "Statistika."

Bennigsen, Alexandre. 1971. "Islamic or Local Consciousness among Soviet Nationalities." In *Soviet Nationality Problems*, edited by Edward Allworth, pp. 168–182. New York: Columbia University Press.

Bennigsen, Alexandre, and Marie Broxup. 1983. *The Islamic Threat to the Soviet State*. New York: St. Martin's Press.

Borisov, V. A. 1976. *Perspektivy rozhdayemosti*. Moscow: Statistika.

Carrère d'Encausse, Helène. 1979. *Deline of an Empire. The Soviet Socialist Republics in Revolt*. New York: Newsweek Books.

Davis, Christopher, and Murray Feshbach. 1980. *Rising Infant Mortality in the USSR in the 1970's*. US Bureau of the Census, series p–95, no. 74 (June).

Demko, E. J., and B. Ball. 1978. "Internal Migration in the Soviet Union." *Economic Geography* 54 (2):95–114.

Eason, Waren W. 1981. "Rising Soviet Infant Mortality in the 1970's: A Closer Look at the Evidence and a Reinterpretation of the Trends." Unpublished manuscript.

Eberstadt, Nick. 1981. "The Health Crisis in the USSR," *The New York Review of Books* (February 19):23–31.

———. 1983. "The Soviet Union's Health Crisis." *Washington Inquirer* (April 1):7.

Ekonomicheskaya Gazeta. 1986. No. 43 (October):6.

Feshbach, Murray. 1979. "Prospects for Outmigration from Central Asia and Kazakhstan in the Next Decade." In *Soviet Economy in a Time of Change*, US Congress, Joint Economic Committee, pp. 656–710. Washington, D.C.: US Government Printing Office.

———. 1982a. "Social Maintenance in the USSR: Demographic Morass." *The Washington Quarterly* (Summer):92–98.

———. 1982b. "The Soviet Union: Population Trends and Dilemmas." *Population Bulletin* 37 (3).

Fuchs, Roland, and George Demko. 1978. "The Postwar Mobility Transition in Eastern Europe." *Geographic Review* 68 (2):171–82.

Goldman, Marshall I. 1982. *USSR in Crisis: The Failure of an Economic System*. New York: W. W. Norton and Co.

Goldscheider, Calvin. 1971. *Population, Modernization and Social Structure*. Boston: Little, Brown.

Grandstaff, Peter. 1980. *Interregional Migration in the USSR: Economic Aspects, 1959–1970.* Durham, N.C.: Duke University Press.

Grunbaum, Adolph. 1953. "Causality and the Science of Human Behavior." In *Readings in the Philosophy of Science*, edited by Herbert Feigl and May Brodbeck, pp. 766–77. New York: Appleton-Century-Crofts.

Grupp, Fred W., and Ellen Jones. 1983. "Infant Mortality Trends in the USSR." *Population and Development Review* 9 (June):213–46.

Hempel, Carl S. 1965. *Aspects of Scientific Explanation.* New York: Free Press.

Janis, Irving L. 1983. *Groupthink.* Boston: Houghton Mifflin.

Jones, Ellen. 1985. *Red Army and Society: A Sociology of the Soviet Military.* Winchester, Mass.: Allen and Unwin.

Jones, Ellen, and Fred W. Grupp. 1987. *Modernization, Value Change and Fertility in the Soviet Union.* Cambridge, England: Cambridge University Press.

Karakhanov, M. K., ed. 1970. *Problemy narodonaseleniya.* Moscow: Izdatel'stvo Moskovskogo Universiteta.

Kennan, George. 1982. "On Nuclear War." *The New York Review of Books* (January 21):2.

Kitagawa, Evelyn M., and Philip M. Hauser. 1973. *Differential Mortality in the United States: A Study in Socioeconomic Epidemiology.* Cambridge: Harvard University Press.

Lewis, Robert A. 1987. "Data Comparability: The Central Statistical Problem in the Study of Soviet Population." In *Research Guide to the Russian and Soviet Censuses*, edited by Ralph S. Clem, pp. 36–47. Ithaca, N.Y.: Cornell University Press.

———. Forthcoming. "Soviet Demographic Policy: How Comprehensive, How Effective?" In *Soviet Geographic Studies in Our Time*, edited by Lutz Holtzner.

Lewis Robert A., and Richard H. Rowland. 1979. *Population Redistribution in the USSR.* New York: Praeger.

Lewis, Robert A., Richard H. Rowland, and Ralph S. Clem. 1976. *Nationality and Population Change in Russia and the USSR.* New York: Praeger.

Lubin, Nancy. 1984. *Labour and Nationality in Soviet Central Asia.* Princeton, N.J.: Princeton University Press.

Mazur, Peter. 1973. "Relations of Marriage and Education to Fertility in the USSR." *Population Studies* 27 (March):105–16.

Meyer, Herbert E. 1978. "The Coming Soviet Ethnic Crisis." *Fortune* (August 14):158.

Nagel, Ernest. 1961. *The Structure of Science.* New York: Harcourt, Brace, and World.

Roland, Richard H. 1982. "Spatial Patterns of Urban In-Migration in Late Nineteenth Century Russia." *Historical Geographical Research Series*, no. 10. Norwich, England: Geo Abstracts, Ltd.

Rywkin, Michael. 1979. "Central Asia and Soviet Manpower." *Problems of Communism* 28 (Jan.-Feb.):1–13.

———. 1982. *Moscow's Muslim Challenge.* New York: M. E. Sharpe.

Schaefer, Fred K. 1953. "Exceptionalism in Geography: A Methodological Examination." *Annals of the Association of American Geographers* 43 (September):226–49.

Silver, Brian D. 1974. "Levels of Sociocultural Development among Soviet Nationalities: A Partial Test of the Equalization Hypothesis." *American Political Science Review* 68 (4):1618–37.

Suplee, Curt. 1983. 'Reds, Feds, and Cheese." *The Washington Post*, p. 01.

Treml, Vladimir G. 1975. "Production and Consumption of Alcoholic Beverages in the USSR." *Journal of Studies on Alcohol* 36 (3):285–320.

United Nations. 1973. *The Determinants and Consequences of Population Trends.* New York: United Nations.

US Congress, Joint Economic Committee. 1982. *Soviet Economy in the 1980's: Problems and Prospects*, part 2. Washington, D.C.: US Government Printing Office.

US Department of Health and Human Services. 1981. *Vital Statistics of the United States, 1977, Volume 11: Mortality Part A*, section 6. Washington, D.C.: US Government Printing Office.

US News and World Report. 1982. "The Population Time Bomb That Kremlin Faces." December 6, p. 28.

Wimbush, S. Enders, and Dmitry Ponomareff. 1979. *Alternatives for Mobilizing Soviet Central Asian Labor: Outmigration and Regional Development*. Santa Monica, Calif.: Rand Corporation (R–2476–AF).

Zyuzin, D. I. 1983. "Causes of Low Mobility among the Indigenous Population of the Central Asian Republics." *Sotsiologicheskiye issledovaniya*, no. 1: 109–17, translated in *The Current Digest of the Soviet Press* 35 (March):2–4.

PART II

Party and People

6

Soviet Society and Communist Party Controls: A Case of Constricted Development

Mark G. Field

There is a Soviet story – apocryphal perhaps – that a class of school-children, while studying Russian history, came to Napoleon's retreat from Moscow. One pupil asked: "Comrade teacher, how could we ever defeat the French when we did not have a [Communist] party?" This naïve question makes good sense when viewed through the prism of contemporary Soviet society, and particularly in the light of the critical importance officially attributed to the existence and functions of the Communist party of the Soviet Union: the Party is the keystone of Soviet society, the alpha and omega, the cement that holds it together, the "organizer of victories," the essential vanguard, the indispensable guide in the march of the Soviet Union toward Communism. This is what the party would like to have the world, including particularly the Soviet population, believe. This self-proclaimed role is a statement of *functionality*: that it is a structure that performs certain tasks or fulfills certain needs indispensable to the existence and survival of society. Conversely, the cessation of the performance of such tasks would have dire consequences that would affect the fate of the Soviet system, its ability to

Note: This is a revised version (1987) of a paper originally published in *Soviet and Chinese Communism: Similarities and Differences*, ed. Donald W. Treadgold (Seattle: University of Washington Press, 1967). I thank the University of Washington Press for permission to use these materials. I want to express my gratitude to Professors Jerry F. Hough and Robert C. Tucker, who critically read this manuscript in its original form and provided many important suggestions. The paper also owes more than I can say to Professor Talcott Parsons and to the ideas expressed in his course on institutional structure and, later, in the *The Evolution of Societies* (1977). I alone bear responsibility for the contents of this essay.

master the environment, and march toward a more perfect social order. It may well be that the Party now does most of what it claims to do. It has become such an integral part of practically every aspect of Soviet society and is so interdigitated with most social processes that its sudden disappearance might throw the Soviet Union, at least temporarily, into serious disarray; there are few alternative forces – or, more important, institutional mechanisms – that could take over the functions the Party has arrogated to itself.

In speculating on what might happen in the event of an anti-Communist revolt, Jerry Hough states:

> A post-Communist regime in Russia could not function without former party members serving in important administrative and even political posts. (Hough and Fainsod 1979, 568)

In my opinion, the Soviet Union would be more dependent on former party members than Germany was in the post-World War II period on former Nazi officials. The absence, of course, of any other "political" groupings that might serve as functional equivalents emphasizes the monopolistic nature of the Party's role, differentiating it from *parties* as the term is commonly used in the West. It is part of its modus operandi, derived from Lenin's definition of its leading role, that alternative forces should *not* be allowed to emerge and challenge its hegemony. If they arise, they usually are either destroyed (as were the Kulaks during collectivization) or incorporated or co-opted into the Party (as the intelligentsia were during the 1930s) or placed under strict party supervision (as the armed forces are). It is the military, incidentally, and the organs of internal security, because of their organizational control of a large number of men and means of violence, as well as a relatively autonomous communications network, that might be able to take over in the unlikely event that the Party should cease functioning or falter. What is remarkable, particularly when compared with the experience of many other countries (especially the developing ones), is the degree to which the Party has been able to hold the military at bay.

And yet the role and the position of the Party cannot, in the nature of the case, remain static. The policies, programs, and purposes it pursues alter, in the course of time, Soviet society; and the Party's modus operandi must, or should, change to keep up with the changes it helps produce. Seen in any evolutionary perspective, given the inevitable petrifaction that accompanies the oligarchic holding of power over a long time, and contrary to the image it wants to maintain, the Party may be, presently and on balance, more a source of retardation, conservatism, and stagnation than of dynamism, progress and vision. Gorbachev might agree with this assessment. Indeed, the further modernization of Soviet society may hinge perhaps not so much on what the Party will actively do to promote the process of development, as on its ability (or inability) to maintain what it feels is adequate control over the unfolding of society, while divesting itself of enough day-to-day supervision over most sectors to permit them to expand without its direct supervision. Thus, the provision of increased freedom to many components of the economy, and the legitimization of market transactions with their automatic adjustment of demand and supply, would eliminate the jobs of thousands of party officials. It is no wonder that Gorbachev is meeting increasing resistance in implementing the reforms that would get the economy going again but at the price of upsetting, or eliminating, thousands of party and governmental bureaucrats who, meanwhile, are quietly sabotaging his efforts. At issue, then, is the ability of the Party to tolerate the further differentiation of Soviet society, the potential formation of interest groups (which have existed in a latent fashion for years), and the articulation of group interests, and to maintain a legitimate role for itself that would continue to justify its retaining the ultimate power of making secular decisions and its privileges.

At the same time, if functions now performed by the Party (in the political, economic, and cultural areas, for example) were to be replaced by fairly autonomous institutional mechanisms (democratic consultation, a market system, an independent judiciary, professional peer review, and so on), this would necessarily mean a lessening of party control, a situation that in itself must be anxiety provoking. This would lead to two unacceptable consequences: first, the system might develop in directions deemed undesirable, because it would lead to that anathema of Lenin and of the Party, spontaneity. (The people, given a choice, might "wrongly" opt for more consumer goods and better housing rather than for investments in heavy industry and the military.) Because, in the eyes of the Party, there is not much evidence that the Soviet population is ruled by consciousness of what is eventually "best" for all (more investments in heavy industry and in national defense), a phasing out of controls, though it might increase efficiency to some degree, is seen as a slippery slope, a dangerous trade-off. Second, the replacement of current functions by other mechanisms and institutions would emphasize the resultant redundancy of the Party's role and affect its legitimacy, since it would become and appear increasingly functionless, and therefore parasitic. The Party might thus become like so many aristocracies or upper classes in the past, a privileged estate with no functional or social contractual justification or reason for that privilege or, for that matter, for its existence as a corporate group.

Functioning organizations, generally speaking, do not fold their tents when they see that the purpose for which they were created no longer exists. Usually they seek new goals, new functions, new mandates to perform in order to justify their existence. It would be absurd, even for a moment, to contemplate the idea that the Party would deliberately rule itself out of existence if it perceived that its role was no longer necessary. It is, however, possible to contemplate, at least in the longer perspective, a restriction and shifting of functions — say toward a general stewardship and oversight of Soviet society and toward keeping the faith alive, a secular equivalent to a return or retreat to the temple. But these are distant speculations. At the conclusion of this essay I suggest how a Marxist interpretation of the workings of impersonal historical forces connotes a rather bleak future for the Party.

At the same time, the possibility exists that when we speak of the Communist party of the Soviet Union we may, in fact (though not in theory), speak of the Communist parties, in that it is difficult — indeed impossible — to conceive of the Party as a monolith. Its many internal elements represent different social forces, interest groups, aspirations, sectors of the economy, conservative and reformist trends, and so on. Thus the competition for positions and priorities, for the commitment of resources — indeed, for policies and programs domestically and abroad — must constantly take place in the inner councils of the party. But these are not public debates; there are no appeals to constituencies. Decisions are taken in executive sessions behind closed doors, and the outside world, including the Soviet population, is served the end product of these processes: the official line.

"Cult of the Personality" or "Cult of the Party"?

The expression, "cult of the personality," with which Nikita Khrushchev and his successors chose to stigmatize Josef Stalin's rule was not fortuitous. Neither was it quite accidental that Khrushchev, after his fall, also was accused of having created a small cult of his own personality.[1] Eventually a cult of the personality of his successor, Leonid Brezhnev, also developed. Brezhnev's two immediate successors, Yuri Andropov and Konstantin Chernenko, did not rule long enough for a full cult to develop (although there were hints of a beginning, for example, the extravagantly hailed publication of Chernenko's public pronouncements). As of this writing (mid-1987) no real cult of the personality of Mikhail Gorbachev has yet developed, although his picture appears almost daily in the Soviet press as befits a head of state. However, once his power is firmly established, which is by no means a certainty, the very nature of the position may lead to some glorification. Hill and Frank have suggested that a certain amount of adulation may permit the leader to exercise substantial influence over policymaking (1986, 95).

The word *cult* has a distinct religious flavor and conveys the impression of a religious type of activity: it denotes the uncritical worship of an individual leader who behaves as if he had divine wisdom and inspiration. Stalin was criticized, ostensibly, because he had cast himself in the role of an omnipotent and omniscient deity who could do no wrong. Implicit in the criticism, however, was another charge: that Stalin had arrogated to himself the role that rightfully belonged to the Party, that he had reduced the Party to a powerless instrument of his personal and unchecked rule, and that he had further degraded it by undermining its hegemony through other organizational instrumentalities, such as the secret police (Brzezinski 1961). Khrushchev's aim, as expressed in his speech at the 20th Party Congress in 1956 and in his subsequent statements, was to restore what he termed "Leninism" but what might better be called the "cult of the party," — that is, respect for and worship of that mystic entity and collectivity constituted by the Party that, for lack of a better term, might be called the Communist living church or the body of Marxism.

Indeed, the main burden of Khrushchev's bill of particulars against Stalin was that he had purged thousands of party comrades. Khrushchev did not shed many, if any, tears about the millions of others (for example, Kulaks) who perished at Stalin's behest.

The resemblance of the Party and its function to that of an organized and established church can serve as a possible model for an examination of the systemic nature of contemporary Communist society of the Soviet type. The use of a church or religious model is not, of course, new or particularly original. What is proposed here is an attempt to follow some consequences attendant on this kind of structural model and to advance the hypothesis that Soviet society, although in many respects and trappings an industrialized, mechanized, and urbanized social system, may lack certain characteristics of other industrialized modern societies. Seen on an evolutionary scale, Soviet society may then fall somewhat short of being a fully modern social system in the terms that are used and defined below.

No value judgment is implied in the adjectives *modern* or *advanced*, any more than such a judgment is implied in saying a society is *primitive* or *preliterate*. These are classificatory terms, and the criteria for their applicability are those of internal differentiation, complexity, and integration, not whether one society is better or more conducive to happiness than another. The judgment, if any, is a functional one, and the ultimate test is an appraisal of the capacities of that social system to adapt and master its domestic and foreign environments.

Societal Evolution and Differentiation

Talcott Parsons, in *The Evolution of Societies* (1977), holds that it is possible to trace the evolution (and transformation) of different social systems from the relative simplicity of the primitive society to the intermediate level (such as ancient Egypt, the Mesopotamian empires, China, India, Israel, and Greece), to the modern societies, whose development was made possible in part by the Renaissance and the Reformation. Whereas Parsons uses a three-stage analysis, other writers use more complicated schemes. The point, however, is that it is possible to order types of societies on a scale of increased internal complexity, and that "socio-cultural, like organic, evolution has proceeded by variation and differentiation from simple to progressively more complex forms" (1977, 24). The most fundamental principle, as Parsons outlines it, is that evolution consists of the improvement of the adaptive capacities of the society or system. This enables it to cope with a range of different conditions and unexpected contingencies.

The development of that capacity comes as a result of the internal differentiation and specialization of mechanisms of the organism, in essence a division of labor between specialized organs or structures. Thus, a relative lack of differentiation, or separation, between the kinship and the economic systems (an arrangement in which economic activities are all carried out within a kinship group, as in primitive agricultural societies or a family firm) is not as efficient as one in which kinship and economic activities are carried out in distinct contexts, and in which recruitment for the different economic tasks can proceed on the basis of ability or achievement rather than of particularistic and ascriptive ties of descent or marriage. Thus, the offsprings of the founder of an industrial firm might not have the managerial capacity or the motivation to operate the company efficiently. The moment will inevitably come when a better-qualified outsider, "not family," will be invited to assume executive or managerial responsibilities. By the same token, the governing of people in today's large-scale nation-state is carried out more efficiently by a separate and differentiated governmental structure, made up of individuals working on a full-time basis, than would be the case if every citizen had to participate (on a part-time basis to be sure) in making every decision and in administering the state (as in the Greek polis). This is also why the monarchical principle of transferring real political power from the monarch to the eldest child (who might be, for all practical purposes, totally incompetent) is rarely found in the contemporary world.

The key concept is differentiation. S. N. Eisenstadt has stated that it is like complexity and specialization: "It describes the way through which the main social functions or the major institutional spheres . . . become disassociated from one another, attached to specialized collectivities, and organized in relatively autonomous symbolic and organizational frameworks within the confines of the same institutionalized system" (1964, 376).

The process of differentiation can be described as the gradual liberation of social processes from rigid kinship, tribal, or ascriptive ties; it implies a fair amount of autonomy for the differentiated spheres and the development of criteria of action specific to these spheres. It also raises the important question of the integration of these different areas through a system of exchange of outputs. If this integration is missing, the process becomes merely one of segmentation rather than of differentiation and may lead to stagnation and breakdown. Differentiation, as Eisenstadt has pointed out, opens up new possibilities for development and creativity – whether in the area of technological development or the expansion of political, cultural, philosophical, religious, or personal powers and rights. Of course, this also poses the question of the delicate balance and interplay between social forces and the functional needs of the society. Indeed, differentiation, according to Eisenstadt, may lead to what he describes as "constricted" development, a situation in which one of the differentiated spheres will attempt to dominate the others coercively by restricting and regimenting their tendencies towards autonomy. More precisely:

> This probability is especially strong with respect to the political and religious (or value) spheres, because these spheres are especially prone to "totalistic" orientations that tend to negate the autonomy of other spheres. Religious and political élites may attempt to dominate other spheres, imposing rigid frameworks based on their own criteria. The aim of such policies is usually an effective de-differentiation of the social system, and they may result in rigidity and stagnation, or precipitate continual breakdowns of the system. These tendencies to de-differentiation are usually very closely related to the specific processes of change that may develop within any institutionalized system. (1964, 381).

In this, precisely, lie some of the dangers presented in the United States and elsewhere (for example, in Iran) by the claims of fundamentalists (like the Moral Majority) who would politically impose their religious and moral views on *all* aspects of society.

It might be posited that the modern world is characterized by the absence of an overarching and necessarily restrictive ideology or religion and of a coercive organization enforcing its tenets, through which every human being and institutional action is screened and evaluated, approved or disapproved. It is further asserted that this absence, the general freedom from totalistic normative evaluation, in the final analysis, improves a society's adaptation and mastery of its environment. This is the ideal Mao Tse-tung once expressed, but did not follow, of "letting one hundred flowers bloom."

Returning to the Soviet case, the basic ethos of that society, its normative base, is the body of ideas and theories generally known as Marxism or Marxism-Leninism. This theory constitutes an ideology and is not simply, as Marx would have claimed, an objective and scientific method of looking at and understanding people, society, and the historical process. It has reached the status of a faith – secular, to be sure, yet endowed, by virtue of its position and role in the Communist world, with the characteristics of religious beliefs, doctrine, and often dogma. As Robert V. Daniels (1962, 349–50) has pointed out, the followers of the faith embrace the doctrine, not because it passes a particular test of metaphysical or historical truth, but because it conveys a sense of the exclusive possession of the truth.

Emile Durkheim argued long ago that religion was not merely a superstructure reflecting material interests (as Marx asserted) but a fundamental matrix for the evolution of culture. Through a process of gradual differentiation, other elements of the culture emerged from that matrix. In primitive society, thus, there seems to exist no sharp break between what is sacred and what is profane, nor is there a clear dichotomy between the natural and the supernatural. In this type of social order, the society as a whole is the "church." Only through a long process of differentiation were boundaries established between the sacred and profane, worlds, and a lay culture arose relatively independent of religious criteria, injunctions, and sanctions. When it is possible, for instance, in the same society and culture, to worship in church and to teach freely that the earth is round and not the center of the universe, or that people did not descend from Adam and Eve, a process of differentiation has taken place. On the other hand, when persons are burned at the stake; questioned by the inquisition; hanged for being witches; sent to jail, concentration camps, or insane asylums; expelled, exiled, shot, or tortured because they hold (and proclaim) views incompatible with the current theology or the state's or party's truth, then the process of differentiation is far from complete.

By the same token, at the societal level (in contrast with the cultural one) the process of differentiation from the church-society led, as in the case of Christianity, to the formation of a specialized, separate, corporate entity – the Church – staffed by full-time religious functionaries, organizationally quite distinct from other spheres, though its claim for competence has tended to be *totalistic*. In the Soviet Union, the analog to that body would be the Party.

It is contended here that Soviet culture and society have become differentiated, but incompletely so. At least as seen on a comparative and evolutionary scale, that society falls short of other, more advanced, pluralistic social systems. The process of differentiation is slowed by the totalistic nature of the value system and the orientation of the Communist party, the guardian of the Soviet *Weltanschauung*.

Following this line of reasoning, it can be argued that in the Soviet Union *partiinost'* (partyness) has often served as a criterion for the judgment of actions in most spheres of activity – that is, as a test of Communist morality, as well as a device to bludgeon nonconformists – and has hindered the development and the expression of autonomous or independent criteria of thought or action so that secular culture has not yet completely emancipated (or differentiated) itself from ideology.[2]

Furthermore, if Marxism has become an official faith, then the Communist party is the guardian, the repository, a differentiated corporate embodiment of that faith; it has become a secular, or nonreligious, but established, official, and unique church — regardless of whether party officials believe sincerely in its tenets.

The question of belief, of acceptance, of internalization of the basic elements of the ideology is a difficult one to document. One tendency is to accept that most people in the Soviet Union, particularly the members of the Party, do not take the Marxist–Leninist ideology very seriously and that they are cynical about it; that it has become a kind of catechism one must learn and formally repeat at certain times and on certain symbolic occasions; and that it certainly is not a guide to action. However, the hold that certain aspects of the tenets exercise on the population and leaders cannot be gainsaid, because they have become part of the general Soviet culture, taught in schools and endlessly repeated. Indeed, some of the more famous dissidents, like P. G. Grigorenko (*The Grigorenko Papers* 1976) and Leonid Pliushch (*The Case* 1976), indicted the regime precisely because they felt it had deviated from and distorted the basic principles on which it claims to base itself.

In addition, ideology and its symbolic link to the charismatic figure of Lenin provide the party with its claim to legitimacy, because this claim can be (to use Max Weber's terms) neither traditional, as in the case of monarchs and ruling houses, nor rational-legal, as it does not rest on the specific and limited mandate of an enfranchised electorate and an effective constitution.[3] The legitimacy of the Party is, thus, a *routinized charismatic* type. The Party claims its right to exercise control and authority because it considers itself the only legitimate representative and interpreter of the fundamental truth. If the Party were to discover, or acknowledge, that its world view is based on false premises (an improbable event), it would logically have no choice but to dissolve itself. It is more likely, however, to assert time and again that the basic premises on which it rests are scientifically correct, in the sense that they rest on a materialistic interpretation of people, society, and history, and thus, by implication, are also "eternal."

Interpretation of the doctrine, however, makes it possible for the Party and its leaders to claim that their doctrine is not dogma, but that it is broad and universal enough to provide answers to a variety of changing situations, and that these answers, while fitting the situation of the moment, are nevertheless faithful in spirit to the original doctrine — to the fundamental law of Marxism. Furthermore, the Party justifies its existence and its role as seen earlier in functional terms by claiming credit for all the achievements of the regime.

As the corporate body of the only true faith, the Party cannot admit the legitimacy or the existence of other faiths or parties and therefore rejects any idea of ideological or political pluralism. This exclusive claim to the truth and its interpretation explain for example the obsessive nature of the regime's concern with dissidents. The number of dissidents in the Soviet Union is microscopic; their support among the large masses of the population is nil (they tend to view the dissidents as either crazy or treasonous). And yet, the regime goes to any and all lengths to silence them. Perhaps the Party fears that some day a charismatic figure will rise and say, "it is written but I say . . ." or a Soviet counterpart of Martin Luther will nail his theses on the door of the Kremlin! The Party's position is that the doctrine on which it rests must and will become universal, that is, embrace all humanity, and its historical function is to help in the promotion of this inevitable march of history. The Soviet Union, as such, is the resource base on which the movement depends – it provides the human and material underpinning for that movement – and the Party is the agency responsible for mobilizing these resources on Soviet soil. Thus, as the proclaimed instrument of history it has acquired a mystique of its own; its existence, its survival, and its perpetuation are the prerequisites and the guarantee for the actualization of the faith at home and in the world. This helps explain the reluctance of such men as Leon Trotsky to attack or split it even though they opposed its leader. There may be bad "popes" who temporarily seize control of the party machinery, but this does not, in any way, bring into question the justifiability and sanctity of Party supremacy.

At this juncture, we need not explore the nature of the Party as an organization of leadership within Soviet society, except to note its resemblance to an established church (it was more of a priesthood under Lenin), with a specific and differentiated membership, and to note (as others have on many occasions) that it does constitute, at least for its leading members, an interest group or perhaps, as Milovan Djilas puts it, a "new class." This class has at its disposal the major instruments of rule, such as the use of political power, mass communication, the control of production means (the equivalent, under Soviet conditions, to their ownership), honorific goods (in terms of patterns of deference and prestige), and real goods (the enjoyment of an affluent life style), that are associated with a privileged caste or an establishment.

Status within the party hierarchy is not, of course, hereditary in the traditional sense, though it could be argued that the children of highly placed and influential party members enjoy certain privileges and career opportunities that other members of Soviet society (and particularly the nonparty majority) do not. Quite simply, most party members in influential positions have an interest in the perpetuation of the status quo, that is, in the continuation of party controls over society, and therefore a vested interest in maintaining the system as now structured, regardless of whether they are sincere, believing Communists and regardless of the functional results of such controls.

The Party, by being the one source of Communist morality, attempts to maintain not only a totalistic hold on Soviet society but also a diffuse, undifferentiated power of control and review. Theoretically, its sphere of influence and competence admits no limitations, constitutional checks, or boundaries; there are no jurisdictions over which it dare not trespass. The distinction, for example, between private and public interests does not hold. What a person is and what a person does at home, on the job, in public life, or in other areas are of legitimate concern to the Party. The activity of a party secretary, according to Seweryn Bialer,

> is restricted only by the territorial limits of his jurisdiction and by the decisions of the next secretary up the line; he may exercise his authority in any sphere, imposing his will on the economic administration, the educational system, the local governmental apparatus, etc ... [his] scope of professional interests and right of interference are virtually absolute and all embracing ... he personifies the omnipotence of party apparatus within the society at large. (1962, 259)

The Party thus tends to operate in terms of a militant certainty and an absolutist outlook about objectively doubtful matters that is a habit, as Bertrand Russell pointed out, "from which, since the Renaissance, the world has been gradually emerging into that temper of constructive and fruitful skepticism which constitutes the scientific outlook" (1920, as cited in Djilas 1957, 127). It is this certainty that permits the Party (or the leader) to say to one person or to a group, "You are right" or "You are wrong"; it gives rise to that simple and classic dichotomy, "Either you are with us, or you are against us"; it makes the principle of a loyal opposition an absurdity (opposition, by definition, is treasonable and should be either in jail or six feet underground). In short, in its frequent inability or unwillingness to recognize that there may be shades of gray in the world, in its not having gone through the painful and sobering emancipation embodied, for example, in the Reformation that reminds people they are fallible and that there are very few absolutes in this life, the Party has tended to assume the cloak of infallibility, without fully realizing that the cloak can also serve as a blinder. Bertram Wolfe once suggested that not only was knowledge power, but also that in the case of Stalin, Khrushchev, and the Party in general, "power became knowledge" – that is, the position of the top leadership led to its pronouncements being considered infallible, whether on abstract art, music, genetics, the chemical industry, poetry, the frequency of the milking of cows, or the declaration of who was or was not an enemy of the people. In some instances this infallibility has not been one of Soviet society's strong suits in solving the multitude of problems facing it.

The Nature of Soviet Society

For convenience and the sake of brevity, I have grouped the plethora of theories on Soviet society into three main (though by no means exhaustive) clusters. The first cluster defines in general terms the culture of Soviet society, and the next two the structure of that society in terms of its political and economic institutions. (In essence, this follows and amplifies the analysis presented by Inkeles and Bauer 1959 and Moore 1954.)

Soviet Culture: National Communism

National Communism can be described as the search, on the part of a nation that has recently emerged as a major power on the world scene, for a national and cultural identity, and it rests on the fusion of the doctrinal bases of the Communist movement and the identification of the interests of that movement (which is, in essence, supranational) with the interests of the Russian nation. (For a description of a similar process for the United States, see Lipset 1963, 61–98). This fusion was born primarily out of the recognition, on the part of the Soviet leadership by the end of the 1920s, that no proletarian revolution (except for the short-lived episodes in Berlin, Bavaria, and Hungary) was in sight, and the resulting decision (primarily Stalin's) to build "socialism in one country." From that point on, according to Stalin, Russia was to be considered the bastion of the Communist movement and, as a corollary, anything that added to the strength of Russia as a nation (industrialization, for example) was good for that movement.

This kind of "reactive nationalism" (the expression is from Rostow 1960), which mobilized sentiments and emotions already established in the culture, was clearly expressed by Stalin (1940, 165–66). His famous and almost masochistic recital in 1931 of the past exploitation of Russia by foreigners mandated that industrialization must be pushed at all costs; it was intensified in the late 1930s, reaching a climax during World War II and the postwar period until the death of Stalin. A strong component of this cultural orientation was, and still is, to an important degree, its antagonism to the West, expressed both in terms of fear of Western intentions toward Russia and a feeling of inferiority toward the West, which often takes the form of a boastful assertion of the superiority of Russian culture and the Russian inventive mind.

The regime, particularly under Stalin, capitalized on these fears and insecurities by pursuing a policy of extreme cultural isolation and chauvinism and by applying strong pressures on the intellectual community; any attempt at objectivity toward the West was branded as potentially (if not actually) subversive. Although the campaign for cultural isolation has receded from its high-water mark of the Stalin years, the regime has continued to look with diffidence and suspicion at the West or at anything "foreign" to the Soviet spirit. Though tempered, the fear of contamination by alien ideas, for example, Western music or abstract art, remains. Although the decrease of that xenophobia since the 1950s can be interpreted as a result of a greater sense of national self-confidence, as well as the recognition (for instrumental reasons) of the need for freer communication with the West, the Soviet Union still remains a closed or limited-access society. Thus, in 1984 two laws were issued that severely penalized Soviet citizens for disclosing unauthorized information of a professional nature to foreigners (Boas 1984, 145) or even inviting foreigners (without official permission) to stay overnight in Soviet homes.

Russian chauvinism, which has reappeared in some circles, takes up the theme of the Slavophiles of the nineteenth century who believed in the special nature and mission of Russia and of the Russian people, who rejected the legalistic and industrial West, and who sought a solution to social and other problems in the Russian soul and particularly among the "uncorrupted" peasantry. Strongly tied to the Eastern Orthodox Church, this doctrine or idea has been expressed, to the surprise of many Westerners, by such a well-known (and expelled) dissident as Alexander Solzhenitsyn.

In summary, an important component of contemporary Soviet society, operating at the cultural level, is the amalgam between the doctrinal bases of Communism and Russian nationalism described here. It remains to be seen to what degree Russian chauvinism can be maintained in the light of demographic changes that are tilting the ethnic balance toward the Central Asian Muslim population, which has, hitherto, been treated more as a colonial people than as an equal member of Soviet society.

Political Structure: One-Party Rule or Monocracy

It is difficult, at the present historical juncture, to give a simple and precise formulation of the Soviet political structure. It is perhaps easier, at least for Westerners, to state what it is not: it is not a constitutional system with checks and balances of the democratic type, nor is it a parliamentary system. The holders of power are not elected by a constituency from whom they might claim legitimacy, nor do they depend on votes of confidence given to a party (or a coalition of parties) to govern as long as they are able to obtain such votes. This is sometimes justified by stating that antagonistic interest groups do not exist.

Earlier, and particularly under Stalin, the expressions of totalitarianism and dictatorship, in the sense of personal and absolute rules, were probably appropriate though often oversimplified. These definitions may no longer be correct (Cohen 1985a). And yet a basic feature of that political philosophy has remained constant: the concept that the role of the polity (in this case the Party, acting directly or through the Soviets) is to decide, to lead, and to govern according to its own lights. The functions of that polity, then, are not primarily to reflect the wishes or the aspirations of the population at large, nor to satisfy their demands or those of groups (united into parties, as is the case in the West). Rather, they are to make secular decisions that affect the entire society and then proceed to realize or implement these decisions. To this end, the Party uses a combination of coercion and persuasion and is committed to the mobilization of human and material resources to accomplish its goals and programs.

In earlier days, the leadership (or leader) manipulated Soviet society in any way it saw fit. It destroyed and created social classes; it arrested, jailed, tortured, shot, expelled, exiled, or declared "unpersons" those it suspected of disloyalty; it controlled what was said over the radio, printed in the press, seen on television, expressed in the classroom, depicted in novels, sculpted in marble, or painted on canvas. It decided to invest in *sputniks* and *luniks* rather than in housing and flush toilets. It, and it alone, determined the correct party line and decided who was antiparty or un-Marxist. Absolute power and control over the population was its first concern, and its unwillingness to compromise and to liberalize the system reflected its fear of the dissatisfaction of the masses and its conviction that government from above by a small, self-selected élite should not perish from the face of the earth.

In today's perspective, and from what we know of Soviet society since Stalin's death, this description reads more like a caricature or some ideal type than like a reflection of contemporary reality. Indeed, in the last few years we have seen a variety of models that modulate, if not modify and transform, the relatively undifferentiated picture of political totalitarianism. Some have defined it as the administered society, totalitarianism without terror; others, as monistic rational tutelage or a variation of the bureaucratic model, the Soviet system being held as a kind of large-scale corporation. Still others talk about an essentially pluralistic society, with various interest groups that are articulated or arbitrated by the regime – the Party (Kassof 1964) – or a society based on nonideological consensus arising from post-Revolutionary consensus. (These different models have been reviewed and summarized by Lowenthal [1976].) Whatever the relevance or the accuracy of these models, they suggest both the growing complexity of Soviet society and the difficulty (for Westerners) of grasping and defining the realities of that system.

Recent developments, under the aegis of Gorbachev, have demonstrated how intricate the Soviet political situation has become, and the apparent fact that the head of the party cannot simply dictate: he must persuade his colleagues in the Politbureau and the Secretariat (and in the Central Committee). Political power, however, remains highly centralized, though it must take into account the latent resistance of entrenched bureaucratic interest groups.

Economic Structure: Industrialism

Industrialism can be described as the form of economic structure derived from the use of a specific type of production. This mode of production, the industrial plant or firm, is an important element of any modernization process and immeasurably increases the national product. It is characterized (regardless of its ownership form) by the concentrated employment of large numbers of workers and employees. Industrialism is usually operated by a professional management, divorced from ownership in the legal sense (but not in the sense of control and use) almost as much as the workers and employees are, and in its operations it applies technology and scientific advances. This contrasts sharply with agricultural production or the family firm of early capitalism mentioned before.

In a society of this type, the individual's primary ties with family, church, village, and small community are weakened and replaced by affiliation with larger reference groups, such as trade unions, professional organizations, employee or worker groups, class, the firm, the party, and the nation itself, as focuses of personal loyalty and emotional commitment.

Industrialization also brings a spectrum of consequences resulting from large urban concentrations of population, the development of mass culture, and the gradual replacement of traditionalism, religious orientation, and family- (or kinship-) centered values and solidarities by new attitudes and commitments consisting of a sort of secular morality. This morality tends to emphasize the importance of occupation and, to some extent, the consumption ethics of the city rather than the production ethics of the countryside, which are rooted in the soil and stress physical toil. It also brings in its wake many social problems characteristic of urban life almost everywhere, resulting from a loosening of family and community controls. They include crime, juvenile delinquency, family disorganization and divorce (Mydans 1985), alcoholism, drug addition, and social deviance in general (Connor 1972).

Occupation, and particularly occupational achievement (including employment in the political sphere), tend to become the central determinants of an individual's life chances and of the society's pattern of social stratification and inequality (Yanowitch 1977). In this respect, Soviet class structure resembles to a considerable degree that of Western industrial society, even to the existence of poverty as an officially defined social problem (McAuley 1979; Matthews 1985). An increasingly important role is played by specialists, particularly by professionals on whose activities the functioning of a modern society largely depends. The rehabilitation of the intelligentsia in the Soviet Union during the 1930s, in connection with the program of industrialization, provided dramatic notice that, in spite of ideological exaltation, manual laborers had become relatively unimportant when compared with specialists not engaged in physical labor. It also brought to light the uneasy relationship between the regime and specialists as a social force on whom the regime has to rely for operations of the system, but whom it also tends to distrust politically because of the power inherent in their activities and because the critical faculties indispensable in their work cannot necessarily be limited to that sphere. A well-known case is that of Zhores Medvedev, a highly qualified geneticist who came to the attention of the security organs because he had written several unofficial studies very critical of the Soviet regime (the Lysenko affair, postal censorship, political controls of scientists, etc). He was forcibly detained in a mental hospital, where psychiatrists questioned why he, a scientist, would concern himself with matters outside his field of professional competence. This they considered a symptom of his "illness" (Medvedev and Medvedev 1971).

Here, increasingly, the problem has been how the party can maintain control over people whose effectiveness and contribution are enhanced by lack of control, that is, by independence.

In general, the physical sciences have been granted significantly more leeway than have the humanities. Specialists and professionals have been considerably emancipated from party supervision so that, for instance, it is now possible to be wrong or to express reservations and criticism in professional matters without incurring the risk of punishment. Failures of a technical nature are no longer, as far as one can judge, seen as the result of "wrecking" or sabotage activities for which people have to be penalized. Given the paralyzing effect of the former situation, one can see the degree to which decreased party supervision, at least in this specific sphere of activities, redounds to the advantage of Soviet society.

As for the social sciences, sociology, in particular, has led a precarious existence since its official reestablishment after Stalin's death. Social science is a double-edged weapon: it provides otherwise unobtainable insights into social processes of all types, yet it also constitutes social (and political) criticism that the party is reluctant to allow. The policy of *glasnost'* has permitted some sociologists to emphasize publicly the importance of their discipline, to deplore the restrictions imposed on them in the past, and to call for the freedom openly to investigate "negative" phenomena that need correction. Without that freedom, they say, it will be impossible to tackle realistically the many social and other problems Soviet society faces. As one prominent sociologist wrote in *Pravda* early in 1987

> If one conceals from people generalized information on the conditions governing their own lives (such as figures on environmental pollution, on-the-job injuries, crime, and so on), one cannot expect them to become more active in either the production or political spheres. (Zaslavskaia 1987, 2–3)

With the development of classes and class consciousness, Soviet society has not escaped such phenomena as the attempt by the upper or middle class to monopolize certain privileges and advantages and to pass these on to their children. In the Soviet Union, as is often true in American society, the wise child chooses his parents accordingly.

Industrialism thus leads to important and largely irreversible structural changes in the society. For example, the increased rationality and education needed to operate an industrial and technological society cannot be limited to a narrow field but will eventually alter the entire nature of Soviet society. Or, expressed slightly differently, the economic system always places a constraint on the political system. As the functions performed by educated members of the middle class (the intelligentsia) become more strategic, the regime will find it difficult to ignore their demands for greater freedom.

In summary, the combination and interpenetration of these three major elements (national Communism in the culture, one-party rule in politics, and industrialism in economics) account for many aspects of contemporary Soviet society.

The Question of Relative Undifferentiation

The Party has undertaken to shape the culture, to rule the society, and to manage the economy. It has done so because its leadership, starting with Lenin, has been imbued with the conviction that nothing less than total control in these spheres would permit it to remain in power and to accomplish its foreordained historical mission.

It may be argued, furthermore, that in the past the Party (and Stalin) played a critical and "objectively" necessary role in the development of Soviet society. It would be difficult, for example, to conceive of the rapid industrialization of Soviet society after 1928 without the existence of the Party and of a Stalin (or some similar organization or man) that would, through control of the three spheres, effect such a rapid mobilization of human, material, financial, and emotional resources in pursuit of that goal, particularly under conditions that made it undesirable, or perhaps impossible, for the Soviet Union to borrow large amounts of capital from abroad. As a result of the Party's decision to industrialize under forced draft and to engage in a process of primitive capital accumulation, the main contours of Soviet Russia emerged. Moreover, because of the diffuse power with which the Party is endowed, it can intervene like a flying squad or a benevolent monarch at almost any point in Soviet society and unravel knotty problems caused, for example, by bureaucratic conflicts or breakdowns in supplies (see, for example, Cocks 1978). However, these often tend to be particularistic ad hoc interventions that need to be activated for a specific problem rather than universal regulative mechanisms of the type more available in pluralistic societies, such as an independent judiciary, the political franchise, or market mechanisms.

There is no doubt, as Jerry Hough (1965, 1969) has pointed out many times, that the Party plays a significant role in many aspects of Soviet political and economic life. Hough argues, and quite soundly, that the role of the Party is functional, particularly at the lower administrative levels, in "getting things done," and that if there were no party, some other agency would have to perform these tasks. In contrast, according to Milovan Djilas, the Party has become a parasite on society. Although this is a politically inspired hyperbole, the Party *has* become, as suggested, in many respects a conservative, if not a reactionary, force in Soviet society. Certainly Brezhnev (Shipler 1979) and his colleagues were devoted to the status quo. His two successors did not rule long enough to effect any substantive changes. It remains to be seen whether Gorbachev, a younger and more dynamic leader, aware of the many problems of the USSR, will be able to move Soviet society from dead center. Perhaps in the twenty-first century, when the Party as we know it today will have passed into history, some student will query the teacher on how it was possible for Russia to win the war against Hitler's Germany *in spite* of the existence of the Communist party!

It is precisely the Party's reluctance to relinquish controls that may further slow differentiation and modernization. This implies that one central authority plans and administers all social, cultural, political, and economic processes, and mutual adjustments between the demands of these different spheres and the supply (conceived in a broad form) continue to be administered rather than allowed to find their own level. This may lead to a situation in which rational planning and administering border on the irrational, uneconomical, and dysfunctional.

One imaginary illustration, from the realm of economic planning but perhaps of broader significance, is the well-known case of the pile of potatoes that must be fitted into a sack so that the maximum amount of potatoes and the minimum amount of waste space occur. The "scientific," "rational," "planned," "administered" way to go about it would be to give each potato a different ordinal number; draw profiles for each potato (let's say six to eight profiles per potato); translate these profiles into codable items; and, with the use of a computer, determine precisely how each potato is to fit with the others to keep the waste space to the irreducible minimum. This plan is feasible; it may entail the work of a team of mathematicians and cost several thousands of dollars, but it can be done. The other solution is simply to dump the potatoes into the sack and shake hard, letting each potato adjust to its neighbor in a spontaneous manner. The difference between the two solutions, in terms of waste space, is not likely to exceed 5 to 10 per cent, or perhaps a bit more. But the overall cost of the entire operation will be considerably less using the second approach, although it would deprive the team (read Party) of employment and involvement in fitting the potatoes to each other. It seems to be precisely Gorbachev's aim to let the Soviet potatoes adjust to each other more spontaneously and more cheaply than when they were painstakingly fitted by hand.

Furthermore, in comparison with the situation that obtained at the time of Stalin's death, there has been, relatively speaking, a substantial amount of loosening or thawing in Soviet society toward decentralization and cautious attempts at some degree of differentiation. This has been accompanied by the increased (though hesitant) willingness to grant certain groups greater latitude.

The Limits of Cultural Differentiation

One such group is undoubtedly the professionals, who need a fair amount of autonomy to pursue their activities at a high level of performance. Because these activities are, in many instances, critically important to the regime in its pursuit of domestic and foreign policies, it is perhaps in the cultural area that the process of differentiation has progressed farthest, though unevenly. It is now possible, as we have seen, for scientists in the physical sciences publicly to espouse principles and theories that were placed on the ideological index a few years ago for being of foreign, Western origins (cybernetics, for example). In the so-called life sciences – in biology and genetics, for instance – the vicissitudes of Trofim Lysenko's career indicate how gradual this process has been and how deeply ingrained was the idea that science must conform to orthodoxy, rather than to scientific criteria of evidence. Lysenkoism was admittedly an extreme case, and yet it illustrates the result of ideological controls over inquiry, the sanctions and punishments meted out to people who did not conform or recant their mistakes, and the price paid by the discipline itself in lost time and advances. Almost twelve years elapsed between the death of Stalin and Lysenko's removal as director of the institute of Genetics. (See Joravsky [1970] for an account of the Lysenko affair.)

In clinical medicine, to take another example, the Central Committee of the Party refused in the 1960s, and presumably ever since, to intervene in the case of a cancer cure that had been judged worthless by the Academy of Medical Sciences and prohibited by an order of the Health Ministry. The Central Committee declared that it "does not consider it possible to take upon itself the role of arbiter in approving methods of medical treatment" (*Pravda*, August 1, 1962, p. 2). In an earlier period, the Central Committee (and comrade Stalin personally) would not have been so reluctant to take a stand. But the Stalinist mode or pattern has not, by any means, entirely disappeared. In psychiatry, for example, a professional area that has become notorious because of its abuses in curbing dissidents, the domination of one man (A. V. Snezhnevskii) and his so-called Moscow school is uncontested. There is little room for people who do not agree with his theoretical premises and clinical methods. Not only does he control the major psychiatric institutions in Moscow, but he is also the editor-in-chief of the only journal of neurology and psychiatry published in the Soviet Union.

Generally speaking the development of the Soviet sociological establishment has been marked by crises, internal conflicts, changes in leadership and directions, and redefinitions of the mission of sociology. These reflect, in all probability, the ambivalence the Party feels toward a discipline that can uncover important insights into the actual workings of society, insights that, at the same time, can easily become, or be interpreted as, social criticism of contemporary conditions. Sociology thus has a potentially subversive role that must be constantly and carefully monitored lest it get out of hand. As a keen observer of the Soviet sociological scene (and a former Soviet sociologist himself) has remarked,

> Today, in the mid-1980s, given their unhappy experiences, Soviet sociologists are quite skeptical about any real renaissance in the field. They certainly have no expectations that the Kremlin will suddenly call on them to reveal the real attitudes of the peoples toward the fundamental problems of Soviet society. Those . . . who have built their careers by telling the leadership what it wants to hear are likely to receive continued support, even though the value of these endeavors can hardly deceive the sponsors. Those with more critical attitudes will continue to muddle along, receiving little official recognition but finding satisfaction inside their science. (Shlapentokh 1985, 113)

Contacts and cooperation with sociologists from the West have been accepted, in principle, but the history of the last few years indicates that this is a thorny question for ideologues, fraught with potential problems and pitfalls.

The question is particularly acute at international sociological congresses held outside the Soviet Union, where the kind of control exercised by the regime at home cannot be duplicated. Thus, international sociological congresses are seen as arenas of battle between socialist and bourgeois sociologists. Delegations come well organized and well led; assignments are made to their members to attend specific sessions, to show the Marxist flag, and to refute and defeat bourgeois views; invited sociologists, whose names appear on the program, may be denied exit visas at the last moment and replaced by unknowns. (For a remarkable insight into what goes on in the wings during such congresses, the reader is referred to "Cultural Détente at Scientific Congresses: The Secret Report of the Çzech Sociologists" 1977.) Thus, the further differentiation of sociology and its autonomy from the political system, and hence its greater ability to contribute to sociological theory and knowledge, will undoubtedly be a long and probably not unilinear process.

The uneasy relationship between the regime and artists and writers, and more specifically the poets (with their Russian tradition of social protest), also illustrates the congenital difficulty the Party has in letting the muses sing without a party-appointed conductor. Although the demands and the straitjacket of socialist realism have been toned down, artists and writers still remain under surveillance; those who exhibit too much independence are likely to find themselves invited to visit the local unit of the KGB, sent to the hinterland to gather materials at the grass roots, or facing deportation. Few, however, are likely to lose their lives or their freedom, as was the case earlier. However, jobs, appointments, and promotions often are affected by party determination. Thus, as David K. Shipler reports

> A Jewish expert on American literature discovered when he applied for a teaching job at an institute that he was to appear not before an academic board but a party committee ... he was asked if he had ever tried to change his citizenship – a euphemism for emigrating to Israel. He replied indignantly that the question, obviously about his intentions rather than his past, had no relevance. He did not get the job. (1979, E3)

At the same time, one cannot discount the impact of the generalized knowledge of what is and is not acceptable to the Party in the realm of art and literature. As a Soviet émigré once put it, the Soviet Union is the country of perfect understanding in these matters: this precensorship thus cannot be held to promote innovation, daring, or the breaking of new ground in the cultural or artistic realms.

Starting in the early 1960s, the regime has added two more instruments of control over intellectuals: the threat of their being brought up on criminal charges of anti-Soviet propaganda or of libelling Soviet reality, and of their being certified as mentally irresponsible or incompetent, requiring placement in mental hospitals for indefinite periods of time (Bloch and Reddaway 1977; Field 1972; Medvedev and Medvedev 1971).

It is interesting to speculate on what would take place if the Party were to remove most or all of its strictures on cultural life. It may be conjectured, on the basis of what has happened since Stalin's death, that Soviet culture would only benefit through such a step, as seen in recent years in the case of movies. On balance, in cultural life the Party impoverishes rather than enriches, constricts rather than promotes.

The Limits of Economic Differentiation

As in cultural life, one might argue that the Soviet economic system has reached a level of development and complexity that requires further differentiation from the party in order to acquire flexibility. In addition to the relative decentralization of many economic decisions, this might mean the introduction of limited market-type mechanisms permitting an automatic or spontaneous adjustment of supply and demand, and rationality in terms of actual costs and customer demand, while keeping the economy responsive to the needs and the interests of the whole nation. The Soviets have recognized the necessity, for example, to calculate interest in the use of capital for national economic decisions. However, two elements prevent, or at least slow, such developments. One is the ideological impact of economic policy and decisions; it centers on the potential doctrinal erosion attendant on the introduction of devices that have been associated with capitalism. In other words, party ideologues are saying, "What does it matter if we become economically more efficient, if this is purchased at the price of compromising our basic value commitments?" The other element is the loss of party functions and power noted earlier that would follow the further differentiation of the economic life from party controls.

Actually, the relationship between the Party and the economy, particularly the industrial sector, is more complicated than stated here. There is every evidence that the Soviet economic system is not working well, despite various reforms proposed and implemented. The reason, perhaps, is that a sophisticated economy of the advanced industrial type needs a fair amount of autonomy and flexibility to perform its tasks and to maintain flexibility under changing demands and circumstances. The Party's tight control on appointments in the economy (through the *nomenklatura*) means that the selection of managers may be based more on political considerations that on professional qualifications (Hill and Frank 1986, 88–89). It should also be noted that, as of this writing Gorbachev who, contrary to widely held opinion in the West, has *not* achieved absolute power, will try to introduce important economic reforms aimed at reducing the control exercised by Moscow, giving the managers more freedom to operate "by economic rather than administrative reforms," and drastically cutting the vast middle-level bureaucracy as "superfluous links" (Stephen D. Cohen 1985b). Whether he succeeds is still a moot question.

Some have argued that the provision of this autonomy – this differentiation and separation from the political power represented by the Party – would, as seems to be borne out by the experiences of the West, increase the efficiency and the productivity of the Soviet economy in its industrial sector and would thus eventually place at the Party's disposal greater aggregate resources with which to pursue its aims. But the provision of this kind of autonomy would mean, in the eyes of the Party, the increased power of managers and, eventually, a situation in which the hold and the control of the Party over industrial production might be jeopardized.

There is, of course, no absolute or definitive answer to the above question. However, the weight of the evidence seems to suggest that this concern about the erosion of its own power has kept the Party firmly in control of all phases of the economic system. This has contributed to retarded development of the economy, particularly when compared with those of the West and of Japan, with which the USSR must necessarily compare itself and with which it competes in the world arena.

By the same token, the state of agriculture, which is perennially in a crisis, might improve if the peasants were given more latitude. However, greater control by the peasants over productive activities, though it might mean more food and feed (and decreased reliance on foreign purchases), would also imply the potential power of the peasantry to dictate its terms to the Party, to enforce its will against the Party's wishes, and to charge prices commensurate with its efforts and supply and demand – to exercise, in short, power and blackmail that the Party would not countenance from peasants any more than from industrial managers, blue-collar workers, or the military. Here again we must wait and see the degree to which Gorbachev is willing to relinquish tight controls for the sake of a better agricultural yield and the political price and risk he is willing to take. Certainly, the Chinese have been much bolder with their "responsibility" system, making it possible for peasants to enrich themselves and at the same time increase food production. The Chinese have also recognized the ideological damage done to their collectivistic ethos by permitting the limited reintroduction of capitalistic devices.

The fusion of economic and party functions may, at the present level of maturation, constrict the further development of the Soviet economy.

The Limits of Political Differentiation

It is in the realm of politics and power that the least differentiation has taken place. The Soviets have continued to remain the political instrument of the Party – ruled, controlled, and managed by the Party – and have not been allowed to be what they claim: the representatives of the people. Nor has the concept of the polity, with citizens given an effective franchise and responsibility for the choice of those who govern them, been allowed to take root in Communist society. The unanimous elections are not expressions of popular suffrage, but contrived symbolic manifestations of the kind of organic (monolithic) unity the Party claims for the society it rules. By claiming to embody the will of the people, the Party has effectively deprived the people of this will. By claiming that it speaks for the interests of all groups in Soviet society, the Party has deprived these groups of the ability to articulate, in public, these interests. (They may, of course, be articulated within the bureaucratic structure of the Party. See, for example, Skillings [1969].) The Party thus has eliminated and constricted public debates and the possible enrichments that might arise from such debates.

The Question of Unsanctioned Differentiation

The loosening up of Soviet society, as part of the general modernization launched by the Party, is bound to continue, whether sanctioned or not by the Party. It is visible in the realm of economics with the existence of a parallel economy and of a grey (or black) market that operates on the principle of supplying (illegally, to be sure) a pent-up demand for consumer goods. In the culture, the growth and flowering of an underground literature (*samlzdat*) permits the expression and the dissemination, however precarious, of texts the Party would not approve for publication. There also are artists who produce paintings and sculptures for a private market. The amount of official corruption regularly reported in the press suggests that the wishes of at least some constituents are satisfied in a kind of rude (and illegal) democracy. And the reported cases are apparently only the tip of the iceberg. But these processes of differentiation are slow and halting, given their often deviant or illegitimate character.

Conclusions

There is no indication that the Party is prepared to wither away or to give up substantial portions of its power in controlling most aspects of the society it inhabits. There is evidence, however, that since 1953 some differentiation has taken place, although very cautiously and probably with mental reservations on the part of the Party. It is possible that, with time, the professionals, specialists, and managers – the members of the intelligentsia – will constitute an ever-increasing and potentially more powerful pressure group in Soviet society, and that the Party will have to grant them more autonomy.

It is also possible that the regime will grant more latitude to the operation of economic forces, particularly if it can convince itself that this would be a prerequisite for the maintenance of the Soviet posture in the world and would not lead to erosion of the Party's power. There is no evidence that the regime will allow a loyal opposition or a second party to develop.

Thus, the Party that (in earlier phases of Soviet history) was an element of strength in the mobilization of societal resources for specific goals may now (on balance) be a source of structural rigidity. This is because, as Hill and Frank point out,

> Such a political system may be a suitable instrument for policy-making in a relatively simple society with one or two overriding goals to which all else is subordinated.... What is by no means certain is that a single party is the ideal instrument for ensuring all-around development and smooth running of a complex, modern, sophisticated and educated society ... a lively political debate is likely to produce a wider range of acceptable and effective policy options. (1986, 3–4)

The archaic nature of Soviet society may be due to a party leadership that believes in centralized control. It tends to stifle initiative and inventiveness that would add immeasurably to the power and efficiency of Soviet society. This is not to deny the possibility that in many instances, as mentioned earlier, the Party is playing the role of expediter. The Party also plays an important role in the articulation of interest groups and is an arbiter among them (but of course not a neutral arbiter, because it has vested interest in the outcomes of interest-group conflicts). The Party has done a fairly good job of surviving and keeping itself in power; it has been able, when necessary, to adjust its structure to admit into its ranks members of society who are most important in reaching the goals it has defined. To some degree it has been responsive to the demands of professionals, industrial workers, and (lately) peasants. However, these responses are necessarily in terms of party interests, party ideology, and party power.

Hypothetically, the Party now may contrive to retard and constrict the society it inhabits and helped to develop, because further differentiation, decentralization, and democratization could be secured only at the cost of ideological erosion and power concessions, a price it is unwilling to pay.

Some in the West and in certain countries of Eastern Europe have commented on the good fortune of having the Communist party at the helm in the Soviet Union, because that party substantially decreases the might and the power of the Soviet Union. Imagine, they say, what the situation would be if that country were run efficiently and if its potentials, now frozen by its conservative party leadership, were unlocked by a new system or a new regime! To reiterate, in radically altered form, the classical statement of a latter-day American cultural hero, what is good for the Communist party may not necessarily be good for Soviet society toward the end of the twentieth century.

To recast the hypothesis presented in this essay in a Marxist perspective: the Party objectively and historically was, on balance, a progressive and liberating force when compared with tsarism; it led to the unlocking and mobilization of resources, both human and material, to industrialize, urbanize, mechanize, educate, and otherwise propel Russia to a higher stage than reached before; it has by now accomplished its historic task, and unless it is willing or able radically to alter its modus operandi, it may become increasingly redundant, superfluous, and dysfunctional to the society it inhabits; and if it has become a ruling class, it is doomed to generate the very instrument of its own destruction.

And yet, as Hough (Hough and Fainsod 1979, 556–76) has cogently pointed out, analysts of the Soviet scene have been particularly unsuccessful in their predictions of the development of Soviet society and unwilling to recognize the significance of the roles of different leaders in imparting new directions in that society. Who can tell what Gorbachev and his successors will be able to accomplish?

Notes

[1] For example, production of a movie entitled "The Chairman" was held up because it portrayed a Khrushchev type. The essence of the type was that the chairman knew it all and trusted no one:

"Before us we have a chairman, a leader, who regards himself as a commander . . . in the sense that he knows only one way of dealing with subordinates, by command. It is no accident that he shouts so much. . . . This is an essential part of his style of leadership. He is the leader who decides everything for all, he does everything for himself, he entrusts nothing to anyone. If he consulted with an experienced peasant, it is only as if he were an obedient 'apprentice,' nothing more." (Cited in the *New York Times*, December 15, 1964, 12.)

[2] It might be argued that in the United States, Americanism has sometimes played a role similar to that of partyness, although its application, and the implications of that application (except in moments of paranoid hysteria such as McCarthyism), are not intense as the more inclusive and universalistic Soviet term.

[3] The fiction is maintained, of course, that Party congresses are means to convey the wishes of the membership to the Party.

References

Bialer, Seweryn. 1962. "But Some Are More Equal Than Others." In *Russia Under Khrushchev*, edited by Abraham Brumberg, pp. 240–62. New York: Praeger.

Bloch, Sidney, and Peter Reddaway. 1977. *Psychiatric Terror: How Soviet Psychiatry Is Used to Suppress Dissent*. New York: Basic Books.

Boas, H. P. 1984. "Soviet Science." *Science* 225 (July): 145.

Brzezinski, Zbigniew. 1961. "The Nature of the Soviet System." *Slavic Review* 20, no. 3: 351–68.

The Case of Leonid Pliusch. 1976. Introduction by Peter Reddaway. Boulder, Colo.: Westview Press.

Cocks, Paul. 1978. "Administrative Rationality, Political Change, and the Role of the Party." In *Soviet Society and the Communist Party*, edited by Karl W. Ryavec, pp. 41–59. Amherst: University of Massachusetts Press.

Cohen, Stephen F. 1985a. *Rethinking the Soviet Experience: Politics and History Since 1917*. New York: Oxford University Press.

Cohen, Stephen D. 1985b. "Gorbachev's Power Struggle," *The Boston Globe*, September, 23, p. 17.

Connor, Walter D. 1972. *Deviance in Soviet Society: Crime, Delinquency and Alcoholism*. New York: Columbia University Press.

"Cultural Détente at Scientific Congresses: The Secret Report of the Czech Sociologists." 1977. Edited and introduced by Lewis S. Feuer. *Orbis* 20 (Spring): 115–27.

Daniels, Robert V. 1962. *The Nature of Communism*. New York; Random House.

Djilas, Milovan. 1957. *The New Class: An Analysis of the Communist System*. New York: Praeger.

Eisenstadt, S. N. 1964. "Social Change, Differentiation and Evolution." *American Sociological Review* 29, no. 3: 375–86.

Field, Mark G. 1972. "Soviet Psychiatry and the Polity: A Study of the Medicalization of Deviance." *Annals of the New York Academy of Medicine* 48, no. 1: 82–92.

The Grigorenko Papers. Writings by General P. G. Grigorenko and Documents on His Case. 1976. Introduction by Edward Crankshaw. Boulder, Colo.: Westview Press.

Hill, Ronald J., and Peter Frank. 1986. *The Soviet Communist Party*, 3rd ed. Boston: Allen & Unwin.

Hough, Jerry F. 1965. "The Soviet Concept of the Relationship between the Lower Party Organs and the State Administration." *Slavic Review* 24, no. 2: 215–40.

————. 1969. *The Soviet Prefects: The Local Party Organs in Industrial Decision-Making*. Cambridge: Harvard University Press.

Hough, Jerry F., and Merle Fainsod. 1979. *How the Soviet Union Is Governed*. Cambridge: Harvard University Press.

Inkeles, Alex, and Raymond A. Bauer. 1959. *The Soviet Citizen*. Cambridge: Harvard University Press.

Joravsky, David. 1970. *The Lysenko Affair*. Cambridge: Harvard University Press.

Kassof, Allen. 1964. "The Administered Society: Totalitarianism without Terror." *World Politics* 26 (July): 558–75.

Lipset, Seymour Martin. 1963. *The First New Nation*. New York: Basic Books.

Lowenthal, Richard. 1976. "The Ruling Party in a Mature Society." In *Social Consequences of Modernization in Communist Societies*, edited by Mark G. Field, pp. 81–118. Baltimore, Md.: Johns Hopkins University Press.

Matthews, Mervyn. 1972. *Class and Society in Soviet Russia*. New York: Walker.

————. 1985. "Poverty in the Soviet Union." *The Wilson Quarterly* IX, 4: 75–84.

McAuley, Alastair. 1979. *Economic Welfare in the Soviet Union: Poverty, Living Standards, and Inequality*. Madison: The University of Wisconsin Press.

Medvedev, Zhores A., and Roy A. Medvedev. 1971. *A Case of Madness*. New York; Alfred A. Knopf.

Moore, Barrington, Jr. 1954. *Terror and Progress USSR: Some Sources of Change and Stability in the Soviet Dictatorship*. Cambridge: Harvard University Presss.

Mydans, Seth. 1985. "Social Revolution Sweeps through Soviet Home." *The New York Times*, August 25, p. 14.

Parsons, Talcott. 1977. *The Evolution of Societies*. Englewood Cliffs, N.J.: Prentice-Hall.

Rostow, Walt W. 1960. *The Stages of Economic Growth: A Non-Communist Manifesto*. New York: Cambridge University Press.

Russell, Bertrand. 1920. *Bolshevism: Practice and Theory*. New York: Harcourt, Brace, and Howe.

Shipler, David K. 1979. "Brezhnev and His Colleagues Are Devoted to the Status Quo." *New York Times*, June 14, p. E3.

Shlapentokh, Vladimir. 1985. *Sociology and Politics: The Soviet Case*. Falls Church, Va.: Delphic Associates.

Skillings, H. Gordon. 1969. "Interest Groups and Communist Politics." In *Communist Studies and the Social Sciences: Essays on Methodology and Empirical Theory*, edited by Frederick J. Fleron, Jr., pp. 281–97. Chicago: Rand McNally.

Stalin, J. 1940. *Problems of Leninism*. Moscow: Foreign Language Publishing House.

Yanowitch, Murray. 1977. *Social and Economic Inequality in the Soviet Union: Six Studies*. White Plains, N.Y.: M. E. Sharpe.

Zaslavskaia, T. 1987. "Questions of theory: Restructuring and Sociology." *Pravda*, February 6, pp. 2–3. (Available in English translation in the *Current Digest of the Soviet Press*, XXXIX (6), 3: 22–23.)

7
Words and Deeds:
CPSU Ideological Work

Thomas F. Remington

Ideology and Political Power

As is the case with other mature "movement-regimes," to use a term introduced by Robert C. Tucker (1971) to describe "revolutionary mass-movement regimes under single-party auspices," the Soviet political regime has changed in character from one dedicated to generating revolutionary power to one concerned with maintaining and managing that power. Historically, the impetus of the Bolshevik revolution reached its peak during Stalin's rule as party general secretary, before being overtaken by the forces of bureaucratization that it launched. Through the often violent collectivization of agriculture, the forced-draft establishment of an industrial infrastructure, and the replacement of most forms of market exchange with a system of central planning and administration in the economy, Stalin fulfilled the Bolshevik vision of a powerful state dedicated to industrial progress and national might and freed of competing political forces. At the same time, through the decimation of the Party, and particularly its older generation, and of military, cultural, and other elites, Stalin went far to replace the Party's institutional authority with personal dictatorship.

Through what Khrushchev later termed his "cult of personality," Stalin sought to establish himself as the only true apostle of Marxism-Leninism – Lenin's faithful follower – and as a brilliant "continuator" of the doctrine who had enriched it through original and profound formulations (Tucker 1973, 483–4). In effect, Stalin aimed at merging ideology and power in his own person. He continued to insist that each policy decision the leadership made was in accordance with the scientific laws of socialism, but, as Soviet dissident historian Roy Medvedev put it, Stalin

> did not derive theoretical positions from concrete reality; he forced theory to fit his wishes, subordinated it to transient situations – in a word, he politicized theory.... No one except Stalin could challenge or correct a theoretical proposition in the Marxist-Leninist classics. This law applied especially to his own propositions. They could only be slavishly repeated without the slightest alteration. (Medvedev 1973, 512)

The death of Stalin in 1953 and the Party's apparently permanent renunciation of terror confronted the post-Stalinist leadership with a different dilemma. If the stultifying rigidity of the policy process and fear of taking initiative or questioning truths identified with the ruler's pronouncements that had characterized the late Stalin era began to disappear, so too did the convergence of party and state authority in a single unchallengeable figure. The end of Stalin's personal dictatorship weakened both ideology and power.

Accordingly, it was politically expedient for Nikita Khrushchev, first secretary of the CPSU from 1953 until he was deposed in 1964, and, subsequently, for Leonid Brezhnev, who succeeded Khrushchev and remained party general secretary until his death in November 1982, to emphasize the *Party*, not the leader, as the preeminent source of political authority in the system ,(Breslauer 1982, 157–60). Khrushchev's risky campaign of de-Stalinization substitued the positive symbols of the Party and its Leninist heritage for the tarnished symbols of Stalin and the "cult of personality" under which serious "crimes" had been committed. By means of a variety of ideologically oriented measures, such as the introduction of a third party program in 1961, Khrushchev sought to reinspire popular faith in the vision of a society advancing to a definite goal, that of communist society, characterized as one of abundance and equality.

Although Khrushchev is often, and rightly, remembered for his dramatic gestures of cultural liberalization – represented, for example, by his intervention in 1962 in allowing the publication of Alexander Solzhenitsyn's gripping portrait of life in a Stalinist labor camp – his efforts to restore Marxism-Leninism to a central place in the outlook of Soviet citizens were a consistent aim of his rule. In his attempt to spread familiarity with the basic tenets of the doctrine among as broad a stratum of the population as possible, he demanded that party propaganda be linked with "life" – that is, it should be practical – and with the building of communism – that is, it should point the way toward the future (Harris 1984). A major party resolution of 1960 attacked the existing propaganda system for failing to educate the masses "in a communist spirit." Propaganda of Marxism-Leninism should be "brought to every Soviet person." Party organizations were called on to organize a system of courses in doctrine at the primary, intermediate, and advanced levels and to enroll as many people as possible in them. The result was a tremendous swelling of the party education system, particularly with nonmembers of the Party (Barghoorn and Remington 1986, 240–41).

Although the Brezhnev-Kosygin leadership quickly changed the orientation of party propaganda from a mass to an elite educational system, it also encouraged other, newer forms of ideological work geared to various segments of the population, all in keeping with the continued effort to emphasize the continuity and legitimacy of *Party* rule. This general goal was all the more pressing in view of the new party oligarchy's criticisms of their predecessor, who was accused of "subjective" and impulsive decision making. The primacy of the party received a further boost with the 1971 decision that the party's right of *kontrol* – which can be translated as the right to verify that party policy is being implemented in a particular organization – was extended from factories and other production-oriented enterprises to educational, medical, design, and research establishments. Some 170,000 Primary Party Organizations (PPOs) thus acquired the power to supervise managerial performance of scientists and other professionals (*Partiinoe stroitel'stvo* 1985, 100). This change corresponded to what Soviet researchers saw as an increase in the Party's active intervention in technical matters and personnel decisions in their institutions during the late 1960s and 1970s (Miller 1985).

The Party's central status in the political system received constitutional standing in the 1977 Constitution. In contrast to the Stalin Constitution of 1936, which had referred to the Party only in conjunction with descriptions of the rights of mass organizations, the 1977 Constitution formalizes the Party's leading role within the political system as a whole. Article Six declares the Party to be "the leading and guiding force of Soviet society, the nucleus of its political system and of state and public organizations" (Sharlet 1978, 12, 78). Similarly, the revised edition of the third party program adopted at the 27th Party Congress in 1986 introduces a new section on the "political system," which employs formulations equivalent to those used in the Constitution. According to the new edition of the Party program adopted at the 27th Party Congress in 1986, the Party

is the core of the political system of Soviet society. All other links in this system function under its direction – the Soviet state, the trade unions, the Komosomol, cooperatives and other public organizations, reflecting the unity and uniqueness of the interests of all strata of the population, of all nations and nationalities of the country. Working within the framework of the Constitution, the CPSU directs and coordinates the work of state and public organizations, seeing to it that each of them fully carries out its particular functions. (*Materialy* 1986, 158)

By describing the Party's distinctive role as that of the leading core of the entire political system – the body coordinating and directing not only government, but also all public and voluntary associations – the new program sets forth a much more ambitious claim for the Party's institutional position than even that laid out by Khrushchev.

The cumbersome, bureacratized political system that Gorbachev and his fellow rulers have inherited is in most essentials still, as Vernon V. Aspaturian puts it, "the house that Stalin built," with the exception, of course, that Stalin's towering personal power and mass terror are absent (1984, 68). Stalin completed the Bolshevik revolutionary drive to concentrate maximum political and economic power in the hands of the party leadership. The problem for Stalin's successors has been to make that power a permanent and regular resource at the disposal of the Party for the accomplishment of centrally determined policy goals.

The Party and Ideological Work

The USSR's transformation from mobilizing to ruling party regime may be compared to the development of other indigenous Communist revolutions, such as that of China, as well as to non-Marxist parties of national revolution, such as the PRI in Mexico and the Congress in India. Many analysts regard the modernization of society as the driving force in the changes that occur in the ruling parties of such systems and in the relations between the ruling parties and their societies. The passage from a predominantly revolutionary value system at the heart of mass politics to that of a complex bureaucratic system challenges a party's ability to maintain its identity as the ruling force. As Barrington Moore put it in an early and prescient analysis of Soviet politics, the criteria for making "good" decisions will always combine the demand for power, the force of tradition, and a rational calculation of cost and benefit, but the relative importance of the last considerations must rise if the party is to guide the system successfully (Moore 1966, 184–185).

In a leading theoretical framework for comparing the development of single-party regimes, Samuel Huntington outlines a succession of three phases. In the first phase, the regime is intent on the transformation of political and social structures, particularly to destroy alternative bases of power and to create new ones. In the second phase, the regime consolidates its power by regularizing procedures and institutions for decision: the party as an organization assumes greater importance than in the revolutionary phase, while the personal power of the charismatic leader or leaders and the force of ideology declines. In the third, or adaptive phase, the party faces the new challenges of maintaining its predominant policy role while acknowledging the claims to power made by the new forces grown up on the native soil of the regime, such as the modernizing demands of specialists and managers, the complexity of organized groups, a more numerous and confident but still critical intelligentsia, and demands by popular groups for participation. Through some combination of exclusion and co-operation, the party responds to these claimants and is itself made over into a more broadly representative body, far removed from the exclusive, revolutionary elite character it possessed in the initial phase (Huntington 1970).

How well does this scheme fit the development of the Soviet political system? While it is the case that after Stalin's death, and again after Khrushchev's dismissal, the leadership emphasized the Party's institutional authority and the *collective* nature of its leadership, it is equally true that in each succession the party leader ultimately came to overshadow his comrades in the leadership and to place ever greater reliance on propaganda as a way of justifying his, and the Party's, authority. Ideological work, far from atrophying, has been successively intensified despite the declining importance of ideology as a directing and unifying force in society. If the 1960 resolution cited earlier represented Khrushchev's effort to revive ideology as an instrument of power, a 1979 party resolution on the need for an overhaul of ideological work was the equivalent under Brezhnev ("O dal'neishem uluchshenii" 1979).

Now, under Gorbachev, ideological policy has been reoriented dramatically. Gorbachev himself has repeatedly demanded that ideological work be harnessed to the urgent demands of economic modernization and social reconstruction.

Specifically, Gorbachev has frequently pointed out that the test of the effectiveness of ideological work is its impact on improving productivity. "The most important field for exerting effort in ideological work, as in all activity of party and people, was and remains the economy," Gorbachev asserted, even before assuming the office of general secretary, in a major address on ideology at a Kremlin conference in December 1984. Insisting that the measure of performance in the ideological sphere is *deeds*, not *words*, he has attacked the reliance on hollow, trite jargon and the bureaucratic reflex of reporting purely quantitative measures, such as the number of official measures taken rather than actual results obtained (Gorbachev 1984). Intent on revitalizing a society that had slipped into stagnation, Gorbachev and his colleagues have pressed the mass media to criticize the complacent, expose the corrupt, and identify solutions to problems. Through the campaign for *glasnost'* – openness, publicity, or disclosure – limits of permissible debate and criticism in the mass media have been sharply expanded.

In many ways the shift in ideological policy under Gorbachev resembles Khrushchev's efforts to eliminate Stalinist dogmatism and open public discussion to new ideas. Two major aspects of Khrushchev's de-Stalinization were criticism of unwanted practices identified with the past and a stress on concepts and values associated with Leninism in an undistorted form. In a similar way Gorbachev has discarded theoretical concepts promoted under Brezhnev and Chernenko — such as the notion that the USSR had entered a "stage" of "developed socialism" that led gradually and inexorably toward the Communist future — that were widely regarded as excuses for slack leadership and ineffective policy. As under Khrushchev, the content of doctrinal teachings has changed to focus attention on the policies of the new leadership, particularly Gorbachev's ambitious program for raising social productivity.

The oscillation of ideological policy between phases of orthodoxy and pragmatism and the Party's continuing need to generate support for policy through propaganda suggest that the Party adapts ideology to current political and policy needs but is unwilling to relinquish its monopoly on the determination of ideological policy. German political scientist Richard Löwenthal has argued that "while a further evolution of Communist regimes ruling mature societies toward an acceptance of ideological erosion may be conceivable, it would also be an evolution away from the monopoly of the party — a step on the road toward democracy" (Löwenthal 1974, 357).

Thus, although Huntington's observations about the greater institutional authority of the Party and the challenges posed by the greater complexity of managing a modern society (not to speak of one with world-wide commitments) alert us to forces acting on the makeup and duties of the Party, we must also bear in mind the ways in which Communist party regimes typically differ from those with broader and more inclusive structures. Specifically, the CPSU claims three principal powers: determination of policy and verification of policy implementation; recruitment, training, and assignment of cadres to leading positions in government and public life; and control over the ideological molding of Soviet citizens through direction of the means of political socialization and communication (*Partiinoe stroitel'stvo*, 1985, 60). These powers explain the Party's predominance within the political system. At the center, the Party Politburo (and in each lesser territorial jurisdiction, the equivalent policy-setting inner core of the governing party committee) determines the broad lines of domestic and foreign policy that party and government agencies must follow. The Politburo is assisted both in formulating policy and in ensuring that it is implemented by the apparatus of the Central Committee, divided into twenty functional departments that oversee lower party and government organs; the apparatus is run by the Secretariat, made up of the full-time party officials vested with responsibility for the day-to-day business of the Party. Similar units perform equivalent roles at lower levels of the hierarchical party system.

The Party's control over cadre selection is the second and highly crucial instrument of political power. Through the *nomenklatura* system (a set of lists of posts, appointment to which requires the approval of a designated party committee), party personnel managers wield the power to control promotions, demotions, and transfers to all "key positions," as the handbook *Party Construction* puts it, in state and society. A party committee may "recommend" that a particular comrade be named to a certain job – and its recommendation is normally treated as binding – or it may simply reserve the right to veto a choice made by another organization. Party recruitment of political elites extends as well to the training of cadres. Each individual admitted to the Party, or to the *reserve nomenklatura* (a back-up pool of candidates eligible for appointment to nomenklatura jobs), or to nomenklatura positions proper, is expected to enroll in an appropriate unit of the party schooling system. Party committees are urged to maintain an adequate pool of reserve candidates, to give them assignments, and to monitor their progress (Harasymiw 1984, 154–9; Cherniak 1984, 110–11).

In return for its many demands of cadres, the Party offers those in nomenklatura posts a number of advantages. Among these are a certain degree of political security: career moves are generally lateral or upward, occasionally downward, but, at least until Gorbachev, such moves rarely threatened nomenklatura status itself. Material privileges and access to internal sources of information complement the security of tenure afforded by possession of a nomenklatura position and also tend to foster the widespread impression that the people in nomenklatura posts form a ruling class, since they are identifiably also the leading *social* elite in Soviet society (Voslenksy 1984).

The final power over which the Party claims and exercises a political monopoly is the ideological function – control over the content of political socialization and political communication. Party ideological responsibility is strikingly broad. It extends to the planning and monitoring of the thematic content of all forms of regular communication on political topics, such as the print and broadcast media, the systems of oral briefings, exhortation, and instruction for general and specialized audiences, and the calendar of anniversaries and holidays and other forms of ceremony. It also encompasses the ideological aspects of many other government and private functions, including military training, popular education, citizen contacts with the outside world, scientific research, and the popular and fine arts. It relies on a small hierarchy of party officials in the agitation–propaganda departments of each party committee for basic supervision. They are supplemented by specialized bureaucracies and agencies of communications and control, including the KGB, which among its many other duties watches over political and ideological leanings of citizens; the censorship apparatus (sometimes called *Glavlit*), which grants approval before publication of all printed or broadcast material; the State Committee on Publishing, which runs the printing and publishing industry; the Journalists' Union and the parallel unions of writers, artists, composers, and other branches of the creative intelligentsia; the Main Political Administration of the Soviet Army and Navy, which supervises the political organs overseeing the armed forces; and the League of Communist Youth, or Komsomol, considered to be the Party's trusted helper and reserve in matters affecting Soviet youth. In each agency, the Party makes its presence felt through an inner core of primary party organizations composed of the party members working in each institution.

Beyond these organizations stands the enormous corps of spare-time speakers and organizers making up the ideological *aktiv* of the party. Activists perform a wide variety of ideological duties, nearly all involving face-to-face interaction between speaker and audience. About four million persons (of whom about 60 per cent are party members) perform "agitation" on a regular or sporadic basis. Agitators, who are often shop foremen, brigade leaders, and leading workers, give relatively simple and straightforward pep talks related to specific tasks, such as fulfilling the production plan or turning out to vote in the elections to the soviets.

More substantive briefings ("political information") are normally carried out by such persons as engineers and technicians, managers, and administrators. Like agitation, these briefings are usually conducted at the workplace, where the familiar atmosphere is used to enhance the credibility of the message. There are about two million political information speakers, of whom some 70 per cent belong to the Party.

Another three million people – usually scholars and ranking specialists – belong to the Znanie (Knowledge) Society, which operates as a nation-wide lecture bureau; to be sure, only a minority of them regularly give lectures. Znanie began as part of the effort to instill an atheistic outlook through imparting scientific knowledge and a scientific world outlook; today the organized lecture system covers a broad range of political, scientific, legal, and other topics. To these regular institutions of oral communication should be added the network of adult political instruction, under which spare-time courses in theoretical issues are offered by party committees and Komosomol organizations. Some seventy million people take courses in the "party education," "economic education," or "Komsomol education" systems, and about two and one-half million trained propagandists take part as teachers and discussion leaders (Nenashev 1985, 6).

To these settings of oral ideological work should be added the many organized contacts between citizens and officials through the practice of "reports." Reporters are managers, specialists, government and party officials, and other ranking elites who are sent out to address groups in a given territory on a given topic, often on what are termed *unified political days*. The Party encourages the opportunity for officials to appear to the public not as faceless and all-powerful bureaucrats, but as servants of the people engaged in solving tasks of major importance. By answering audience questions they may help squelch rumors or reduce dissatisfaction with existing conditions; at the same time, as is the case with all the enumerated forms of oral political contacts, the monitoring of questions and comments raised from the public serves as an important source of feedback information for party and government officials about current performance.

All told, as many as eleven million or so individuals, a majority of them party members, serve as ideological activists by taking part at least occasionally in one of these activities. They help ensure that the authority the party leadership maintains in the ideological sphere is upheld in the many channels of organized communication, in part to serve in molding the character and consciousness of the "new Soviet person" by shaping the influences exerted in every collective setting of socialization, and in part to ensure that the party can monopolize the processes of articulation and aggregation of political demands. The ideological *aktiv* helps radiate the Party's authority, as leading force of the political system, outward into the society and to funnel information and demands back to the inner party apparatus and up the chain of party command. So great a degree of saturation of society by oral ideological work inexorably engulfs spontaneity in stultifying organizational routine. The Party must constantly fight the tendency for lower party organizations to claim success in ideological work by reporting the number of lectures read, listeners reached, meetings held, activists enrolled. Judging from the experience of the late 1950s and early 1960s, the effort to fight ideological decay by promoting *glasnost* will generate expectations that are hard to meet.

Revitalization of party ideological work has been identified as an urgent task in view of two disturbing trends reported by a number of surveys. One trend is that despite rising educational levels and media use, a substantial part of the population, often though not exclusively people with lower educational attainments, poorly comprehend the political messages to which they are exposed in the media and oral communications networks; they rely instead on conversations with coworkers, family, and friends for their information and interpretive cues (Kokorev 1973, 114–18; cf. Dridze 1975, 1979). At the same time, at the upper end of the educational spectrum, studies have found that individuals with high levels of education and background knowledge tend to be critical and discriminating users of official information sources: for them, increasing exposure to the media system even brings negative marginal returns, prompting them to "escape its effect and begin to satisfy their information needs in other forms and with the help of other means" including "ideologically hostile sources," such as samizdat and foreign radio broadcasts (Manaev 1984, 43; Komarovskii 1985, 186–97).

In view of these persistent findings, it can be little comfort to the Party's ideological managers that the surveys have also identified a third tendency: that the people who are most active in official social and political life, whether as executives or as party activists, also are likeliest to hold views congruent with the official line. As one study put it, the person in a position of political responsibility tends to "speak and think in the language [of the media] himself" (Kokorev 1973, 116). The correlation between education and social status, on the one hand, and involvement in or acceptance of regime attitudes on the other, is not linear. People with the lowest levels of background knowledge often lack the cognitive skills to absorb media messages and hence reflect the common wisdom of their peers and families. Higher on the social hierarchy, some individuals, particularly among the intelligentsia, treat official sources critically and independently and seek outside information. Still another sizable group, above all those who occupy positions of political responsibility as executives or activists, themselves become conduits of ideological influence into their surroundings. All of these patterns help explain the continuing importance of face-to-face communication, not only in maintaining particular social milieux, but also in communicating information and forming opinion in Soviet society.

Party as Elite of Elites or Ideological Priesthood?

We have described the organization of party ideological work in greater detail to illustrate the point that the rather small inner apparatus of the Party exercises its powers over *policy*, *personnel*, and *ideology* through an array of organizations and institutions that transmit and apply its authority, noting as well that party influence permeates all other organized settings of social life. This raises an important question. When we say that these are the party's exclusive powers, what do we mean by *the Party*? Is the Party the 19 million individuals who (as of 1986) enjoyed full, voting membership? Is it the large body of activists who back up the Party in its oversight and organizing functions? Or is it the 150,000 to 200,000 or so individuals who, at any given time, are employed as paid party officials?

Certainly one should take account of vast differences in status within the Party and even among the Party's paid staff. One would surely exclude from the listing of influentials the category of instructors, who rank lowest in the hierarchy and who carry out the vast bulk of liaison and administrative work.

At the same time, those officials in important bureaucracies who hold nomenklatura positions should probably be recognized as members of the "political elite" as much as party staff officials (Voslensky 1984, 94–5). These considerations suggest that the Party as an institution corresponds only roughly to the social base of the Soviet political elite.

The problem is compounded by the fact that membership policy helps the Party serve two competing aims: that of "representing" society, and that of leading it. The first principle is expressed in the current formula that the Party is a "party of the whole people, while remaining in ideology and class essence a party of the working class" (*Materialy* 1986, 188.) It is therefore a matter of concern to the party's personnel managers to ensure a rough correspondence between the proportions of workers, peasants, and white-collar employees in the workforce and in the party, as well as to bring membership levels of women and national minorities up to levels approx-imating their shares in the all-union population. On the other hand, it is also vital to the maintenance of the Party's claimed position leadership in society that it take in people holding decision-making positions as well as people at local levels who are key communicators, organizers, and opinion leaders (Miller 1982, 2–4). As a result, a dispropotionately high percentage of the country's most highly educated persons are party members, and the Party itself is a much more highly educated group than the population at large (Harasymiw 1984, 75, 188).

If we also consider that men have entered the Party at a higher rate than women, we find that for the educated male segment of the Soviet population, party membership is a good deal less exclusive than it might seem. To be sure, the Party constitutes only about 9.7 per cent of the adult Soviet population, but, as Jerry Hough writes, "with approximately half the men over thirty with a college degree being members and over a third of men over thirty with a high school degree alone being members, we are, indeed, using the word 'elite' in a very broad sense if we continue to speak of the party in such terms." Thus, for Hough, "There is no possibility that one-fifth of the male population of any country can be a special ideological priesthood, a group that can arise above occupational and other parochial interests in any single-minded dedication to the party" (Hough and Fainsod 1979, 344–45).

Judging from the Party's composition, then, we might agree that the Party is tending to become "an elite of specialized elites," to use Zygmunt Bauman's term (1976, 91). The tendency for the Party to become trans-formed in this way is accelerated by the decreasing relevance of Marxist-Leninist doctrine – or indeed of any dogmatic belief system – to the complex problems the society faces. With the erosion of ideology, according to Samuel Huntington, comes a lowering of the old tension between "red" and "expert," or political loyalty and pragmatic rationality, as criteria for policy making;

"the political needs as seen by the party elite and technical-administrative needs endorsed by the managerial specialists" grow closer (1970, 33–34). To be sure, some ideology specialists might be found defensively arguing that if only managers and line administrators would wholeheartedly back the Party's ideological efforts, they might expect improved performance and productivity. But the demands on the party for rationalization of decision making and for accommodation of the interests of technical and managerial elites make this the rearguard struggle for survival of an increasingly obsolescent section of the Party.

The conception of adaptive change this line of argument advances is one of the increasing spread of modernization, that is, the differentiation and specialization of political and social institutions, the diffusion of rational-technical rather than traditional or political criteria of decision making, and the growth of influence of expert and managerial elites. As these are incorporated into the Party, they transform it into an arena in which professional politicians are brokers among powerful outside interests but not themselves representative of a single, unified political will. The problem with this point of view, though, is that it treats one important *tendency* as the predominant direction of change, ignoring forces that stimulate the reinforcement of party authority and cause the party to fall back on the threadbare, but still indispensable, doctrine of Marxism-Leninism to justify the demands for social unity and discipline.

Among these demands perhaps the most important factor is the international situation. Soviet pronouncements make it clear that global politics continues to be a mortal struggle between contending political forces, most sharply between the camps of socialism and capitalism. The complexity of the world arena and the aggressiveness of imperialism are cited to justify the demand for unity of perspective and centralization of decision making in foreign policy, although these demands do not preclude an increasing reliance by senior decision makers on military, intelligence, foreign area, and other specialists, the latter influence policy largely to the extent that policy makers open a "window" for their advice, normally within their defined spheres of competence (Gustafson 1981, 82). Direct challenges to the policy line of the leadership are sharply suppressed, whether these emanate from factional rivalries or as popular protest. Although clear differences in the interpretation of foreign affairs do emerge from the writings by Soviet specialists, using a foreign policy or national security issue to mobilize opposition to incumbent leaders is taboo. A corollary is the intensification of *counterpropaganda*, which refers both to the use of ideological means to combat the effects of Western influences on Soviet society as well as to foreign propaganda that meets "the ideological enemy on his own territory" (Zasurskii 1984, 6). In the sphere of foreign policy and national security, the Party's efforts are directed toward preventing opposition to the basic policy line of the central leadership and building public support for it.

A second factor tending to raise the salience of party-political authority is the nationality problem. To be sure, the extent to which ethnic cleavages pose a threat to the stability of Soviet society is often exaggerated: apart from the trends toward increased representation by ethnic minorities in the social and political leadership of the national republics and standardization of living conditions and career opportunities for non-Russian nationalities, the *competitive* quality of nationality interests keeps ethnic demands from cumulating and thus paradoxically increases the legitimacy of centralized rule (Hodnett 1978; Jones and Grupp 1984).

Nevertheless, the continuing strength of national consciousness on the part of most larger nationalities in the union remains a strong reason for retaining the class and internationalist content of Marxist–Leninist doctrine (Gitelman 1983; Karklins 1986). Egor Ligachev, the Politburo member and Central Committee secretary in charge of ideology and cadres, has warned against "localism" and "regionalism" among the national minorities and attacked as well, the propensity for "bourgeois nationalism" to cloak itself in "religious attire," such as Islam and Catholicism ("XXVII S"ezd" 1986; Ligachev 1986, 18). The fear that giving in to minority ethnic nationalism would lead to social disintegration probably unites many ethnic Russians around values of centralism and a statist, even imperial, Great Russian nationalism (Barghoorn 1986). Moreover, the nationality issue is tied to the international situation, both through the ties ethnic groups maintain with their kin abroad, as well as through their religious heritage. Each large religious creed in Soviet society belongs to a world-wide community, requiring that party work take care to separate national identification from religious (without offending, according to party ideological specialists, the feelings of believers) and also instill the sense of dual nationality – local plus Soviet – that reinforces regime unity. While Russification may be an alternative to Marxist–Leninist indoctrination as a tool for creating a unifying culture, it is also fraught with serious risks. The absence of an alternative ideological framework for the multiethnic Soviet state is one of the most powerful rationales for party ideological work.

Finally, ideological work counteracts pressures for pluralism. Here, again, ideological policy alternates between reformist and conservative phases. Encouraged by the Khrushchev thaw, post-Stalin reformers tested the limits of permissible expression in the late 1950s and early 1960s with spontaneous poetry readings, daring literary almanacs, and attempts to publish material abroad. The Brezhnev regime signalled its tolerance of such experiments by arresting two writers, Sinyavsky and Daniel, in 1965 and trying them for anti-Soviet propaganda in 1966. The suppression of a liberal–reformist regime in Czechoslovakia in 1968 produced a further retrenchment, and throughout the détente era, strenuous efforts were made to prevent any harmful spillover from the political and economic contacts between the USSR and the West into intellectual culture (Barghoorn 1976). The restrictive climate under Brezhnev widened the gap between critical intellectuals and the political elite. Now, under Gorbachev, cultural policy has been significantly liberalized again as part of the general drive for social reconstruction. The mass media are urged to publish constructive criticism and to press for change; but, as Ligachev indicated at the Twenty-seventh Party Congress, criticism of negative phenomena must be balanced by praise for what is positive ("XXVII S"ezd" 1986). Moreover, some of the remarkable, probing assaults on bureaucratic self-interest that have been published have had the effect of strengthening the Party's claim to the status of an overarching, politically disinterested, unifying force in society (Zalygin 1987).

These points merely illustrate that, alongside modernizing forces opening the political elite to multiple social interests, there exist strong pressures strengthening its specifically ideological identity. The demand for a continued monopoly on political power, coupled with a fear that external pressure might exploit domestic disunity to blackmail or defeat the state, helps enable the Party to retain its distinctive status as the political source of social elitehood in Soviet society. The emphasis on the political is borne out as well by recent trends in party recruitment policy. Whereas in the past there was a practice of co-opting technical specialists in their mid-career into the Party, this declined in the 1970s, while admission directly from Komsomol increased. This has now been further reinforced by the new rule in the new party by-laws that youth under twenty-five years old may *only* be admitted via the Komsomol. If admission policies in the 1960s tended to emphasize technical qualifications, current policy appears aimed at combining technical *and* political criteria. Indeed, according to Bohdan Harasymiw, the emphasis on political reliability and working-class representation has meant that some highly educated sectors of the population are falling behind in their rates of party membership (1984, 190, 45–6).

So long as the CPSU remains the one uniquely political organization in Soviet society, ideological work will be an indespensable means of identifying the Party in the public mind with all the highest aspirations and values of the system, justifying the foreign and domestic policies set by the leadership, and eradicating particularistic instincts. Although ideological work accordingly upholds the purely political side of the Party's authority, it cannot be performed except by delegating shares of responsibility for ideological work to a wide range of social elites. This in turn poses the two problems we have discussed. One is the difficulty of distinguishing the party per se from the entire fabric of socio-political authority in the state. The party is concerned to ensure that social privilege flows as much from proximity to political power as political power from social privilege: through admission policy and the cultivation of the *aktiv*, the Party seeks less to incorporate social elites, as T. H. Rigby puts it, than to "overlap" with them (1968, 453). The other problem is the degeneration of ideology into dogma and ritual, which in turn prompts phases of renewal. Whenever the ceremonial, bureaucratic character of party ideological work grows so acute that party leaders regard it as a handicap for the accomplishment of overriding system-level goals (victory in war, restructuring of society), there will be renewed calls to make words the servants of deeds. Loosening the ideological constraints on public communication, however, releases new energies from society at the expense of centralized political control.

References

Aspaturian, Vernon V. 1984. "The Stalinist Legacy in Soviet National Security Decisionmaking." In *Soviet Decisionmaking for National Security*, edited by Jiri Valenta and William C. Potter, pp. 23–73. London: George Allen & Unwin.

Barghoorn, Frederick C. 1976. *Detente and the Democratic Movement in the USSR*. New York: Free Press.

———. 1986. "Russian Nationalism and Soviet Politics: Official and Unofficial Perspectives." In *The Last Empire: Nationality and the Soviet Future*, edited by Robert Conquest, pp. 30–77. Stanford, Calif.: Hoover Institution Press.

Barghoorn, Frederick C., and Thomas F. Remington. 1986. *Politics in the USSR*, 3d ed. Boston: Little Brown.

Bauman, Zygmunt. 1976. "The Party in the System-Management Phase: Change and Continuity." In *Authoritarian Politics in Communist Europe: Uniformity and Diversity in One-Party States*, edited by Andrew C. Janos, pp. 81–108. Berkeley, Calif.: Institute of International Studies.

Breslauer, George W. 1982. *Khrushchev and Brezhnev as Leaders: Building Authority in Soviet Politics*. London: George Allen & Unwin.

Cherniak, A. V., compiler. 1984. *Tovarishch Instruktor*. Moscow: Izdatel'stvo Politicheskoi literatury.

Dridze, Tamara. 1975. "Lingvosotsiologicheskie aspekty massovoi informatsii," *Sotsiologicheskie issledovaniia*, no. 4 (October–December):52–61.

———. 1979. *Organizatsiia i metody lingvosotsiologicheskogo issledovaniia massovoi kommunikatsii*. Moscow: Izdatel'stvo moskovskogo universiteta.

"XXVII S"ezd Kommunisticheskoi partii Sovetskogo Souiza." 1986. *Pravda* (February 28).

Gitelman, Zvi. 1983. "Are Nations Merging in the USSR?" *Problems of Communism* 32 (September/October):35–47.

Gorbachev, Mikhail S. 1984. *Zhivoe tvorchestvo naroda*. Moscow: Politizdat.

Gustafson, Thane. 1981. *Reform in Soviet Politics: Lessons of Recent Policies on Land and Water*. Cambridge, England: Cambridge University Press.

Harasymiw, Bohdan. 1984. *Political Elite Recruitment in the Soviet Union*. New York: St Martin's Press.

Harris, Jonathan. 1984. "After the *Kratkii kurs*: Soviet Leadership Conflict over Theoretical Education: 1956–1961." In *The Carl Beck Papers in Russian and East European Studies*, no. 401. Pittsburgh: University of Pittsburgh.

Hodnett, Grey. 1978. *Leadership in the Soviet National Republics: A Quantitative Study of Recruitment Policy*. Oakville, Ontario: Mosaic Press.

Hough, Jerry F., and Merle Fainsod. 1979. *How the Soviet Union Is Governed*. Cambridge: Harvard University Press.

Huntington, Samuel P. 1970. "Social and Institutional Dynamics of One-Party Systems." In *Authoritarian Politics in Modern Society*, edited by Samuel P. Huntington and Clement H. Moore, pp. 3–44. New York: Basic Books.

Jones, Ellen, and Fred W. Grupp. 1984. "Modernisation and Ethnic Equalisation in the USSR," *Soviet Studies* 35 (April): 159–84.

Karklins, Rasma. 1986. *Ethnic Relations in the USSR: The View from Below*. Boston: Allen & Unwin.

Kokorev, I. E. 1973. "K probleme tipologii auditorii massovoi kommunikatsii." In *Materialy nauchnogo seminar 'Semiotika sredstv massovoi kommunikatsii'*, edited by A. G. Volkov, pp. 114–18. Moscow: Izdatel'stvo moskovskogo universiteta.

Komarovskii, V. S. 1985. "Metodika sotsiologicheskogo issledovaniia vozmozhnogo vozdeistviia burzhuaznoi propagandy." In *Voprosy teorii i praktiki ideologicheskoi raboty*, compiled by Zh. T. Toshchenko et al., pp. 186–97, vyp. 17. Moscow: Mysl'.

Ligachev, Egor. 1986. "Uchit' po-novomu myslit' i deistvovat'." *Kommunist* (October): 8–23.

Löwenthal, Richard. 1974. "On 'Established' Communist Party Regimes." *Studies in Comparative Communism* 7 (Winter): 335–58.

Manaev, O. T. 1984. "Vkliuchennost' lichnosti v sferu vliianiia sredstv massovoi informatsii." *Sotsiologicheskie issledovaniia* (October–December): 37–44.

Materialy XXVII S"ezda Kommunisticheskoi partii Sovetskogo Soiuz. 1986. Moscow: Izdatel'stvo politicheskoi literatury.

Medvedev, Roy A. 1973. *Let History Judge: The Origins and Consequences of Stalinism*, trans. Colleen Taylor. New York: Vintage.

Miller, John H. 1982. "The Communist Party: Trends and Problems." In *Soviet Policy for the 1980's*, edited by Archie Brown and Michael Kaser, pp. 1–34. Bloomington: Indiana University Press.

Miller, Robert F. 1985. "The Role of the Communist Party in Soviet Research and Development," *Soviet Studies* 37 (January): 31–59.

Moore, Barrington, Jr., 1966. *Terror and Progress – USSR*. Cambridge: Harvard University Press.

Nenashev, M. F. 1985. "Nasushchnye voprosy sovershenstvovaniia organizatsii i stilia ideologicheskoi raboty." In *Voprosy teorii i praktiki ideologicheskoi raboty*, compiled by Zh. T. Toshchenko et al., pp. 3–17, vyp. 17. Moscow: Mysl'.

"O dal'neishem uluchshenii ideologicheskoi i politiko-vospitatel'noi raboty." 1979. *Pravda* (May 6).

Partiinoe stroitel'stvo: Nauchnye osnovy partiinoi raboty. Kurs lektsii, vol. 1. 1985. Moscow: Mysl'.

Rigby, T. H. 1968. *Communist Party Membership in the U.S.S.R.*, 1917–1967. Princeton, N.J.: Princeton University Press.

Sharlet, Robert. 1978. *The New Soviet Constitution of 1977: Analysis and Text*. Brunswick, Ohio: King's Court Communications.

Tucker, Robert C. 1971. "On Revolutionary Mass-Movement Regimes." In *The Soviet Political Mind: Stalinism and Post-Stalin Change* by Robert C. Tucker, pp. 3–19. New York: Norton.

————. 1973. *Stalin as Revolutionary, 1879–1929: A Study in History and Personality*. New York: Norton.

Voslensky, Michael. 1984. *Nomenklatura: The Soviet Ruling Class*, trans. Eric Mosbacher. Garden City, N.Y.: Doubleday.

Zalygin, Sergei. 1987. "Povorot. Uroki odnoi diskussii." *Novyi mir*, no. 1 (January): 3–18.

Zasurskii, Iasen. 1984. "Problemy effektivnosti sovetskoi zhurnalistiki v 1983 godu v svete reshenii iiunskogo (1983 g.) Plenuma Ts.K. KPSS." In *Vestnik moskovskogo universiteta*, series 10, "Zhurnalistika." (July/August): 3–8.

PART III

Everyday Life and Social Problems

8

The Sacred and the Secular in the USSR

Jerry G. Pankhurst

The USSR is the first modern nation to have declared the promotion of atheism as an official policy. Although the government is statutorily neutral on questions of religion, as required by the clause of the Soviet Constitution that guarantees "freedom of conscience,"[1] the Communist party (CPSU) claims no such neutrality (Timasheff 1960, 437). Thus, the CPSU's control of the government organs insures that the state, in fact, is not totally neutral in regard to religion. Through state and party operations, religious institutions are limited in the scope of their activities, and the religious consciousness of the population is combated.

It is a great irony that this "first atheist nation" should nevertheless contain within its borders large and active religious communities, including representatives of four of the world's great religions: Buddhism, Judaism, Christianity, and Islam. Even after some seventy years of communist rule, sociological evidence indicates that about 45 percent of the population remain believers (Fletcher 1981, 212).

How is this possible? How can official atheism and active religious groups relate to each other? Is the USSR experiencing the ethno-religious resurgence evidenced elsewhere? Is a "Polish phenomenon" possible in the Soviet Union? What will Gorbachev's reforms mean for the faithful in the USSR? These are a few of the questions this chapter contemplates.

Major Soviet Religious Groups

Even though the Soviet Buddhist community is small, numbering perhaps 400,000 followers (Barrett 1982, 689; cf. Antic 1976), it is important because it is located near the strategic border with China. Buddhism also has influenced some Soviet intellectuals. However, the other religious groups require greater attention here.

Identification with Judaism or Islam connotes ethnic ties as well as religious group adherence. (See the chapter by Ralph Clem in this volume.) The international importance of the Arab–Israeli conflict, the apparent strengthening of religio-political concern among Muslims all over the world, the war in Afghanistan that pits Soviet atheism against traditional Islam, and the worldwide mobilization of concern for Soviet Jewish immigration – all of these factors have given the situation of Soviet Jews and Muslims great international significance.

According to several commentators, the Soviet military incursion into Afghanistan was at least partly motivated by the fear that the conservative religious ideology of the rebels might spread into the Islamic Central Asian region of the USSR. There are approximately fifty million nominal Muslims in the USSR (Bennigsen 1984), and although not all are active believers, the spread of the Islamic revival into this sector of the Soviet population could have enormous consequences for economic and political development (Feshbach 1979). (See Bennigsen 1975, 1977.)

Since the late 1960s the emigration of Jews from the USSR has been a focal concern of the international human rights movement. In fact, until the early 1970s the Soviet Jewish population exceeded even the population of Israel, the US Jewish population being the largest in the world. With emigration and assimilation reducing the Soviet Jewish community – it dropped from 2.15 million to 1.81 million between the census years of 1970 and 1979 (Ts.S.U. 1980, 24) – it has now assumed third place in size. Even though the majority of Soviet Jews are highly secularized, they pose a major problem for Soviet domestic and foreign policy, and the world attentively watches how the USSR treats this religious–ethnic minority group. (See Gitelman 1977; Davis 1976.)

Christianity is the traditional faith of the Russian core of the Soviet Union, as well as of the western frontier regions from the Baltic republics through Belorussia and into the Ukraine and Moldavia, and of Georgia and Armenia. Virtually every major variant of Christianity is represented in the USSR – Barrett (1982, 696) counted 152 different denominations in 1980, with a total of 96.7 million nominal members. By far the largest denomination is the Russian Orthodox Church. Celebrating its 1000th anniversary in 1988, it includes more than 70 million baptized members. In fact, the Russian

Church is the largest Eastern Orthodox Church in the world. Pospielovsky [1984] and Ellis [1986] have recently published important scholarly works on this church.

Roman Catholicism is concentrated along the western frontier of the Soviet Union, with at least 2.25 million Latin-rite Catholics in Lithuania (Vardys 1977) and as many as 4.8 million in the entire USSR (Barrett 1982, 689, 692). The Lithuanian Catholics have been at the forefront of religious dissent and since 1972 have published an underground journal, the *Chronicle of the Lithuanian Catholic Church* (Bociurkiw 1975; Bourdeaux 1979). Besides the regular Roman Catholics, the USSR also contains large numbers of Eastern-rite Catholics (Uniates) who, although their church was abolished and officially absorbed into the Russian Orthodox Church after World War II, remain active. This group must operate entirely underground and has become a focus for Ukrainian nationalism (Markus 1975a, 1975b).

With their own ancient national churches, the Georgians and Armenians hold a unique place in the religious developments in the USSR. The Georgian Orthodox Church has experienced a severe decline in recent years (Reddaway 1975). Barrett (1982) estimates that the church has some 800,000 nominal members in 80 parishes. Conversely, the Armenian Apostolic Church – a Monophysite Church that went into schism from most of the rest of Christianity after the Council of Chalcedon in 451 – has some security and strength, although it is under official pressure. A strong relationship exists between Armenian national identity and the Armenian church, which provides support for the church, even among many nonbelievers. Barrett (1982, 695) counted 1.4 million adherents in 1980.

Soviet Protestants are extremely varied in composition. They range from the traditional Lutherans, found primarily in Latvia and Estonia, who number about 850,000 (Antic 1976), to Adventists, to small and scattered groups of Jehovah's Witnesses. The most important and widespread Protestant group in the Soviet Union is the Evangelical Christians and Baptists (often called simply Baptists or ECB). The ECB church is, in fact, a composite of several Protestant strains, including the regular Baptists, the more Methodist-like Evangelical Christians, the Pentecostals, although their union with the others has been particularly precarious, and some groups of Mennonites. Within the recognized denomination, the ECB probably number about three million adherents, including those who are regular participants in ECB activities but who may not have met the stringent requirements for membership (Lane 1978, 140; Barrett 1982, 695–96). In addition to this three million are an undetermined but large number of ECB believers who are not associated with the official ECB organization in the USSR. Their very important role is explained later.

Finally, mention should be made of the native Russian religious groups scattered throughout the Soviet Union. Largest among these is the Old Believers, who probably total somewhat more than two million adherents today (Barrett 1982, 695–96). There are also groups of Molokans, True Orthodox Christians, Dukhobors, and some others. (See Lane 1978 for thorough discussions in English of these various groups.) In general, the Russian sectarian groups have not fared well under Soviet rule, and they seem to be dying out rather quickly, their place being taken in part by the evangelical Protestant groups (Klibanov 1969, 1973).

It must be recognized that any count of members or adherents of these religious groups in the USSR is only a very rough estimate based on various official and unofficial statements. No government data on religious affiliation are available, and it is clear that the churches themselves are partly involved in self-censorship describing their own denominations. Nevertheless, these figures indicate that a very large number of believers remain in the Soviet Union whose denominations represent a broad range of religious persuasions.

Soviet Atheism and Interest Group Conflict

As we have had more and more opportunities since the mid-1950s to look closely at the state and society of the USSR, it has become clear that simplistic notions regarding the Soviet system as fully totalitarian, a dictatorship, or a police state do not adequately serve the purposes of objective comprehension of that nation. However appropriate such ideas may have been for the era of Josef Stalin's rule, since his death Soviet society has revealed itself as one in which various groups vie for influence, prestige, and power. Although there is near monopolization of the police power and other political power resources by the state organs and the Communist party, the latter has increasingly revealed its own internal diversity, and other groupings have emerged to declare their legitimacy and their ability to promote special interests both within and outside of official structures. (See, for instance, Skilling and Griffiths 1971; Hough 1977.) Such groupings may be found in intellectual, nationality, and religious affairs, as well as elsewhere.

Although the official acceptance of these movements of diversification and development of semiautonomous areas of influence depends on many factors, the broader political dynamism of the situation calls for a closer look at some of its facets. Even lacking official sponsorship or recognition, some movements may influence Soviet politics through representing popular interests and preferences in the sociopolitical arena. (See McCarthy and Zald 1977.) Such interests may be quite inchoate or subtle, or they may be explicit and well developed.

The process whereby group interests become articulated to the degree that we can term the group an *interest group* is of central importance here. The concept of interest group has many meanings in the sociological and political science literature: this discussion adopts the usage specified by Ralf Dahrendorf (1959, 237, 289–95). According to this approach, latent interests are those that can be identified by an outside observer but that are not fully recognized by group members. The opposition of other groups can cause individuals to become activated in pursuit of common interests, and this changes the interests from latent to manifest. Whole categories of people may be drawn together by the emergence of shared manifest interests; the resulting group is termed an *interest group*.

For the USSR, an *antireligious group* that has developed clear manifest interests in opposition to religion can be identified. It is called the *state/party* here because it is largely through state and party means that its activities are realized. There are many denominations that can be seen as specific religious interest groups. However, there is only an incipient *religious group* in the sense of an interest group devoted to the pursuit of general religious interests. The following discussion clarifies these designations and the interrelationships between these groups.

From the start it must be noted that the religion-related interests of the state/party are fairly well established insofar as the state/party adheres to the Marxist ideology of atheism. In addition to the ideology, Bociurkiw (1973, 38–40) has pointed out that three underlying attitudes of the Soviet elite tend to motivate it toward more severe antireligious measures. These are the "historical memory," in which the church is associated with the oppressive tsarist state and with the support of counterrevolutionary activities in the early post-Revolution period; the "ideological legacy" of Lenin and his followers, which interpreted Marxist atheism in a militant way under the influence of the Russian anticlerical tradition; and the "authoritarian aspirations" of the leadership, which aimed to integrate all aspects of society under the purview of the Party and attempted to transform them into the Party's "conveyor belts." The latter was a very difficult task, because religion was a distinctly non-Marxist orientation, and the result of attempts to integrate religion into the party-led institutional framework often was suppression of religious activities.

Since the Revolution of 1917, the state/party has maintained an antireligious campaign, although its virulence and focus have varied from period to period. Furthermore, there has developed a cadre of professional and amateur atheists, perhaps six to ten million in number (Antic 1977), who are devoted to antireligious activities and represent a clear occupational interest group centered on these activities. They work in the communications media, in the schools and other educational institutions, in factories and offices, and even in private homes, where they carry out "individual work" among believers to help free them from the allegedly harmful effects of their faith.

Whereas the "antireligious group" advocates opposition to all forms of religiosity, one cannot easily describe a *religious group*. Instead, there are many separate religious traditions and organizations, each of which puts forward its own claims to legitimacy and autonomy aimed not only against the state/party, but also, to a certain extent, against each other. Were these diverse groups to come together in cooperative or ecumenical activities directed at fostering religious interests, they would provide a more viable counterinfluence to the state/party's antireligious campaign. Such a religious interest group might fight for greater publication rights for religious literature or for fewer bureaucratic requirements when a new congregation wishes to organize, or it might fight for less harassment of religious activists or for the right to proselytize. In addition, it might struggle for a school curriculum in which scientific atheism was an optional subject instead of a required one. All of these interests clearly unite the various denominations on a latent level, although they are seldom articulated openly except by dissidents.

Why are these shared latent interests not made manifest interests? First, of course, are the pressure and restrictions of the state/party. To espouse these ends openly means to jeopardize, to a greater or lesser extent, one's status and way of life. For energetic advocacy in this area, many religious dissidents have found their way to prison on charges of antistate activity (Keston College 1987). Indeed, such activities present a fundamental challenge to accepted ways of Communist party administration. However, there are very significant reasons other than state strictures why (until very recently) an ecumenical movement has not developed to protect religious rights. Although all of these reasons cannot be reviewed here, a brief overview will indicate the more important ones.

During the 1930s the state/party attempted to abolish all religious organizations, hoping thereby to end religious influence in Soviet society. This effort was probably doomed to failure in any event, but the invasion by Nazi Germany intervened to require that the state/party reorganize the churches in support of the war effort. The new organizations, however, were given their lease on life fully at the sufferance of the state/party, and therefore the leadership became, in certain regards, obliged to fulfill state/party ends. Harvey Fireside (1971) has termed the postwar religious leaders "junior partners" to the state because in certain ways they took on state functions. This has meant that the life style of the religious leadership has become entangled with its state/party functions and interests, and its members are thus hard pressed to mount a campaign against the state/party, their benefactor. The seeming co-optation of the official All-Union Council of

Evangelical Christians-Baptists (AUCECB) led to a major schism in the 1960s that formed itself into the unofficial Council of Churches of the ECB (CCECB). (See Bourdeaux 1968.) Major protests against leadership co-optation are also found among the Orthodox (Bourdeaux 1970). Nevertheless, the leadership's state involvements hinder religious interest group development. (See Murvar 1968.)

But we can delve even deeper to understand the lack of ecumenical spirit in the Soviet Union and the reluctance to mount a religious civil rights campaign. Historically, the Russian Orthodox Church has not been a compromising church. In its historical isolation it evolved the ethnocentric theology of "Moscow, the third Rome" and the idea of the Russian Church as the Church Universal. As Vatro Murvar (1971) has shown, Russian sectarian groups further emphasized Orthodox tendencies toward seeing the world as seamless and undifferentiated, with groups designated only as good or evil according to a single measure of worth. In general, Russian Orthodox religious culture fostered a "take it or leave it" attitude, and often forced the taking.

Along with these blockages to ecumenical relations among the churches, the Russian Orthodox Church never fostered an intellectualized faith, but instead stressed the magic of the rite. (See Lane 1975.) The ritualist orientation tends not to stimulate religious activism, except as directly related to the ability to carry out the rites, and the latter is essentially maintained in the USSR, although with some limitations.

Finally, the established Orthodox were not ready for the disestablishment brought about by the February Revolution in 1917. They had not digested this fact when the October Revolution placed in power a directly antagonistic party of Bolsheviks. A reaction of conservative retrenchment was almost inevitable, in spite of significant earlier strides in a liberal direction. The protracted attack on the church as a counterrevolutionary force further squelched movements for reform within it. Only since about 1970 do we see the beginning of reformist thinking once again in the Russian Church. In the meantime, the exclusivist orientation has predominated.

With the Russian Orthodox Church as the central religious institution in the Soviet Union, the smaller or more localized religious groups, though varying in their tendency to accept ecumenical or cooperative activities, could not themselves mount a viable nationwide religious rights movement. (There are important movements for the special rights of various groups, such as the Baptists and Lithuanian Catholics, but they are on a lower level of analysis than the type of movement of concern here.)

Thus, it is clear that there are many sources of lack of unification among the religious groups that are more complex than simple state/party pressure against such unification, however important such pressure has been. Since a major antireligious campaign in 1958–64, a protest movement of major dimensions has developed in the USSR. Prominent among Soviet dissidents are religious activists, and since approximately 1976 we have seen some clear movements among them toward the sort of cooperation based on common interests that may presage the beginning of a cooperative or ecumenical religious interest group. In part, these developments are undoubtedly the simple result of time, that is, the religious groups have had a long period without war in which once again to become well organized. (This has perhaps provided the Orthodox, in particular, the opportunity to begin a reexamination of their position.) It is perhaps inevitable that they should begin to mount protests against the constraints of the Soviet system.

On the other hand, there are clear indications that the emerging cooperative activities of the religious groups are responsive in some ways to international relations. An understanding of the processes involved here is necessary, so that we can properly evaluate the effects (intended or otherwise) of the human rights activities that have become a part of international diplomacy. This question is addressed later in the chapter. (See also Pankhurst 1978c.)

Options for Antireligious Policy

What are the options for antireligious policy in the USSR? What organizational options for adaptation to the antireligious program are open to and taken by the religious movements? And what effect do the religious movements themselves have on the state/party? Although complete and final answers cannot be given here, these questions can be examined by briefly reviewing the situation of the Russian Orthodox Church and the Evangelical Christians and Baptists.

Imagine that the antireligious motivations of the regime were unchecked by other contingencies. In such a situation, one would expect all organized religious activities to be outlawed, and there might be attempts to suppress even individual and private religious observances. Although this would not eliminate many aspects of personal belief in supernatural forces, religious superstitions, and such, it could succeed to a great extent in removing the influence of religion on policy formation. With no organized leadership to speak for religious group interests, religious considerations would be eliminated. This, in large measure, appears to be the case in Albania (Prifti 1975). To a comparable, though somewhat less severe, degree, this approach was carried out during the 1930s in the USSR. At that time all religious bureaucracies were eliminated, and the churches were left with only informal and seemingly illegal central leadership. For the Russian Orthodox, on the eve of World War II, only the dioceses of Leningrad and

Moscow retained any open coordinating activities. The Baptists and Evangelical Christians had no such activities.

One can also imagine a situation in which the imperative of Marxist atheism involves for the Party only a sort of expansive exemplariness. That is, the Party would see itself as the exemplar of the alleged good of atheism and minimize direct suppression of religious activities. The East European Marxist nations provide examples of this type of approach, as in Poland (Heneghan 1977), East Germany (Howard-Johnston 1978; Ward, 1978; Oestreicher 1978), and Hungary (Kovats 1977; Aczel 1977; Cserhati 1977). In these countries the major religious groups have some meaningful input into policy development, and some church–state dialogue occurs. To a certain extent this condition existed in the USSR in the period between the end of World War II and 1958; in relations with many non-Orthodox groups, it was also the case in the 1920s. (The Orthodox Church in the 1920s did not experience this relatively benign treatment largely because of its association with the previous government and its connection with counterrevolutionary activities both inside and outside the Soviet state.)

Although we have not yet mentioned the most recent periods in Soviet policy, these considerations indicate the variety of responses to the problem of religion taken by the policy makers. In general, the periodization of church–state relationships described by Nicholas Timasheff (1942, 1946), writing during World War II, seems appropriate. Timasheff identified six distinct phases of policy before the war, three aimed at eradicating religion and three in retreat from that aim because of popular resistance. The last retreat, he stated, was also stimulated by the threat of war at the end of the 1930s. Because he treated only policy toward the Orthodox Church, this perhaps oversimplified the dynamics of the 1917–28 period, during which the Orthodox Church faced an increase in pressure until 1923 and then a decrease, while the sectarians experienced a fairly consistent low pressure (and even some support) from the state and party. Nevertheless, this indicates, in a very general way, the pattern of relationships through the war years. As mentioned earlier, the rapprochement with the churches begun during the war lasted until 1958.

Contrary to Timasheff, these policy variations need not be seen as a "retreat" from Communist principles. As Bociurkiw (1973) has shown, these variations and the ones occurring into the 1960s and 1970s (which will be discussed later) are consistent with an overriding principle of "the Leninist formula subordinating the struggle against religion to the 'interests of the class struggle of the proletariat'." More specifically, Bociurkiw sees these variations as responsive to considerations related to internal and external security, peasant policy, nationality policy, and foreign policy. He finds these considerations sometimes require a moderation of the attack on religion in order not to undermine efforts in these policy areas. During times when these policy areas are not so crucially related to antireligious activities – that is, when a more "pragmatic" approach to the antireligious struggle is not justifiable in terms of greater ends – then the ideological "fundamentalists" exert a stronger influence on the topmost leadership that is shaping policy and stimulate a more repressive approach to religion.

Bociurkiw and other commentators have recognized the influence of the religious believers, their reactions to repressive policy, and their organization on the policy formation process. Further analysis suggests that a direct relationship exists between the organizational forms of the churches and the policy options adopted by the authorities. In particular, it appears that the stronger the repression of religious practices, the greater the tendency for schisms or variant sects to develop among believers, and thus the greater the difficulty in surveillance of religion as it becomes organizationally fragmented. This is particularly the case when the schisms are illegal in the Soviet context and are forced to carry on their activities clandestinely. Because this sectarian tendency occurs in response to the repressive policies of the regime, it can be called *responsive sectarianism.*

Paradoxically, however, if the regime adopts a very benign approach to religion, it also finds itself faced with schisms. This seems to be increasingly the case as the hold of the Orthodox hierarchy on the faithful becomes weaker through secularization, and as some of the Orthodox believers move to other sectarian faiths (most importantly the Baptists). Related most directly to internal religious evolution, this type of sectarian formation can be called *theological sectarianism*.

Figure 8.1 portrays these relationships graphically. Because the curve relating state antireligious pressure to religious organizational differentiation seems to approximate a hyperbola, the pattern is labeled the *hyperbolic principle* of church–state relations. (There is no exact calculus possible, so perhaps a parabola or other bowl-shaped curve would be as applicable.)

Surveillance of the condition of religion is the minimal condition required for a Marxist antireligious program that expects to witness and guide the "withering away" of religion. Therefore, too much organizational differentiation among religious believers is undesirable, because it makes surveillance more complicated and difficult. Optimum antireligious policy should seek to maintain sufficient pressure to safeguard its own "militant atheist" identity, while not exerting so much pressure as to cause extreme organizational fragmentation, which would undermine the surveillance capability.

Though never formulated in this way as a specific principle, the Soviet state/party seems generally to be aware of the problems indicated here by the hyperbolic principle. For example, in a 1936 resolution the Commission on

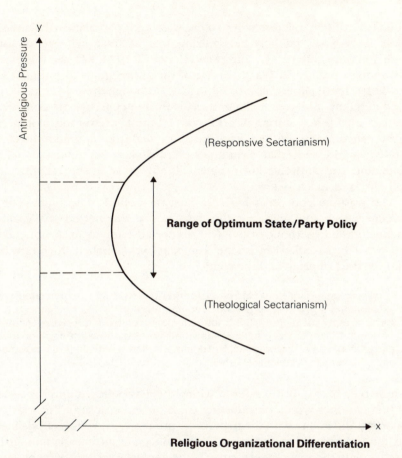

y

Antireligious Pressure

(Responsive Sectarianism)

Range of Optimum State/Party Policy

(Theological Sectarianism)

x

Religious Organizational Differentiation

Source: Jerry Pankhurst, "The 'Hyperbolic Principle' in Church-State Relations in the USSR" (1978b), Figure 1.

Figure 8.1. The Hyperbolic Principle of Church–State Relations in the USSR

the Affairs of Cults, attached to the Presidium of the Central Ideological Commission, reported that

> administrative practices with the violation of laws, as facts and materials of [our] inquiry show . . . [are] not forwarding the overcoming of religiosity, frequently lead to activity of sectarianism, its partial growth, the appearance of new religious rites, and to the organization of underground religious sects which provide favorable soil for counter-revolutionary activities of anti-Soviet elements. (Quoted in Lialina 1977, 118–19)

The commission, it appears, was grappling with the problem of responsive sectarianism. The coercive approach had simply driven religion underground toward sectarianism, where there was even "partial growth." Atheist leaders were soon publicly recognizing that at least half of the total population were believers (Anufriev and Kobetskii 1974, 17), and this paved the way for a pre-World War II easing of the antireligious campaign. (See Fireside 1971, 167; Konovalov 1974, 11–13.) Although there were additional, and certainly more compelling, reasons for the church–state concordat that was established during World War II, these prewar developments indicate an attempt by the state/party to find the optimum level of antireligious pressure that would lessen the sectarian tendency while maintaining the antireligious program in force at a subjectively and ideologically satisfactory level.

The wartime concordat led to a postwar period of accommodation between church and state, but the dynamics of this period give further evidence of the hyperbolic principle. This period came to an abrupt end in 1958, when the so-called Khrushchev campaign was launched. Bociurkiw has attributed the campaign to three elements:

> It was an important political resocialization undertaking in connection with [Khrushchev's] grand design to "build communism" in the "present generation"; it was an aspect of his "destalinization" course – a return of the original "Leninist principles" in the Soviet religious policy; and, possibly, it was a concession to the party "ideologues" disconcerted and demoralized by his ideological innovations and pragmatic experiments in other policy spheres. (1973, 49)

To these possible motivations for initiating the new policy, it must be added that the churches were consolidating gains made because of the wartime concordat. And in line with the hyperbolic principle, the return of prisoners from the Stalinist prison camps had induced significant unease among the churches, with the apparent growth of some unofficial variants of theological sectarianism (Bourdeaux 1968, 1971). In particular, although the state had hoped for a single Protestant church under the officially recognized All-Union Council of ECB (AUCECB), major problems of group unification had not been solved (Mitrokhin 1974; Lialina 1977; Rowe 1975; Simon 1974, 157; cf. Klibanov 1969, 104).

The Khrushchev campaign lasted from 1958 through 1964. During that time more than half of the remaining Orthodox churches were closed, the number of theological seminaries was reduced from eight to three, and the number of monasteries dropped from sixty-nine to between ten and fifteen (Bourdeaux 1971, 29–31; Bociurkiw 1971, 135; Conquest 1968, 37–38; Simon 1974, 73, 112, 115). Among the ECB the state/party pushed for dissolution of nonregistered congregations and even the closing of many of the officially registered AUCECB congregations, as well as the formalization of the nondemocratic structure of the AUCECB, which had been hastily established in the war years (Bourdeaux 1968, 20–21; Bociurkiw 1971, 135; Conquest 1968, 104–08; Simon 1974, 154–55). Jews and Muslims also suffered severe setbacks, as did other religious groups. (See, for instance, Conquest 1968, 67–127.)

After the fall of Khrushchev in 1964, there was a reassessment of the campaign (discussed in Bociurkiw 1971; Blane 1974). What has ensued is an anomalous phase in which the official groups have regained some lost privileges and have made advances in some ways, while the pressure on unofficial groups, which surfaced with considerable vigor during the campaign, has been maintained at a fairly high level through the mid-1980s. This appears to be the most complex stage of church–state relations in the Soviet era.

Detailed accounts of the Khrushchev campaign can be found elsewhere; it is necessary to review here only a few major events and their consequences. These will form the basis of a clear understanding of the present relationships between church and state in the USSR.

The Khrushchev Campaign and its Effects

As is evident from *samizdat* (underground literature) documentation, the Khrushchev campaign made clear to many believers the extent of state/party meddling in the affairs of the churches. The authorities mounted the attack on religion in many ways, but the manipulation of the church leadership that took place was the measure that most directly launched the large religious dissent movements of the 1960s and 1970s. (Documentation of the following can be found in Bourdeaux 1968, 1970.)

For the Orthodox, the major occasion was an unusual synod of bishops in 1961. The synod was unusual because there was less than twenty-four hours' notice of its convening. The essential point of the decisions of the irregular synod was to revise the Church Regulations of 1945 by depriving the parish priest of the right to serve on the parish *dvadtsatka* (the founding and general decision-making group) and the executive council, three persons who run the parish's day-to-day affairs. These resolutions of the synod specifically limited the priest's activities to the spiritual service of the parish, especially the proper fulfilling of the sacramental duties. Thus, for all administrative matters, the priest was at the mercy of the *dvadtsatka* and especially the small executive council. He became, in essence, only an employee of the parish; thus he could be much more easily removed, and his influence in administering parish affairs could be minimized. Through the elaboration of the control functions of the Council for Russian Orthodox Church Affairs and the manipulation of the composition of the parish administrative bodies (see Secret Instructions 1973; Sawatsky 1976), the state apparently hoped to control any independent-minded priests who might wish to implement innovative programs or otherwise protect or increase the appeal of the church. In short, these developments created the circumstances by which the state/party could carry out its massive campaign.

In response to these happenings, in the summer of 1965, Archbishop Yermogen led a delegation of eight bishops to visit Patriarch Alexi. They gave him a declaration recounting the problems with the 1961 synod and demanding that a general church council be called to rectify the situation. An open letter also was circulated by the priests Eshliman and Yakunin that further described the church's difficulties with the state and charged the church administration with not fulfilling its duty to protect the church in the face of attack. For their actions Eshliman and Yakunin were banned from all priestly functions and Yermogen was involuntarily "retired" to the Zhirovitsy Monastery. However, the dissent movement that they began continued to grow in scope through the end of the 1960s and into the 1970s. Among the movement's major spokesmen were Anatoli Krasnov-Levitin, Boris Talantov, Aleksandr Solzhenitsyn, and Archpriest Vsevolod Shpiller.

The experience of the ECB Church was similar to that of the Orthodox church. For the ECB the precipitating incident comparable with the 1961 synod of bishops came in 1960, when the AUCECB promulgated the New Statutes (constitution) for the denomination and distributed a Letter of Instructions to the senior presbyters regarding the implementation of the New Statutes. The New Statutes made official a hierarchical order for the ECB bureaucracy with no democratic checks on its incumbents, a situation that contradicted the orientation of many of the groups within the ECB communion. There were also several stipulations or omissions regarding common activities that were unacceptable to many (see Bourdeaux 1968, 28–31). The Letter of Instructions directed, among other things, that missionary and proselytizing activities were to be restricted and that work with children and youth was to be limited. Overall, the letter tended to limit the prerogatives of local ministers and their congregations, and it strengthened the role of the centralized bureaucracy through a hierarchical organization of presbyters.

Following the promulgation of the New Statutes and the Letter of Instructions, a group led by Alexei Prokofiev and Gennadi Kryuchkov began to meet to consider needed changes in the statutes and to develop an agenda for a proposed national congress of the ECB to revise the statutes and establish a policy for implementation. This group took the name Action Group or *Initsiativnaia gruppa*. From this, its members are often referred to as *Initsiativniki*. After failing in their efforts to have a congress called to revise the statutes, and later failing to gain representation at the ECB congresses that did so, the *Initsiativniki* denounced the AUCECB leadership and claimed they should be the proper heads of the ECB Church. After a successful mobilization effort, this group in 1965 formed the Council of Churches of ECB (CCECB), a direct schismatical contender with the AUCECB for the allegiance of the ECB faithful. (See Mitrokhin 1974, 82–83.) Because of their efforts, during 1961–64 at least 197 of their number were imprisoned.

The CCECB has remained in existence as an illegal Protestant church in the USSR. Allied with it is the group called the Council of Prisoners' Relatives, which has maintained an information network among the ECB concerning problems of persecution experienced by Soviet Baptists. Both the CCECB and the Council of Prisoners' Relatives have made massive contributions to *samizdat*, both for their own edification and for the information of a broader public about the difficulties of religion in the USSR.

Now let us reconsider the hyperbolic principle in light of the developments of the 1960s. According to that principle, the increased state/party pressure of a campaign such as that of 1958–64 should have caused an increase in sectarian movements of the responsive type. This is clearly what happened for the ECB, where various strands of diffuse differentiation in the movement focused in the formation of the CCECB, a group providing an alternative to the AUCECB for individuals and congregations of evangelical Protestants.

The political importance of this schism became most evident in 1965, when the CCECB directed its attention more toward the authorities, seeking legitimation from them, than toward the AUCECB. Nevertheless, from the very start the schismatic movement was based on an understanding of its problems as rooted in the interference of the state/party, as allegedly sanctioned by the AUCECB.

So far, this supports the hyperbolic principle, but when the developments of the Orthodox Church are considered, the principle becomes less clear, as discussed earlier. Certainly, Yermogen, Eshliman, Yakunin, Levitin, and others have not started an Orthodox sect. It is possible that the closing of a church or the removal of a priest has led some believers to shift their allegiance to one of the indigenous sects, but we do not have any information on this. However, there is strong evidence of a move toward the ECB by some (Pankhurst 1978a, ch. 5). In any event, this is not sect creation, but movement among the possible options already in existence.

Although there are ample signs of popular Orthodox dissatisfaction with the church–state relationship in the 1960s, there are few signs of the coalescence of a movement in response, except among the intelligentsia. This latter movement is clearly responsive sectarianism. It is possible that, if the intelligentsia took a fully schismatic stand, they would find some followers among the larger category of Orthodox adherents.

The leaders of the ECB schism proved to be among the intellectuals of the ECB, not the fanatics portrayed in the Soviet press. Their writings promoted arguments very similar to those of the Orthodox dissidents, and Michael Bordeaux (1970) has convincingly argued that the Orthodox were directly influenced in their opening of protest by the activities of the Baptists. It is important to note that the CCECB movement was fully mobilized by the time the first major Orthodox protests were made in 1965.

These considerations lead to the conclusion that the state/party pressures have had different effects on the Orthodox and the ECB, not because the pressure was experienced in significantly different ways, but because the two groups possessed different resources whereby they could mobilize social movements in response to these pressures and could develop such mobilization in the form of effective social movement organizations. (See McCarthy and Zald 1977.)

The hyperbolic principle, as qualified here, describes important dynamics in the interest group conflict involving the Baptists, the Orthodox, and the state/party. The considerations discussed here suggest that the ECB has an advantage in relation to the Orthodox as both groups face the state/party. The ECB has a greater flexibility of response to state/party pressure that is built on its structural resources, which allow for increased autonomy of action on the part of individual adherents and clergy in contrast to the Orthodox. This autonomy may be exercised in the formation of partially legitimated movements of protest against church policy as it becomes too tied to state/party control.

In turn, such development may lead to revitalization of the church's religious message and provide a foundation for continued expansion of the number of adherents. Some expansion may come at the expense of the Orthodox because of their comparative weakness on this dimension. The revitalization of the religious message implies that the understanding of the religious interests of the ECB, and the comprehension of the opposition of those interests to the state/party's antireligious interests, are strengthened for ECB adherents. In other words, those interests become more manifest, and the Baptist group as an interest group is thereby strengthened. Thus, it may challenge more directly the state/party or antireligious group.

In large measure, these developments became possible only after the World War II change of policy by the state/party that allowed the reconstitution of the religious bureaucracies and the unification of the Evangelical Christians and Baptists. The reasons for that policy change were clearly compelling for the state/party, but they nevertheless laid the groundwork for the present organization-based interest group conflict.

For religious groups, schisms or other forms of splintering usually are not desirable. However, these considerations of the hyperbolic principle suggest that it is not necessarily so undesirable in the context of Soviet society. This is a context characterized by high secularization of the population, and the tasks of religious groups are to protect themselves from further erosion and to grow wherever they can. Clearly, the formation of schisms would not be desirable if there were a larger and stronger religious base in such a society. The example of Poland, where more than 90 percent of the population is counted nominally Catholic, indicates the importance of size for a religious group to prosper in the face of an officially atheist controlling elite.

But in the Soviet case, religious organizational differentiation presents policy makers with a dilemma: How do you exert antireligious pressure without decreasing your ability to abet the "withering away" of religion? In the post-Khrushchev era, we see the state/party trying to conquer this dilemma by strengthening the official church organizations in some ways, while maintaining continuing pressure on schismatics and dissidents. (This was reflected in legislation changes in 1975; see Steeves 1977.) However, the dissidents and schismatics of the Orthodox and the ECB tradition have been able to persist, often with startling success. As long as that is so, the state/party will continue to be on the horns of this dilemma, and religious faith will continue to be a real option in Soviet society.

Current Religious Conditions

It was earlier asserted that a religious resurgence is occurring in the USSR. It is now possible to put such a resurgence in perspective. The events briefly reviewed indicate that one form of that resurgence is the increased amount of religious dissidence since the end of the Khrushchev antireligious campaign. This dissidence has been a major component in the diverse dissenting activities that have been witnessed in the USSR since the mid-1960s, including literary protests, nationalist protests, and other movements seeking political, social, or economic reorganization of the USSR.

These dissenting movements have arisen at the same time that the government has reached out to other nations, seeking better relations and greater cooperation through the policy of detente. This has allowed much more information to become available about Soviet society, and some of it has aroused protests in the West. Strengthened and emboldened by foreign support and attention and perceiving the Soviet government as constrained by such attention, the protest movements within the USSR have become very sensitive to international relations.

This sensitivity has clearly contributed to the development among religious dissenters of greater cooperative, ecumenical relationships, often even involving nonbelieving dissenters like Andrei Sakharov. For example, after the Helsinki pact of 1975, there grew up in the USSR groups of dissenters seeking to keep track of the Soviet record on human rights. Called the Helsinki Monitoring Group, one of their central concerns was the religious situation (Monitoring Group 1977). Also in 1975 the World Council of Churches initiated an investigation of religious conditions in the USSR. In 1976 an ecumenical Christian Committee for the Defense of Believers' Rights was organized in the USSR; one of this group's early protests concerned the refusal of permits for dissidents to go to Geneva for a meeting of the World Council of Churches.

These and other developments dating from the mid-1970s attest to the incipient growth of a true religious group (in the sense outlined earlier) that could act as a more significant counterbalance to the antireligious group of the state/party. It is clear that such developments have been very responsive to international interest in human rights in the Soviet Union. While most of the major leaders of the ecumenical dissent efforts were spending time in prison camps or exile, there were others who were becoming active. As long as the hyperbolic principle constrains antireligious policy and mediates against a return to the conditions of the Khrushchev years, it is unlikely that the state policies alone can eliminate these movements. Their continuation depends on several factors. Most important are continued international attention that supports dissent and the induction of additional believers into protest activity.

This last factor, which would support the development of a religious group counterbalancing the antireligious group, indicates the final issue to be considered in this essay – the state of religious faith in general in the USSR in the face of all the pressures for secularization.

The first and most important fact to consider is that without a doubt there has been a high degree of secularization in the USSR since the 1917 Revolution. Before 1917 atheism was unthinkable except for a few radical intellectuals (although religious faith may have been of little consequence for many people). As noted earlier, by the late 1930s the official point of view was that about half of the population could still be considered religious believers. This group included about one-third of the urban population and two-thirds of the rural population (Anufriev and Kobetskii 1974, 17). Soviet sociological estimates currently place the percentage of the population who are believers at 15–20 percent of the adult population, with 10–15 percent of the urban population and 20–30 percent of the rural population in that category (Kobetskii 1978, 24; Lane 1978, 223–34). It is probably the case that such estimates, made by professional atheist investigators, underestimate the number of people who hold at least some positive relationship to traditional religious conceptions and religious organizations. Indeed, Fletcher's extensive analysis of Soviet sources led him to estimate that the proportion of believers in the Soviet population has dropped only from 56 percent in 1937 to 45 percent (1981, 212), a proportional drop that would imply an actual growth in the number of religious citizens in the USSR. However, even taking this into consideration, there has been a significant decline in the amount of religious adherence of the population.

Given other major changes in the Soviet Union – for example, massive urbanization, industrialization, and increased educational attainment – and the lack of societal support for religion, perhaps such a decrease in religious involvement is not surprising. Using several indicators of religiosity, Christel Lane (1975) found that Orthodox believers were very similar to members of national or established churches of Europe, such as those in England or Sweden. "The majority of Orthodox are . . . traditional Christians who believe and/or practice because their fathers and forefathers did so for centuries" (136). They scored low on all religiosity indexes except participation in rites of passage, such as baptisms, confirmations, weddings, and funerals. Lane concluded that "Religious commitment of Orthodox in its present configuration is thus shaped by the interaction of influences emanating both from the characteristics of a [national] church-type organization and a militantly atheist socialist society." Obviously, the apparent popular decline of the Orthodox Church is not fully attributable to state/party policy.

By comparison, although 86 percent of Americans indicated in a 1984 survey that their religious beliefs were "very" or "fairly important" to them, and 40 percent attended church in a typical week (Gallup 1985, 22, 42), many scholars would contend that this religious involvement is nevertheless very shallow and represents a generally pro-religion situation in the United States. One sociologist has speculated that there may be greater religious faith in the USSR than in the United States because the Soviet Union retains more "features of a traditional peasant society (of which religion is usually a part)" (Hollander 1973, 187).

It is important to note that the process of secularization is not inevitable and not unidirectional. Robert Nisbet (1970) has theorized that secularization processes are cyclical. Moreover, he has argued (1979) that we are in the midst of a historic transition that will reverse secularization. He asserts that the allure of the secular political order has faded, leaving room for the religious order to reassert itself and establish a new world predominance similar to that which it held during the Middle Ages. Whether Nisbet is correct, we obviously cannot take secularization for granted. Nor should we think that secularization must be linked with progress, for the nature of progress is defined in varying ways by varying secular ideologies (cf. Martin 1978). Thus, the process of secularization must be understood in a limited, though still very useful, way. (See the critical review of the debate over secularization by Robertson 1974; cf. Berger 1969, 105–07.)

Even though the long-term trend seems to indicate a decrease of religious involvement in the Soviet Union – and this is supported by much Soviet sociological research – there are significant developments within this pattern of decline. It is possible that they could presage a reversal of the secularization process, although they do not necessarily indicate this at present.

In the face of secularization, the strength of the ECB and other Protestant groups is noteworthy. Their vigor may represent a major readjustment in the religious allegiances of the Soviet population. Over the period of Soviet history, there has been a clear shift among believers toward Protestantism. Table 8.1 provides illustrative data from one region of the USSR.

Table 8.1
Religious Organizations and Groups in Rostov Oblast, 1917 and 1972

| | 1917 | Number in 1972 | |
		Registered	Not Registered
Russian Orthodox churches	401	64	–
Russian Orthodox monasteries	3	–	–
Russian Orthodox ecclesiastical schools	2	–	–
Old Believer churches	16	4	12
Armenian–Gregorian churches	16	2	–
Roman Catholic churches	3	–	–
Jewish synagogues	12	1	–
Muslim mosques	2	1	–
Baptist houses of prayer	2	8	33
Seventh-Day Adventist houses of prayer	–	2	15
Christians of Evangelical Faith prayer houses (*Piatidesiatniki*)[a]	–	–	25
Jehovah's Witnesses groups	–	–	2
True Orthodox Christian societies[b]	–	–	10
"Ioanniti" societies[c]	–	–	5
"Khristovovery" groups (*Khlysty*)	–	–	1
Skoptsi groups	–	–	1
Total	457	82	104

Note: In a footnote to this table, Voroshilov notes that it was "composed from archive materials of the Official Committee for Religious Affairs attached to the Council of Ministers of the USSR for Rostov oblast and from the current archives of the Rostov oblast house of scientific atheism, taking into account changes in the borders of the Don Army oblast."

[a] Pentecostals

[b] An underground Orthodox group, True Orthodox Christians do not accept the present hierarchy of the Russian Orthodox Church.

[c] The Ioanniti are an Orthodox sect that appeared during the last two decades of the nineteenth century. They are named for St. John of Kronstadt, whom they especially revere. The Ioanniti operate clandestinely.

Source: A. S. Voroshilov, "Religioznost' kat predmet sotsiologicheskogo issledovaniia (opyt) konkretno-sotsiologicheskogo issledovaniia v Rostovskoi oblasti" (1974), 75–76.

The shift towards evangelical Protestantism may represent a "normative reaction to normlessness" (Becker 1957, 1960) within the Soviet context of secularization and antireligious activities. Such a reaction does not necessarily imply the incipience of real normlessness but, rather, a perception or feeling by some people of severe threat to what they consider sacred values. In response, social movements arise to reassert, perhaps in a modified form, the values at issue through the establishment and dispersal of what they consider a stronger normative system. The particular growth of the Western sects, especially Baptist, in view of the weakening of the Russian Orthodox Church, seems to fit such a pattern of normative reaction. Stephen and Ethel Dunn (1964) have pointed out the shifting functions of the sects in Russia, and specifically the shift toward the Western sects, that now seem to represent the most viable platform for protest against the regime.

The normative reaction to normlessness is a natural process engendered in situations of social change that dislocate and disorient the people involved. The Soviet leadership and Communist Party are embarked on an attempt to build a new society, a communist society, that requires overthrowing present conditions and replacing them with new social forms. Recognizing that new social forms require some normative or ethical anchorage, the state/party promotes *communist morality* and the communist upbringing of the population. In this connection, in the 1960s and 1970s, socialist rites of passage were established to commemorate major stages in the life cycle (Lane 1979). These rites, coupled with the mass political holidays celebrated since the Revolution of 1917, make up a set of rituals and ceremonies directly opposed to similar religious practices (Lane 1981). (See the comments by Mark G. Field on the "secular faith" of Marxism-Leninism in his chapter in this volume.)

Jennifer McDowell (1974) and Christel Lane (1979, 1981) find increasing support among the population for the new ceremonies for birth and marriage, although Soviet funeral rites are still quite infrequent. Urban populations have accepted the rites more quickly than have rural populations. However, "there is a possibility that ritual involvement is merely motivated by a desire to mark important events in personal life in an elevated form and that the rhetoric of Marxism-Leninism is not more than an acceptable backcloth" (Lane 1979, 275).

Whether this is the case, or whether there is sincere interest in linking the ideological orientation with the life cycle is an important question for the future of religion in the USSR. The state/party would prefer that the population shift its observances to the socialist ceremonies, and though this shift has partially been achieved, it is not clear how far it will go. If these state/party alternatives to religious rites are successful in the long run, they would severely undermine the appeal of religion. Viewed as functional alternatives to religion, their acceptance could also be related to a resurgence in religious interest that is refocused on these socialist rites.

At present we can discern no certainties about the future of religion and atheism in the Soviet Union. However, there is no doubt that the program of reform being implemented by Mikhail Gorbachev will affect religion directly or indirectly. As a minimum, it seems that the orientation of the new leadership in the Sovet Union is not as ideological as that of previous leaders and is more pragmatic (compare the chapter by Remington in this volume), a pattern that should improve the religious situation. In fact, Gorbachev seems single-mindedly intent on economic reform, and his economic focus seems to have little room for concern about religion. Insofar as religion is of interest, it may be seen as a positive support for the work ethic. Or perhaps the religious energy of the population will be harnessed for social welfare improvements. In any event, as I have argued elsewhere (Pankhurst 1986), the present stage of religious development in the USSR should suggest to Soviet leaders that the persecution of believers is counterproductive (have they learned the lesson of the hyperbolic principle?) and that the resources of religious groups can be put to socially profitable use.

The Brezhnev era saw the excesses of the Stalin and Khrushchev eras reduced. This meant a moderated, though still militant, atheist program. It also meant the reinvigoration of certain strands of religious activity. Religious dissent was the clear expression of a renewed interest in religion among intellectuals and some other groups of the population. Under Gorbachev, will the general stagnation of the Brezhnev years be overcome? If so, the process of change will undoubtedly invigorate the religious side of the Soviet people as well.

In general, since the mid-1960s the question of religion and atheism has become politicized, especially because believers have begun the processes of interest group development. Processes that were driven completely under-ground in the 1930s began to consolidate after World War II: they were submerged during the Khrushchev campaign but emerged with real impetus in reaction to that campaign. Although this interest group development is not a mass movement, it does insure that religion will continue to be a real alternative in Soviet life.

Note

[1] Article 52 of the 1977 Soviet Constitution reads as follows:

Citizens of the USSR are guaranteed freedom of conscience, that is, the right to profess or not to profess any religion, and to conduct religious worship or atheistic propaganda. Incitement of hostility or hatred on religious grounds is prohibited.

In the USSR the church is separated from the state, and the school from the church. (As translated in Topornin 1980, 254)

The "incitement of hostility" clause is new in this constitution, but the rest of the article is only slightly revised from the earlier (1936) version. The most noteworthy feature is the guarantee of atheistic propaganda without a similar guarantee for religious propaganda. This is the basis on which religious missionary or evangelization activities are prohibited in the USSR.

References

Aczel, Gyorgy. 1977. "The Socialist State and the Churches in Hungary." *New Hungarian Quarterly* 18, no. 66:49–62.

Antic, Oxana. 1976. "Numbers of Religious Persons in the USSR." *Radio Liberty Research* RL 158/76 (February 2).

———. 1977. "The Promotion of Atheism in the Soviet Union Today." *Radio Liberty Research* RL 258/77 (November 8).

Anufriev, L. A., and V. D. Kobetskii. 1974. *Religioznost' i atiezm (sotsiologicheskie ocherki)*. Odessa: Maiak.

Barrett, David B., ed. 1982. *World Christian Encyclopedia: A Comparative Study of Churches and Religions in the Modern World, A.D. 1900–2000.* New York: Oxford University Press.

Becker, Howard P. 1957. "Current Sacred–Secular Theory and Its Development." In *Modern Sociological Theory in Continuity and Change*, edited by Howard P. Becker and Alvin Boskoff, pp. 133–85. New York: Holt, Rinehart, and Winston.

———. 1960. "Normative Reactions to Normlessness." *American Sociological Review* 25:803–10.

Bennigsen, Alexandre A. 1975. "Islam in the Soviet Union: The Religious Factor and Nationality Problem in the Soviet Union." In *Religion and Atheism in the USSR and Eastern Europe*, edited by Bohdan R. Bociurkiw and John W. Strong, pp. 91–100. Toronto: University of Toronto Press.

———. 1977. "Modernization and Conservatism in Soviet Islam." In *Religion and Modernization in the Soviet Union*, edited by Dennis J. Dunn, pp. 239–79. Boulder, Colo.: Westview Press.

———. 1984. "Islam and the USSR." *Geopolitique* 7 (Fall):53–60.

Berger, Peter L. 1969. *The Sacred Canopy*. Garden City, N.Y.: Doubleday Anchor Books.

Blane, Andrew. 1974. "A Year of Drift (Part I)." *Religion in Communist Lands* 2, no. 3:9–15.

Bociukiw, Bohdan R. 1971. "Religion in the USSR after Khrushchev." In *The Soviet Union under Brezhnev and Kosygin*, edited by John W. Strong, pp. 135–55. New York: Van Nostrand.

———. 1973. "The Shaping of Soviet Religious Policy." *Problems of Communism* 32, no. 2:37–51.

———. 1975. "Religious Dissent in the USSR: Lithuanian Catholics." In *Marxism and Religion in Eastern Europe*, edited by Richard T. DeGeorge and James P. Scanlan, pp. 147–75. Boston: D. Reidel.

Bolshakoff, Serge. 1950. *Russian Nonconformity*. Philadelphia: Westminster Press.

Bourdeaux, Michael. 1968. *Religious Ferment in Russia:, Protestant Opposition to Soviet Religious Policy.* New York:, Macmillan.

———. 1970. *Patriarch and Prophets: Persecution of the Russian Orthodox Church Today*. London: Macmillan.

———. 1971. *Faith on Trial in Russia*. London: Hodder Stoughton.

———. 1979. *Land of Crosses: The Struggle for Religious Freedom in Lithuania, 1939–1978*. Chulmleigh: Augustine.

Chrypinski, Vincent C. 1975. "Polish Catholicism and Social Change." In *Religion and Atheism in the USSR and Eastern Europe*, edited by Bohdan R. Bociurkiw and John W. Strong, pp. 241–55. Toronto: University of Toronto Press.

Conquest, Robert. 1968. *Religion in the USSR.* New York: Praeger.

Cserhati, Jozsef. 1977. "Open Gates." *New Hungarian Quarterly* 19, no. 67:48–62.

Dahrendorf, Ralf. 1959. *Class and Class Conflict in Industrial Society*. Stanford, Calif.: Stanford University Press.

Davis, Moshe. 1976. "Jewish Spiritual Life in the USSR: Some Personal Impressions." *Religion in Communist Lands* 4 (Winter):20–23.

Dunn, Stephen, and Ethel Dunn. 1964. "Religion as an Instrument of Culture Change: The Problem of the Sects in the Soviet Union." *Slavic Review* 23:459–78.

Ellis, Jane. 1986. *The Russian Orthodox Church: A Contemporary History.* London: Croom Helm.

Feshbach, Murray. 1979. "Prospects for Outmigration from Central Asia and Kazakhstan in the Next Decade." In *Soviet Economy in a Time of Change*, vol. 1, pp. 656–709. Washington: Joint Economic Committee of the U.S. Congress.

Fireside, Harvey. 1971. *Icon and Swastika: the Russian Orthodox Church under Nazi and Soviet Control*. Cambridge: Harvard University Press.

Fletcher, William C. 1981. *Soviet Believers: The Religious Sector of the Population.* Lawrence: The Regents Press of Kansas.

Gallup, George, Jr. 1985. "Religion in America." *The Gallup Report* 236 (May).

Gitelman, Zvi. 1977. "Judaism and Modernization in the Soviet Union." In *Religion and Modernization in the Soviet Union*, edited by Dennis J. Dunn, pp. 280–309. Boulder, Colo.: Westview Press.

Heneghan, Thomas E. 1977. "The Loyal Opposition: Party Programs and Church Response in Poland." In *Eastern Europe's Uncertain Future*, edited by Robert R. King and James F. Brown, pp. 286–300. New York: Praeger.

Hollander, Paul. 1973. *Soviet and American Society: A Comparison.* New York: Oxford University Press.

Hough, Jerry F. 1977. *The Soviet Union and Social Science Theory.* Cambridge: Harvard University Press.

Howard-Johnston, Xenia. 1978. "Editorial." *Religion in Communist Lands* 6, no. 2:74–75.

Keston College. 1987. *Religious Prisoners in the USSR.* Keston, England: Keston College.

Klibanov, A. I. 1969. *Religioznoe sektantstvo i sovremennost'.* Moscow: Nauka.

———. 1973. *Religioznoe sektantstvo v proshlom i nastoiashchem.* Moscow; Nauka.

Kobetskii, V. D. 1978. *Sotsiologicheskoe izuchenie religioznosti i ateizma.* Leningrad: Leningrad State University.

Konovalov, B. N. 1974. *K massovomu ateizmu*. Moscow: Nauka.

Kovats, Charles E. 1977. "The Path of Church–State Reconciliation in Hungary." In *Eastern Europe's Uncertain Future*, edited by Robert R. King and James F. Brown, pp. 301–11. New York: Praeger.

Lane, Christel. 1975. "Religious Piety among Contemporary Russian Orthodox." *Journal for the Scientific Study of Religion.* 14:139–58.

———. 1978. *Christian Religion in the Soviet Union: A Sociological Study.* Albany: State University of New York Press.

———. 1979. "Ritual and Ceremony in Contemporary Soviet Society." *Sociological Review* 27, no. 2:253–75.

———. 1981. *The Rites of Rulers: Ritual in Industrial Society – The Soviet Case.* New York: Cambridge University Press.

Lialina, G. S. 1977. *Baptizm: illiusii i real'nost'.* Moscow: Politizdat.

Markus, Vasyl. 1975a. "Religion and Nationality: The Uniates of the Ukraine." In *Religion and Atheism in the USSR and Eastern Europe,* edited by Bohdan R. Bociurkiw and John W. Strong, pp. 101–22. Toronto: University of Toronto Press.

———. 1975b. "The Suppressed Church: Ukrainian Catholics in the Soviet Union." In *Marxism and Religion in Eastern Europe,* edited by Richard T. DeGeorge and James P. Scanlan, pp. 119–32. Boston: D. Reidel.

Martin, David. 1978. *A General Theory of Secularization.* New York: Harper Colophon.

McCarthy, John D., and Mayer N. Zald. 1977. "Resource Mobilization and Social Movements: A Partial Theory." *American Journal of Sociology* 82:1212–41.

McDowell, Jennifer. 1974. "Soviet Civil Ceremonies." *Journal for the Scientific Study of Religion* 14:266–79.

Mitrokhin, L. N. 1974. *Baptizm,* 2d ed. Moscow: Politizdat.

Monitoring Group. 1977. "Monitoring Group Reports on Religious Discrimination." *Religion in Communist Lands* 5, no. 2:126–27.

Murvar, Vatro. 1968. "Russian Religious Structures: A Study in Persistent Church Subservience." *Journal for the Scientific Study of Religion* 7, no. 1:1–22.

———. 1971. "Messianism in Russia: Religious and Revolutionary." *Journal for the Scientific Study of Religion* 10, no. 4:277–388.

Nisbet, Robert. 1970. *The Social Bond.* New York: Knopf.

———. 1979. "Progress and Providence." *Society* 17, no. 1:4–7.

Oestreicher, Paul. 1978. "Postscript." *Religion in Communist Lands* 6, no. 2:95–96.

Pankhurst, Jerry G. 1978a. "The Orthodox and the Baptist in the USSR: Resources for the Survival of Ideologically Defined Deviance." Ph.D. dissertation, University of Michigan.

———. 1978b. "The 'Hyperbolic Principle' in Church–State Relations in the USSR: Natural Restraints on Soviet Antireligious Policy." Paper presented at the annual convention of the American Association for the Advancement of Slavic Studies, Columbus, Ohio, October 12–15.

———. 1978c. "Human Rights Diplomacy and Religious Dissidence in the Soviet Union." Paper presented at the annual meeting of the Society for the Scientific Study of Religion, Hartford, Conn., October 27–29.

———. 1986. "Soviet Society and Soviet Religion." *Journal of Church and State* 28 (Autumn): 409–22.

Pospielovsky, Dimitry. 1984. *The Russian Church under the Soviet Regime, 1917–1982.* 2 vols. Crestwood, N.Y.: St. Vladimir's Seminary Press.

Powell, David E. 1975. *Antireligious Propaganda in the Soviet Union: A Study in Mass Persuasion.* Cambridge: M.I.T. Press.

Prifti, Peter. 1975. "Albania – Towards an Atheist Society." In *Religion and Atheism in the USSR and Eastern Europe,* edited by Bohdan R. Bociurkiw and John W. Strong, pp. 338–404. Toronto: University of Toronto Press.

Reddaway, Peter. 1975. "The Georgian Orthodox Church: Corruption and Renewal." *Religion in Communist Lands* 3 (July–October):14–23.

Robertson, Roland. 1974. "Religious and Sociological Factors in the Analysis of Secularization." In *Changing Perspectives in the Scientific Study of Religion,* edited by Allen W. Eister, pp. 41–60. New York: Wiley.

Rowe, Michael. 1975. "Pentecostal Documents from the USSR." *Religion in Communist Lands* 3, nos. 1–3:16–18.

Sapiets, Janis. 1970. "The Orthodox Church in the Soviet Union and Eastern Europe." In *The Soviet Union and Eastern Europe: A Handbook,* edited by George Schöpflin, pp. 467–71. New York: Praeger.

Sawatsky, Walter. 1976. "The New Soviet Law on Religion." *Religion in Communist Lands* 4, no. 2:4–10.

Secret Instructions. 1973. "Secret Instructions on the Supervision of Parish Life" (directed to local authorities regarding the surveillance and supervision of religious activities in their area). English text in *Religion in Communist Lands* 1, no. 1:30–33.

Simon, Gerhard. 1974. *Church, State and Opposition in the USSR*, translated by Kathleen Matchett. Berkeley: University of California Press.

Skilling, H. Gordon, and Franklyn Griffiths, eds. 1971. *Interest Groups in Soviet Politics*. Princeton, N.J.: Princeton University Press.

Steeves, Paul D. 1977. "Amendment of Soviet Law Concerning Religious Groups." *Journal of Church and State* 19:37–52.

Timasheff, Nicholas S. 1942. *Religion in Soviet Russia, 1917–1942*. New York: Sheed and Ward.

———. 1946. *The Great Retreat*. New York: Dutton.

———. 1960. "The Inner Life of the Russian Orthodox Church." In *The Transformation of Russian Society*, edited by Cyril Black, pp. 425–37. Cambridge: Harvard University Press.

Topornin, Boris. 1980. *The New Constitution of the USSR*. Moscow: Progress Publishers.

Tsentral'noe Statisticheskoe Upravlenie pri Sovete Ministrov SSSR (Ts. S.U.). 1980. *Naselenie SSSR*. Moscow: Izdatel'stvo politicheskoi literatury.

Vardys, V. Stanley. 1977. "Modernization and Latin Rite Catholics in the Soviet Union." In *Religion and Modernization in the Soviet Union*, edited by Dennis J. Dunn, pp. 348–81. Boulder, Colo.: Westview Press.

Voroshilov, A. S. 1974. "Religioznost' kak predmet sotsiologicheskogo issledovaniia (opyt konkretno-sotsiologicheskogo issledovaniia v Rostovskoi oblasti)." Candidate dissertation, Rostov-on-Don University.

Ward, Caroline. 1978. "Church and State in East Germany." *Religion in Communist Lands* 6, no. 2:89–95.

9

Crime and Criminals in the USSR

Louise I. Shelley

Crime has changed the way many Americans live (U.S. Department of Justice 1978). Many individuals do not go out at night, and others go out only in groups. Furthermore, the fear of crime has spawned a huge private security industry to protect individuals and their property. At various times, American leaders have initiated a war on crime, promising a reduction in one of the United States' most enduring social problems (Murray 1984, 121–23). But never has any leader promised the citizenry that crime would be eliminated.

Marx, however, predicted that crime would disappear with the achievement of communism. Soviet leaders cannot then engage in an occasional war on crime. They must continually fight for the elimination of crime. Consequently, the maintenance of public order is one of the basic guarantees that the Soviet leadership has made to its population (Cohen 1985). Fedorchuk, recently replaced as head of the Ministry of Internal Affairs, claimed that one basic advantage of the Soviet system is that it has a lower crime rate than Western societies (Fedorchuk 1983). Yet no nationwide statistics on Soviet crime exist to support this statement, and, in fact, no national crime statistics have been published officially since 1928 (Juviler 1976, 131), although Soviet legal scholars are now calling for their issuance (Iakovlev and Gamaiunov 1986, 13). Although Soviet crime rates may indeed

Note: This paper was completed while the author was a Research Scholar at the Kennan Institute of the Wilson Center at the Smithsonian Institution.

be lower than those of the United States, there is strong evidence that the USSR, like most capitalist societies, is facing a growing crime problem.

In speeches preceding the 1986 Party Congress, Soviet leaders in diverse regions of the country proclaimed that there was not even basic order in the streets (Patiashvili 1985). What kind of crime problem now exists in the USSR that would prompt such an overt admission of failure in fulfilling one of the state's primary ideological commitments? Certain generalizations about contemporary criminality based on reading the Soviet criminological literature of the last decade begin to answer this question. For example, the crime problem has worsened, especially among juveniles (Smirnov 1985, 14; Gusev 1985, 25). Crime is no longer primarily an urban problem but encroaches on the daily lives of rural residents as well. The measures taken against criminals have been of limited assistance in controlling crime. Alcohol figures in the development and perpetration of the majority of criminality. In this respect the anti-alcohol campaign initiated in 1985 ("New Drive" 1985) represents a major step to combat the increasingly pervasive criminality.

Are there any Soviet explanations as to why they have succumbed to what appears to be one of the most pervasive problems of contemporary society? Do Western theories provide any insight into the distinctive crime patterns of this major socialist state? This chapter answers these basic questions by examining the nature and extent of adult and juvenile crime, the character of the offender population, and the measures taken by Soviet authorities to control criminals.

Explaining Soviet Crime

Western criminological theory examines crime from the sociological, psychological, and biological perspectives. Preeminent among these approaches has been the sociological method that draws on Durkheim's view that crime is normal and necessary for society. Consequently, few Western scholars seriously entertain the idea that crime can be eliminated from society. Instead they have explained the etiology of crime in terms of the environment and social conditions affecting the individual.

Soviet criminologists, assuming the Marxist perspective on crime, have stated that there is "nothing in the nature of Soviet society which could give rise to crime" (Gertsenzon 1960, 52). Consequently, for most of the Soviet period biological explanations of criminality have been taboo. Furthermore, Soviet writers have generally dismissed the relevance of Western criminological scholarship to their research (Connor 1972, 11).

The last five years have seen a remarkable shift in the explanations given by Soviet criminologists for the endurance of criminality in their society. Gone are the broad ideological pronouncements that characterized so much of their studies in the early post-Stalin period. This has given way to a much more sophisticated approach to criminality where the causes of crime are seen to lie very much in the developmental process (Alimov 1983, 33), the anomie that characterizes contemporary urban life (Reznik 1985, 52), and the psychological and sociological problems of socialization (Iakovlev 1985, 84–198). Soviet analyses of juvenile delinquency explain the growth and increasing seriousness of youth crime in terms of the influence of poor home environment, peers, and schools that fail to provide adequate education and supervision (Volkov and Lysov 1983). In these areas Soviet theorizing seems to be converging with Western thought on the origins of crime. Furthermore, biological explanations of crime prohibited in the USSR and long out of vogue in the United States are enjoying a similar resurgence in both societies (Osipov 1978, 42–43; Wilson and Herrnstein 1985).

The following discussion focuses on the major trends in criminological research. It also provides some insight into how crime problems have changed in the most recent decade.

Nature of Soviet Crime

The 1917 Revolution profoundly changed the nature of society including the crime problem. Although the years of civil war and revolution created many homeless youth (*bezprizorniki*) who terrorized the Soviet population through their criminal acts (Volkov and Lysov 1983, 7), the impact of revolutionary change on crime was much more longlasting. New categories of crime were created, and the national policies to urbanize and industrialize society determined the geographical distribution of crime that has remained to this day. The socialization of the means of production, the outlawing of private enterprise, and the requirement that all citizens work have led to the creation of such offenses as speculation (the purchase and resale of goods at a profit) and parasitism (malicious refusal to work). Thus, socialism has placed its special stamp on the nature of crime in contemporary Soviet society. But these so-called "socialist crimes" represent a small share of total crime commission.

Apart from the offenses unique to socialist society, crime patterns in the USSR are not notably different from those in societies that are not fully industrialized. The reason is that even though much of the western part of Russia and the Baltic republics are quite developed, many of the other parts of the country have not acquired the social patterns associated with industrialization (Shelley 1981).

Important evidence on the distribution of convictions for major crimes is shown in Table 9.1. The table includes current national data for some categories of crime in column 3. (Though incomplete, the publication of any such data represents a partial opening up of the criminal justice system.) Recently published research on sentencing in different republics suggests that the distribution of offenses has remained quite similar in many respects in more recent decades (van den Berg 1985, 331–33; Gabiani and Gachechiladze 1982). The only category of crime whose proportional contribution to total criminality has increased is vehicular crime, a consequence of the significant growth in the number of new cars and drivers on the road (*Kurs* 1985, 194). The proportional contribution of crimes against the person has decreased, possibly an indication of the impact of development on patterns of criminality.

The Soviet crime statistics reveal that a significant share of the crimes committed involve attacks against the person. As development of a nation proceeds, crimes against the person become relatively less frequent in

Table 9.1
Distribution of Convictions for Different Categories of Criminal Activity (Percent of all Crimes)

	USSR (1966)	Georgian SSR (1982)	USSR (1985)[a]
Stealing of social property	17	12.27	15–18
Crimes against public order	*	30.27	*
Hooliganism	24	11.38	18–25
Traffic crime	5	10.64	*
Other	*	8.25	*
Crimes against private property	16	12.10	14–16
Crimes against the person	17	14.68	6–7[b]
Economic crimes	5	15.36	*
Official crimes	4	6.64	*
Crimes against the Administration of Justice	1.5	2.11	*
Crimes against the Order of Administration	4	3.65	*
Other	6.5	*	*

Source: Col. 1, S. Ostroumov, *Sovetskaia sudebnaia statistika* (Moscow: Iuridicheskaia literatura, 1970, p. 248; col. 2, A. Gabiani and R. Gachechiladze, *Nekotorye voprosy geografii prestupnosti* (Tbilisi: Izd, Tbiliiskogo universiteta, 1982, pp. 86–108; col. 3, *Kurs* (Moscow: Iuridicheskaia literatura, 1985, p. 194.

* Source provides no data for this category.

[a] Though very incomplete, the national data in the third column are very significant, because they are the first such data published in the USSR since the 1920s.

[b] This seeming reduction in crimes against the person as compared with data in the other columns is artifactual. It represents the diversion of petty crimes against the person, those based on private accusation, to "Comrades Courts" that are noncriminal courts (van den Berg 1985, p. 68).

comparison with crimes against property. For that reason, developed countries as a whole indicate that only 10 percent of the crimes committed are against the person, whereas in developing countries a comparable figure is 43 percent (United Nations 1977, 12–14).

Soviet authorities provide no figures on the total crime rate in their country. But even if such statistics were available they would not provide an accurate assessment of the crime problem as most crimes remain unrecorded. Although the problem of latent criminality (*Kurs* 1985, 163–68), unreported and undetected crime, exists in all societies, the problem is particularly acute in the USSR as the police are under pressure to solve 95 percent of all reported crimes (Kuznetsova 1969, 183). Consequently, many cases of petty theft, economic crime, and violations of labor safety rules never enter into the crime reports (van den Berg 1985, 14). Furthermore, many crimes committed by party members are never prosecuted as the Party must expel an individual before he is allowed to stand trial (Shtromas 1977, 307).[1] Despite the large number of crimes that never enter the official reports, approximately three-quarters of a million individuals are sentenced annually to a variety of penal sanctions (van den Berg 1985, 11). Considering the large number of unrecorded crimes, the conviction figure represents a crime problem of significant proportions.

There is much variation in the crime rate within the USSR. Furthermore, certain forms of criminality are more charactreristic of one region than another. This differentiation – explained by ethnic differences, level of urbanization, and population controls – is discussed in greater depth in the section on the geography of crime.

Certain general characteristics differentiate crime commission in the USSR from that in most other societies. First, a very high percentage of all crimes are perpetrated while the offender is intoxicated. Although alcohol is highly correlated with crime commission in all societies, particularly northern nations, the problem is especially acute in the USSR. Fifty percent of all convicted persons were drunk at the time of their offense. Since most perpetrators of economic and administrative offenses should be excluded (such crimes are not typically committed in a bout of drunkenness), it suggests that the correlation between crime commission and drunkenness is much higher for other categories of crime commission (Shtromas 1977, 304). Recent Soviet statistics indicate that more than 80 percent of all people who committed premeditated murder and other violent crimes, as well as hooliganism, armed robbery, and theft, misused alcohol (*Kurs* 1985, 318). These figures exceed the correlation between alcohol use and crime in most countries for which data are available (Connor 1972, 47). The widespread problem of alcohol abuse among the offenders in these types of street crimes suggests the retreatist behavior identified by Merton in his theory of anomie.

Individuals who cannot achieve society's goals retreat from the society. Often, according to Merton's theory of anomie, their frustration leads to acts of violence (Merton 1938, 1968).

Second, a significant percentage of all offenses are perpetrated in groups. Adult criminals rarely operate in organized gangs, yet in the period from 1963 to 1968, between 21 and 28 percent of all crimes were committed by groups (Criminal Personality 1971, 83), a pattern that appears to have been maintained to the present. Among juveniles the figure is much higher, reaching 80 percent in some studies (Soldatov 1981, 81). Fraud, embezzlement, and other financial manipulations involving large amounts of state capital are more frequently committed by groups than are petty thefts. Violent crimes against property are almost always committed by more than one offender, whereas this is the case in less than one-fifth of all thefts of personal property. Crimes against the person often also take this form. The extent of group crime is surprising as organized crime was almost completely eradicated under Stalin (Chalidze 1977; Shtromas 1977, 301) when almost all professional offenders died in labor camps.

To understand the distinctiveness of Soviet crime patterns and the imprint of socialist conditions on criminality, it is necessary to examine the major categories of crime commission. The following section analyzes the nature and reasons for the perpetration of hooliganism, crimes against the person and property, economic offenses, victimless crime, and political crime.

Categories of Crime Commission

Hooliganism

Hooliganism is the most widespread of all criminal acts in the Soviet Union and represents about 18 to 25 percent of all prosecutions in the USSR (*Kurs* 1985, 194). There is no Western equivalent for this offense that is much more wide-reaching than disorderly conduct. Petty hooliganism is defined in the criminal code as "intentional actions violating public order in a coarse manner and expressing a clear disrespect toward society"; malicious hooliganism can involve the use of a weapon and can carry up to seven years institutional confinement. Hooligans can be arrested for screaming in public or for beating their spouses or lovers (Sootak 1977). Occasionally, even anti-Soviet activity is dealt with under this offense when officials are attempting to mask the extent of political crime in their community. Data from both Azerbaidzhan and the Russian Republic (RSFSR) indicate that in the majority of hooliganism cases physical violence is used (Kafarov and Musaev 1983, 36–37).

More than 90 percent of all prosecuted offenders nationwide have committed the offense while intoxicated (Kydyralieva 1981, 123), and a significant share of those accused of malicious hooliganism are chronic alcoholics (Sootak 1977, 28; Kafarov and Musaev 1983, 101; Kalmykov 1979, 88). In Central Asia and the Caucasus misuse of narcotics also contributes to the rate of hooliganism (Kydyralieva 1981, 123; Kafarov and Musaev 1983, 189). Often the victim of the hooligan attack is also drunk – in some areas two-thirds of victims of hooliganism are drunk (Frank and Konovalov 1975, 263) – and his vulgar language and aggravating remarks may have been the precipitating factor in the beginning of a fight (Kafarov and Musaev 1983, 150). Although drugs and alcohol are important contributing factors to the perpetration of this offense, Soviet authorities state that these are not the root causes (Kydyralieva 1981, 122).

Much of the literature seems to suggest that a subculture of violence exists in Soviet society. According to this theory of Wolfgang and Ferracuti (1967), individuals who belong to this culture are socialized to accept violence as a natural part of their lives and their interpersonal relationships. Examination of the location of most hooligan attacks indicates that they are closely linked to the personal, daily lives of the perpetrators. Studies indicate that more than 33 percent of reported cases of hooliganism occur in homes and apartments, another 30 to 35 percent in streets and courtyards, and a further 25 percent in such public places as stores, cafeterias, and parks (Kafarov and Musaev 1983, 46). The location of these offenses reflects the impact of the physical environment on crime commission. Since many of the offenses are committed in communal apartments, it suggests that the tensions of daily life in the city are more than some individuals can handle. Also indicative of this problem is that the victims of hooligan acts are not strangers but individuals who belong to the same subculture as the perpetrators, for example, spouses, girlfriends, relatives, and acquaintances (Kafarov and Musaev 1983, 72). Although almost all hooligans are male, nearly half the victims of their crimes are female (Frank and Konovalov 1975, 261). Often the offenders join with others of similar backgrounds to commit hooliganistic acts together. (Kalmykov 1979, 86).

Soviet sources suggest that the anomic conditions of urban life contribute to high rates of hooliganism (Kafarov and Musaev 1983, 156). The long working hours of parents with little time to spend and educate children are very different from the conditions in rural communities where children work closely with their parents. Some people, unable to adjust to urban life, become parasites, that is, individuals unwilling to work or study. Research carried out among hooligans shows a close link between parasitism and hooliganism, with approximately 20 percent of hooligans labeled as parasites (Kafarov and Musaev 1983, 150).

Furthermore, some individuals are unable to use their free time appropriately, committing most of their hooligan acts in after-work hours. Part of the reason for the poor social adjustment of the urban residents is that many communities lack the sport and recreational facilities needed to occupy their free time (Kafarov and Musaev 1983, 154).

Recent American research has suggested that changes in routine activity have contributed to increased opportunities for criminality. The increase in the number of working mothers and the large number of hours spent away from home facilitate crime commission (Cohen and Felson 1979). Although even Soviet sources acknowledge that the long hours of parental absence from the home contribute to increased rates of hooliganism, most of the data they present on the circumstances surrounding hooliganism and the background of the offenders suggest a growing subculture of violence and anomie as major causes of hooliganism, rather than changes of routine activity in contemporary urban life.

Crimes against the Person

Crimes against the person are divided into three main categories of criminality – homicide, grave injury or aggravated assualt, and sex crimes. These offenses contribute 8 to 9 percent of all criminal convictions in the USSR or 70–80,000 cases annually (van den Berg 1985, 69). The totality of all sex crimes represents 2 to 3 percent of all crimes in the Soviet Union (van den Berg 1985, 71).

Almost all acts of violence are directed against private individuals rather than against the state as there are few acts of terrorism that result in injury or loss of life. Furthermore, in all categories of violent crime the offense has a domestic character as the victims are rarely strangers and the offense is committed close to home (Frank and Soboleva 1975). Often the individual has initially been convicted as a youthful hooligan and moves on to commit more violent offenses in the adult years (Soldatov 1981, 82).

Homicide is a relatively rare offense in most societies. The same is true in the Soviet Union, but homicide rates are relatively high in the USSR, amounting to about 8 per 100,000 for intentional and unintentional homicides, or approximately 20,000 per year.[2] The Soviet homicide rate almost equals the American figure for the same period, but both are approximately three times greater than the average homicide rate for the developed countries during the same time period.[3]

There are several reasons for the large number of homicides. First, the vast majority of homicides are committed while the offender is intoxicated. Research also indicates that a large number of the victims are drunk at the time of the offense and may contribute to its commission (Frank 1971, 155).

With both victim and offender intoxicated, the restraints that might prevent the perpetration of the crime are not operating (Kudriavtsev 1960, 31). Second, the means by which many homicides are committed contributes to the large number of fatalities. As firearms are not readily available, most homicides are committed using ordinary household instruments, such as knives and axes. Unfortunately, individuals who suffer large losses of blood may not receive the proper emergency medical care that keeps an aggravated assault from becoming a homicide.

Research indicates that in more than three-quarters of the cases the murderer is acquainted with the victim (Frank 1966, 143). Infanticide – which was a significant problem in the 1920s (Shelley 1982) – has not entirely disappeared in the contemporary period despite the liberalization of abortion laws. It still contributes to 3 to 4 percent of all homicides (Frank 1966, 143; van den Berg 1985, 70).

Research on rape reveals that this offense is usually committed while the offender is intoxicated, a fact even in the Moslem republic of Uzbekistan (Akhmedov and Blinder 1964, 69).[4] Data indicate that between 28 and 37 percent of all rapes are committed by multiple assailants. This percentage is down from a figure of over 50 per cent for the pre-Revolutionary period (Criminal Personality 1971, 84). At present, rape is an increasing problem among juvenile offenders (Criminal Personality 1971, 122–23) and is often committed in groups (Soldatov 1981, 84). Those who commit the offense are often recidivists who have led "wanton" lives (Akhmedov and Blinder 1964, 70–71).

Violent offenses contribute a significant proportion of the total crime problem, a fact explained by the still strongly rural character of Soviet life and the significant national problems of alcohol abuse. The urban–rural distribution of crimes against the person is discussed more fully in the section on the geography of crime.

Property Offenses

Property offenses represent about a third of all Soviet crime commission. Soviet authorities carefully differentiate between theft of individual and state property, although each area of criminality contributes about equally to the total amount of property crime. The latter category of criminality is considered much more severe as the individual's offense is considered harmful to the general welfare of society. But more differentiates the two categories of property crime than the nature of the victim. There are significant differences in the geographical distribution of these offenses, the age and background of the offenders and the treatment of these forms of criminality that are discussed in greater depth in the following sections.

Crime rates for these offenses are affected by the police's perception of their ability to apprehend the offender as well as by the party campaigns launched against particular areas of criminal activity (Smith 1979). For example, many cases of pickpocketing are never recorded as there is little chance of locating the perpetrator (van den Berg 1985, 68). Furthermore, significant oscillations in state policy affect prosecutions for such offenses as theft and embezzlement of state property. But no campaigns are launched against people who steal private property as the authorities merely respond to reports of criminal conduct and do not initiate their own investigations.

The losses attributable to theft of state property are significantly greater than those involving individuals. Most citizens steal small amounts from their workplace (Los 1983, 47). This activity is similar to what has been referred to in the United States as occupational crime – "acts of theft, pilferage and fraud that are acceptable practices among fellow employees" and are carried out in groups at the individual's place of employment (Thomas and Hepburn 1983, 309–310). Many cases of large-scale theft are reported as having a crippling effect on the economy. For example, one Soviet newspaper reported that more than 50 per cent of new farm machines are delivered in an unusable state, having had numerous parts removed while in shipment on the railroads (Tenson 1980, 1). Similarly, large losses are reported from warehouses and factories. Soviet authorities explain these crimes in terms of the inadequate social conscience of the citizenry. They generally fail to acknowledge that the shortages created by the system of centralized planning force many people to resort to illegal activity to obtain necessary goods that cannot be acquired through legitimate means.

Official and Economic Crime

Many of the crimes that fall under this category are either unique to socialist society or their importance is escalated by the fact that almost all production and service institutions are now under government ownership. As in the case of theft of socialist property, prosecutions in this area are very much affected by political circumstances and the initiation of campaigns against such forms of criminality as bribery (van den Berg 1985, 61), or the buying up of bread and other produce by collective farms to feed livestock (Osipenko 1985). Although many Soviet officials could be prosecuted for these crimes, few are. Prosecutions often originate to remove officials deemed no longer useful or are "aimed at mobilizing official agencies and public opinion in support of general goals fixed by the party and central planning agencies" (Los 1983, 52).

The most frequently prosecuted of all the official crimes is neglect of, followed in frequency by abuse of, official position (van den Berg 1985, 60).

However, most reported cases of these offenses are not prosecuted, but are handled administratively or in other ways. When losses are large, managers can be removed from their positions, sanctioned by the party, or eventually tried (Kairzhanov 1963, 93). Bribery makes up only 13 percent of all official crimes (van den Berg 1985, 60–61) but is a subject of considerable concern as it is seen to undermine the legal system and social and economic institutions in Soviet society. In extreme cases it can result in the execution of the offender (Fuller 1980). Furthermore, those who are prosecuted for bribery are multiple offenders having committed most of their offenses while performing their jobs or while conducting supervisory work (Kvitsinia 1980, 126–127). The other major category of economic crime is overreporting of production and goods (leading to the illegal payment of unearned bonuses), which is infrequently prosecuted (Demin and Khalin 1985, R4).

Much of this economic crime remains undetected, the extent to which it is uncovered determined by the type of organization in which the crime takes place (Utkin 1980, 130). Often the individual is able to perpetrate an economic offense, such as production of substandard goods, for decades without detection. Even when the individual's guilt is brought to light, the investigation may not be adequate to disclose all the collaborators (Mel'nikova, Oreshkina, and Beliaeva 1984, 38–39).

These official and economic offenses (bribery, issuance of substandard goods, and neglect) might be considered to conform to Sutherland's definition of white collar crime as "crimes committed by persons of respectability and high social status in the course of their occupation" (Sutherland and Cressey 1974, 45). But as one Western scholar points out, up to 95 per cent of the people prosecuted for these offenses are representatives of the medium and lower level of the Soviet administrative apparatus (van den Berg 1985, 62), a figure not inconsistent with their representation in the work force, but hardly the image of Sutherland's white-collar offender. Only in the post-Brezhnev period has an anti-corruption campaign been initiated against more high-level personnel.

The tendency to spare upper-level management from prosecution is not confined to the Soviet Union; it is discussed by Clinard in his work on capitalist corporate crime (Clinard and Yeager 1980). Although the reasons for official and economic crime differ in capitalist and socialist societies (Los 1983, 39), the treatment of the offenders is similar in both types of societies.

Victimless Crime

The concept of *victimless crime* has been used in the West for several decades to denote such activity as prostitution, drug addiction and gambling. Such offenses have generally not been recognized in the USSR, and the concept that there are no victims for certain offenses has not been acknowledged. With the recent "openness" campaign of Gorbachev, the problems of prostitution, drug addiction, and drug trafficking have been acknowledged, and wider actions have been urged against these behaviors.

Soviet authorities long denied that prostitution existed in the USSR. But now they contend that it is an increasing problem (Konovalov 1986). The new criminal code that is now in preparation will probably contain criminal sanctions for those who engage in prostitution (Yakubovich 1986, 21–22).

The problem of drug addiction has been exacerbated in the past decade by the large number of Soviet soldiers who have fought in Afghanistan. Many of the young soldiers have become addicted there, and on their return they have required drugs for themselves and have introduced them to young people. Soviet addicts are increasingly youthful (Albats 1986, 1–3), and many are turning to crime to finance their habits (Karatygina 1986, 3–4). Although the problem has traditionally been treated as a medical problem, its proliferation has led to increased involvement by the law enforcement authorities (Mostovoi 1986, 1–3, 23; "Growing Concern" 1986, 1–4; "Events and Opinions" 1986, 20–21). But citizens complain that the police are not being sufficiently vigilant in dealing with the problem (Sergeev 1987, 12).

Political Crime

Soviet authorities claim that there is no political criminality in the USSR, and no particular criminal code concerned with this form of behavior exists. Instead, crimes against the state and the system of administration are subsumed under the standard criminal code and encompass such acts as anti-Soviet agitation and propaganda, attempts to exit illegally from the Soviet Union, libel and slander against the Soviet state, and insults to representatives of Soviet authority. Offenders accused of these acts are processed differently through the legal system. Political defendants require special defense attorneys, and courtrooms are often closed during these proceedings (Kaminskaya 1982).

Convictions for crimes against the state represent only a small fraction of total Soviet offenses, probably much less than 1 percent. A careful analysis of Soviet statistical reports suggests "a number of between 5,000 and 10,000 sentences for crimes of this type annually during the 1970s in the entire USSR" (van der Berg 1985, 59). Knowledge of the harsh treatment of political offenders may help deter crime commission.

The absence of Soviet research makes it difficult to construct a picture of the political offender. But an analysis of known dissidents divides them into national, religious, and human rights groups (Alekseeva 1984). The celebrated defendants of the human rights movement are not typical of those prosecuted under the political articles of the criminal code. Members of the nationalist and religious movements often lack the training and positions of their counterparts in the human rights movement. Furthermore, not all those prosecuted for antistate activity are members of organized movements. Labor camp memoirs by former political prisoners reveal that many of their fellow inmates in special prisons for political criminals were simple workers who naïvely told anti-Soviet anecdotes in public or attempted to cross the Soviet border without permission (Marchenko 1969; Bukovsky 1978).

The previously discussed categories of crime commission represent the major forms of illegal conduct. The analysis indicates that there is a significant range of criminal conduct that has been affected by the conditions of socialist society. The following discussion focuses on the distribution of crime within Soviet society.

The Geography of Soviet Criminality

Most mainstream criminological research in the United States has focused on the impact of urban life on crime (Merton 1938; Sutherland and Cressey 1974). But some comparative and historical research has focused on the impact of industrialization and urbanization on crime, suggesting that these social forces are major determinants of patterns of criminal conduct (Tobias 1967; Shelley 1981; Zehr 1976). Although Soviet scholars rarely acknowledge the relevance of Western research or follow the same lines of inquiry, there is a striking convergence between Western and Soviet scholarship on the relationship between crime and development.

Soviet criminologists in the past fifteen years have studied the relationship between internal migration, urban growth, and crime. In the last five years the application of the development perspective to analyses of the geography of crime has become a major focus of researchers not only in the RSFSR, but also in many of the non-Slavic regions of the country. Through quantitative analyses they have constructed a theoretical framework to explain the relationship among urbanization, industrialization, and observed crime patterns. Recent Soviet research has attempted to understand the differences between urban and rural crime and the nature of crime in the diverse cities of the USSR (major metropolitan areas, medium-sized cities, ports, resorts, and newly established communities) (Kurs 1985, 239). With surprising frankness that distinguishes this work from many other areas of criminological research, scholars have concluded that industrialization and urbanization usually result in higher rates of crime commission. Their research leads to the implicit (rather than explicit) conclusion that despite the planning of the developmental process, urbanization and industrialization have resulted in serious changes in the pattern of crime commission, not very different from those observed in Western societies that have followed the capitalist form of development.

The general conclusions of Soviet research are that high rates of property crime against personal property are characteristic of urban areas, whereas crimes against the person are more frequent in rural areas (Gabiani and Gachechiládze 1982, 110). This observed pattern is consistent with the criminological findings of Western researchers who have concluded that a major sign of development is the diminution of crimes against the person relative to property crime (Zehr 1976; Shelley 1981).

Other significant differences characterize urban and rural patterns of crime commission. Rural areas are not characterized simply by higher rates of violent crime. Theft of socialist property and homebrewing are also disproportionately rural crimes (Antonian 1978, 79). This is true because state and collective farm workers have very ready access to governmental property. Second, peasants working on these farms have an acute need for grain for their privately owned animals. Because they frequently cannot acquire this grain legally, they resort to theft of governmental crops. Third, Soviet authorities suggest that this form of criminal activity is a manifestation of the traditional peasant practice of salvaging anything they see lying around (Reznik 1985, 55). The state has always been relatively tolerant of this form of criminal conduct, and relatively few cases are prosecuted.

Traditional peasant culture affects rural crime patterns in other ways. First, tightknit rural communities ensure that many cases of hooliganism, assault, homebrewing, and rape are not reported to the authorities but are handled by the community (Antonian 1978, 79).[5] Second, the drinking accompanying religious holidays still celebrated in the countryside results in elevated rates of hooliganism and crimes against the person (Antonian 1978, 80). Third, traditional peasant distrust of outsiders exacerbates crime rates for the same offenses at sowing and harvesting time when nonresidents come to help plant and gather the crops (Reznik 1985, 55).

Bootlegging is the only traditionally rural crime that continues on a mass scale. This offense, usually the domain of older women, has been one of the most common female offenses since the prerevolutionary period (Gernet 1924, 185–86). Women with limited financial resources, the result of low monthly salaries or even lower retirement pensions (sometimes as low as $30 a month) turn to this form of crime as an easy means of increasing their income. The launching of the anti-alcohol campaign has made this form of criminality more risky but also more profitable. The authorities have attempted to combat bootlegging by raising the pensions of collective farm workers (Gerasyuk 1985, 10), thereby removing some of the incentives to engage in this form of crime.

Urban criminality is characterized by offenses against private property and in certain areas by high rates of violent offenses. The property crimes of theft, *grabezh* (open stealing), and *razboi* (armed robbery) are overwhelmingly urban offenses. Burglary has become an increasing urban problem often committed by juveniles during school hours (Sootak 1977; Pankratov, Arseb'eva, and Kulicheva 1984). The disproportionate frequency of crime against personal property in cities and resort areas compared to rural areas – a sevenfold difference in the Republic of Georgia (Gabiani and Gachechiladze 1982, 123–24) – is explained by the greater concentration of wealth in cities and the paucity of material possessions in the countryside. The process of development has strongly differentiated the character of urban and rural property crime.

Significant change has occurred during the Soviet period in the relationship of urban to rural crime. During the 1920s crime rates were three and one-half times higher in cities than in the countryside (Gertsenzon, 1928), and significant differences were observed up until the late 1960s (Reznik 1985, 54). At that time it was reported that the number of crimes per capita in urban areas exceeded that in rural communities by 40 per cent (Connor 1972, 174). This pattern was fully consistent with that of other nations in the world that had undergone industrial development. In rural areas family and neighbors usually exercise greater social control over individual behavior, limiting levels of crime commission. But more recently selected Soviet studies have found that only a slight majority of all crimes are now committed in urban areas and that certain rural areas have crime rates that exceed those of urban areas (Reznik 1985, 54–55).

Closer examination of particular Soviet conditions explains this deviation from the generally observed relationship between crime and development. Georgian and Slavic researchers (Gabiani and Gachechiladze 1982; Antonian 1978, 81) have found that there has been an urbanization of rural life. The prosperity of agricultural life in Georgia has brought many more urban workers into the countryside than in other parts of the Soviet Union, increasing levels of rural criminality (Gabiani and Didebulidze 1982, 106). Furthermore, research has indicated that in certain agricultural areas where some of the population has a higher education, the level of crime is higher than in urban areas (Kurs 1985, 196). Consequently, rural areas have acquired some of the problems of urban life without acquiring its amenities (Reznik 1985, 53–54). The growth of rural crime in the Slavic regions of the USSR is explained by a different phenomenon. As is discussed more fully later, released offenders and parasites are forced to settle in rural areas, adding to the rural crime rates. The urbanization of rural life has led to a dramatic narrowing of the gap between urban and rural areas, and according to a Soviet scholar, fundamental differences between crime in these two areas do not now exist (Reznik 1985, 55).

Examination of literature from the different Soviet republics and ethnic regions of the USSR presents a very different picture. Research in traditionally Moslem areas, as well as in Estonia, shows that strong differences still exist between major urban centers and rural areas in levels of crime commission. This suggests that the generalizations on the convergence of urban and rural areas applies specifically to the Slavic regions of the country. Research in Georgia indicates much lower crime rates in the remote mountainous areas of the republic than in the ethnically diverse urban centers and resort areas (Gabiani and Gachechiladze 1982). Studies in Kazan, the capital of the Tatar ASSR, reveal that juvenile crime is concentrated in the largest cities of this region and is highest in the industrial areas of the city (Volkov and Lysov 1983, 27). Furthermore, the farther one gets away from the main cities and the railroad connections to these locations, the lower are the rates of juvenile criminality. Consequently, 70 per cent of the republic's juvenile crime is committed in the major cities settled by Slavs, whereas juvenile crime is minimal among the indigenous population (Volkov and Lysov 1983, 26). Studies in Estonia indicate that no rural area is represented among the parts of the republic with the highest rates of criminal activity (Leps 1980, 126).

The geography of Soviet crime differs in certain important respects from that observed in other societies. Not only are the traditional differences between urban and rural crime not established in all parts of the country, but also the usual correlation between degree of urbanization and the level of criminality is not observed in the USSR. Furthermore, even within individual republics it is not always the largest cities but often the secondary and tertiary cities that have higher rates of crime (Leps 1980, 126; Gabiani and Gachechiladze, 1982; Volkov and Lysov, 1983).

The current distribution of crime in the USSR is so different from that of most industrialized and industrializing countries because the regime restricts the internal mobility of its population to achieve the goals of a centralized planned economy. These population controls include the internal passport system and registration system, the removal from major cities of convicted offenders, and the closure of major urban centers to new residents. Furthermore, the recently initiated anti-alcohol campaign (Powell 1985) has intensified the process of purifying the city at the expense of the countryside. The measures that limit entry into the cities and expel those who are undesirable have produced a different urban environment in the USSR from other countries that do not control the process of urban settlement. Consequently, the highest rates of criminality are not found in the largest cities, such as Moscow, Leningrad, and Kiev, but are recorded in the medium-sized cities of the North, Siberia, and the Far East (Shelley 1980).

The unique geography of Soviet crime is not a consequence of recent social developments but has come about as a result of deliberate social policies introduced over the past five decades. The internal passport and registration system was introduced in 1932 as a result of the soaring urban crime rates attributed to the large numbers of homeless youth and the large number of rural emigrants fleeing the countryside during collectivization. Consequently, much internal movement has been channelled for the last half century away from major urban centers into more recently developed cities.

The dynamics of Soviet criminality are, therefore, closely associated with the degree of internal migration of the Soviet population. Between 4 and 6 percent of all Soviet citizens move annually (Babaev 1974). Migrants from rural areas go either to heavily populated regions or to sparsely populated areas that Soviet authorities believe would benefit from an increase in population (Babaev 1968, 86–87). The destination of rural Russian migrants is frequently other republics or areas of the Russian Republic with non-Slavic inhabitants of totally different cultural, linguistic, and ethnic backgrounds. Serious adjustment problems of migrants have often resulted in criminality. Not surprisingly, half of all urban residents sentenced for open stealing and armed robberies were born in rural areas (Antonian 1978, 83) at a time when less than half of their age group were born in the countryside.

Crime research conducted in the Russian republic indicates that the highest crime rates exist in the regions in which migrants constitute an especially large proportion of the population. Studies conducted in 1963, 1965, and 1968 suggest that this relationship is due to the crime among migrants and show that regions experiencing population decline due to out-migration are less crime prone (Babaev, 1968).

Soviet criminologists have made significant efforts to study ways to decriminalize the migration process ("Nekotorye" 1980). Recently there has been a significant change in the relationship between migration and crime. This has occurred as the nature of the rural migrant population has changed. In contrast to earlier periods, the most educated and professionally qualified of the rural residents are now leaving for the city. Consequently, the new arrivals in the city are well informed about the conditions of urban life and are prepared to adapt to its environment. Research from the late 1970s and early 1980s reveals that in two major urban centers the criminality of recent emigrants from rural areas has declined and is now exceeded by that of immigrants from major urban centers (Reznik 1985).

The Offender Population

The criminal population consists of both youthful and adult criminals.

Whereas Soviet authorities report a stabilization of the problem of adult criminality, there has been a marked increase in juvenile crime in many regions of the country (Fursev 1968; Raska 1978, 185; Gelishchanov 1979). This is particularly alarming as the earlier the age at which the individual embarks on a criminal career, the more likely he or she is to remain criminal (Soldatov 1981, 82). Although juvenile delinquency is overwhelmingly a male phenomenon, there has also been a growth in the criminality of female youth. Although females are responsible for only 2 to 3 percent of the juvenile delinquency, they often function as instigators of criminality (Volkov and Lysov 1983, 31). The most common juvenile offense is hooliganism (Smirnov 1985, 14), but both male and female delinquents are participating increasingly in violent crime, many of them senseless acts.

Research conducted by Soviet scholars among delinquents indicates that their poor home (Polozov 1984, 210) and school environments contribute to the etiology of their criminal conduct. Many of them reportedly come from homes with alcoholic parents where the abuse of alcohol is so severe that it leads not only to physical defects among children, but also to deep-seated psychological problems. Often their parents are promiscuous, floating in and out of relationships. Not only do they fail to devote time to their children, but many parents of delinquents also feel that education is unimportant (Kormshchikov 1981, 51–55). In such homes, where violence is a common occurrence, it is nine to ten times more likely than normal that the children will become delinquent (Smirnov 1985, 14).

Delinquents have traditionally come from the least privileged strata of Soviet society. Research conducted two decades ago suggests that the income levels of the families of delinquents were below the established minimum standard (Criminal Personality 1971, 256). Furthermore, many offenders report that they feel materially deprived (Gabiani et al. 1981, 125). Although the standard of living of the families of many offenders remains low (Ostroumov 1966), more recent research indicates that many come from homes that are far from being materially deprived (McNeill 1980, 4). Rather like the affluent delinquents studied by American researchers (Matza 1964), the cause of their criminality lies in their peer relations and feelings of social inadequacy.

Research established that the attitudes and orientations of juvenile delinquents are very different from those of law-abiding youth. They are oriented toward immediate satisfaction and unable to defer their pleasures for longer-range objectives (Raska 1978, 14). Furthermore, many delinquents are poorly adjusted at school and are behind their grade level. Many leave school and are unable or unwilling to find work in a field that interests them (Volkov and Lysov 1983, 31–35). Consequently, a significant percentage of juvenile offenders are not only criminals, but "parasites" as well.

Soviet criminologists are particularly disturbed by the age of onset of criminal career. Their research on the age and the seriousness of the crimes of the youth offenders recalls the analyses of American youth crime in studies of birth cohorts (Wolfgang, Figlio, and Sellin 1972). Among recidivists, 81 percent had commenced their criminal careers at ages eleven and twelve (Soldatov 1981, 82). Furthermore, Soviet authorities seem unable to stem the criminality of many youthful offenders as recidivism rates for juvenile delinquents themselves remain significant.

Youth offenders commit their offenses overwhelmingly in groups (Volkov and Lysov 1983, 27), and their crime differs significantly from that of their adult counterparts. Their offenses are confined primarily to the theft of private and state property, open stealing, armed robbery, and hooliganism. Individuals not only spontaneously form groups to perpetrate their offenses, but some also belong to organized bands of thirty or more members who reside in the same area of the city. Gang members commit such serious offenses as intentional homicide and armed assaults (Volkov and Lysov 1983, 53). Often these groups of youths operate in conjunction with more seasoned adult criminals (Volkov and Lysov 1983, 48–64). Soviet studies of the group nature of youth crime recall the research of such American scholars as Cohen (1955) and Cloward and Ohlin (1960) on the impact of peers in the etiology and perpetration of criminal conduct. The importance of adult offenders in the criminality of juvenile delinquents (Dremin 1982) suggests the applicability of Sutherland's theory of differential association and the learning of criminal behavior (Sutherland 1947, 5–9).

Western Marxist scholars have suggested that the surplus population created by the growth of technology in modern capitalist societies has produced a body from which criminals and other forms of deviants are drawn (Spitzer 1975). Still other critical criminologists suggest that juvenile theft is motivated by the desire to participate in social activities when the funds needed to finance this activity by legitimate means are absent. Furthermore, juvenile delinquency is a direct result of labor market conditions of advanced capitalist societies because little employment is available to teenagers despite their training (Greenberg 1977). But the same phenomena identified as causing criminality in capitalist societies also seem to be operating in socialist society as many of the youths who commit crimes are neither working nor studying. Soviet research indicates that the material gains from their criminal acts are being used to finance drinking bouts and other forms of recreation. The problem of a surplus youthful population in the USSR does not appear to be tied to one economic system but is a problem common to economically diverse societies that have a certain element of the population that cannot conform to the demands of contemporary society. (See the chapter by Lane in this volume.)

Table 9.2
Types of Crime in Percentages of all Persons Found to Have Committed a
Crime, Estonia, 1976–1980

	Men	*Women*	*Total*	*Belorussia (1974)*
Intentional homicide	1.5	1.1	1.1	1–1.5
Intentional infliction of especially grave injury	1.8	0.7	1.7	1.4–2.1
Rape	1.9	–	1.7	1.4–2.1
Open stealing, robbery	8.5	2.2	7.7	4
Theft of state property (excl. petty theft)	14.0	10.4	13.6	10–10.5
Embezzlement of state property	2.0	15.2	3.6	3.3
Theft of personal property	15.3	20.2	15.9	7.2–7.5
Hooliganism	12.5	2.0	11.2	21.1
Joyriding	6.9	0.5	6.1	2.5
Traffic crimes	8.5	2.4	7.8	5.4
Other crimes	27.1	45.1	29.2	32.6

Source: Ger. van den Berg, *The Soviet System of Justice* (Dordrecht: Martinus Nijhoff, 1985), p. 333.

Female offenders contribute 12 to 15 percent of total criminality in the USSR (Kurs 1985, 157). Like juvenile delinquents their criminality is concentrated in only a few areas of crime commission – primarily property crimes and crimes connected with their jobs. (See Table 9.2) Female offenders are most frequently prosecuted for cheating customers in stores, and they are heavily represented in prosecution for such crimes as slander and homebrewing (Shelley 1982). In accordance with Western theories of female crime commission, women's crime has grown with increased female involvement in the labor force and women's assumption of more responsible positions (Simon 1976). In Estonia, one of the most westernized of Soviet republics, women's level of participation in economic crimes grew four times in the period between 1976–81 (Kil'g 1982, 99). Furthermore, the criminality of women is higher in urban than in rural areas. This suggests that the relationship between development and female crime observed elsewhere in the world also exists in the Soviet Union (Shelley 1981, 56–57).

Female offenders not only commit different crimes, but they also commit them at a different age. Whereas most male criminals are youthful, women are most criminogenic between the ages of thirty and forty-nine, a fact explained by the strong linkage between their criminality and their employment. But like their male counterparts, they are generally more poorly educated than the general population (Kil'g 1982, 100).

Women criminals are treated differently from men. Female offenders receive lighter sentences than men (Kil'g 1982, 99), a fact that seems to be explained not only by the lesser severity of their criminality but also by the feeling that the removal of women from the community may be harmful to their children and the nature of family life (Serebriakova 1979, 22).

The picture of the typical adult offender is little different from that just constructed of the juvenile counterpart. While the offenders in a few categories of crime, such as theft of socialist property, have comparatively better financial and social positions than the average Soviet citizen (Criminal Personality 1971, 89), most offenders have had a disadvantaged home life. Criminals in the USSR, as in many other societies, are frequently the product of broken homes, alcoholic parents, and family incomes below the Soviet-determined poverty level. For example, research among sex offenders in Azerbaidzhan found that 41 percent of them came from homes with only one or no parent (Daniel'bek 1968, 90).

The average educational level of offenders lags behind that of the general population. Murderers, hooligans, and recidivists have an even lower level of educational attainment than does the average Soviet offender. In a study of hooligans, two-thirds were found to have only elementary or incomplete secondary education (Kalmykov 1979, 87). In the 1960s, 67.8 percent of murderers had only a seventh-grade education, whereas the comparable figure for the general population was 59.5 percent in 1959 (Criminal Personality 1971, 65, 115).

The problem of parasitism, an identifiable phenomenon in all Soviet republics (Gusev and Bakhitov 1971), is even more pronounced among the adult criminal population. In some urban areas parasites contribute almost 30 percent of all crime (Gabiani and Gachechiladze 1982, 133). Nationwide, 20 to 30 percent of all property convictions involve unemployed individuals (Criminal Personality 1971, 100), and parasites also contribute significantly to those convicted of hooliganism (Kalmykov 1979, 87). Interestingly, a larger proportion of female than male offenders are parasites (Kil'g 1982, 99), suggesting that many women are prosecuted as parasites for prostitution-related crimes because prostitution per se is not an officially recognized offense in the USSR. (See the section on Victimless Crimes, however, regarding possible new legal interpretations.)

Soviet authorities have traditionally dealt severely with offenders and even more harshly with recidivists. Although sentences have been reduced significantly since the Stalinist period, individuals stand a better than even chance of being sentenced to some form of incarceration when they stand trial (van den Berg 1985, 95–97). The average length of sentence is about three (van den Berg 1985, 98) or four and a half years (Dement'ev 1982, 9). Part of the justification for the harsh treatment of offenders is that research reveals that the fear of existing sanctions deters many would-be criminals (Sarkisova 1975, 38).

Despite the severity of the punishments imposed, Soviet authorities still face a significant problem with recidivism. Recidivism rates are given as between 25 to 30 percent of all offenders (Iakovlev 1985, 151). Although this is considerably below the estimated rates of 30 to 70 percent in the United States, Soviet figures are depressed by certain methods of calculating recidivism (van den Berg 1985, 50).[6] Furthermore, for certain categories of criminality, such as hooliganism (Kalmykov 1979, 87–88) and property crime, rates are even higher.

Conclusion

Crime and delinquency have become problems of increasing concern to Soviet authorities. The Soviet Union, despite its ideological commitment to the elimination of crime, is facing a growing problem of crime from juvenile offenders, parasites, and recidivists located in remote urbanizing regions of the country.

Soviet authorities have developed increasingly sophisticated theories to explain the persistence of illegal behavior long after its scheduled disappearance. In many ways they have abandoned their effort to explain the endurance of criminality in terms of vestiges of the past. Although they dismiss the validity of Western theory, their current explanations of the continued existence of crime have a familiar ring. The source of contemporary criminality is seen in urbanization, industrialization, and problems of schools and family.

Regardless of the means by which Soviet criminologists attempt to explain the endurance of crime within their society, they must contend with a situation that is partly of their own creation. Not only have Soviet laws created new categories of criminals, such as speculators and parasites, but they have also produced a distinctive geography of criminality. The unique distribution of Soviet criminality that has resulted in the relocation of crime from major urban centers and rural areas to the developing cities of the Far East and Far North is a direct consequence of Soviet police and demographic policies. The dispersion of criminality, while eliminating some of the tensions of urban life in major cities, has made regions in desperate need of more workers increasingly undesirable places to live. Furthermore, the increased production of alcohol under Soviet rule has had a negative impact on all elements of life, particularly that of the Slavic and Baltic populations. Consequently, crime has grown more in those areas in which the impact of alcoholism is greatest.

The Soviet system is ideologically committed to fostering the development of the "new Soviet person," and the criminal justice system, through its capacity to educate and coerce, is viewed as a fundamental institution for achieving this end. But not all citizens conform to this model. Whereas the methods of control have reduced crime in some regions, they have failed to realize the Marxist prediction that "crime will wither away under socialism." Indeed, the evidence presented here supports Durkheim's view of the normalcy of crime and its inevitability within society.

Notes

[1] Many party members who have committed crimes are subjected to party sanctions rather than the punishments meted out by the criminal courts. Evidence for this is presented in the column "V komitete partiinogo kontroliia pri Tsk KPSS" (in the party control committee) of the party journal *Partiinaia Zhizn'*.

[2] The Soviet intentional homicide rate is 4 per 100,000 (van den Berg 1985, 70) and represents half of the total homicide rate.

[3] The American figure is 9.1 per 100,000 (U.S. Department of Justice 1977, 397), while that of Western developed nations is 2.7 (United Nations 1977) for the years 1970–75.

[4] The Uzbek data were collected from Tashkent and the Tashkent oblast where there is a heavy concentration of Slavs. The problems observed might then not represent much linkage between drinking and crime among Uzbeks.

[5] The endurance of traditional patterns of justice in rural areas and the lack of support for the established legal system indicate a lack of faith in the criminal justice system.

[6] The low recidivism rate may be explained by the division of criminal law into criminal law and administrative criminal law. Recidivism rates are only calculated for criminal law, whereas many violations fall into the second category (van den Berg 1985, 50).

References

Akhmedov, B. A., and B. A. Blinder. 1964. "Prichiny i usloviia, sposobstvuiushchie soversehniiu iznasilovanii i puti predotvrashcheniia etikh prestuplenii." *Nauchnye trudy, Tashkenstskii gosudarstvennyi universitet* 267:66–73.

Albats, Ye. 1986. "Profile of an Ailment." *Current Digest of the Soviet Press* 38(32):1–3.

Alekseeva, Liudmila. 1984. *Istoriia inakomysliia v SSSR*. Benson, Vt.: Khronika Press.

Alimov, S. B. 1983. "Aktual'nye voprosy preduprezhdeniia nasil'stvennykh prestuplenii." *Voprosy bor'by s prestupnost'iu* 38:29–33.

Antonian, Iu. M. 1978. "Osobennosti prestupnosti v sel'skoi mestnosti i ee preduprezhdenie." *Sovetskoe gosudarstvo i pravo* 8:78–85.

Babaev, M. K. 1968. "Kriminologicheskie issledovaniia problem migratsiia naseleniia." *Sovetskoe gosudarstvo i pravo* 3:86–89.

———. 1974. "Demograficheskie protsessy i problemy territorial'nykh razlichii prestupnosti." *Voprosy bor'by s prestupnost'iu* 21:9.

Bukovksy, Vladimir. 1978. *To Build a Castle*. London: Andre Deutsch.

Chalidze, Valery. 1977. *Criminal Russia*. New York: Random House.

Clinard, Marshall, and Peter Yeager. 1980. *Corporate Crime*. New York: Free Press.

Cloward, R. A., and L. E. Ohlin. 1960. *Delinquency and Opportunity*. Glencoe, Ill.: Free Press.

Cohen, Albert. 1955. *Delinquent Boys: The Culture of the Gang*. New York: Free Press.

Cohen, Lawrence E., and Marcus Felson. 1979. "Social Change and Crime Trends." *American Sociological Review* 44:588–608.

Cohen, Stephen. 1985. "Soviet Domestic Affairs." School of Advanced International Studies, Johns Hopkins University, January 28.

Connor, Walter D. 1972. *Deviance in Soviet Society: Crime, Delinquency and Alcoholism.* New York: Columbia University Press.

Criminal Personality. 1971. *Lichnost' prestupnika.* Moscow.

Daniel'bek, B. V. 1968. "Pravil'noe polovoe vospitanie – vazhnoe sredstvo predotvrashcheniia seksual'nykh prestuplenii." *Uchenye zapiski Azerbaidzhanskogo gosudarstevennogo universiteta* 1:88–93.

Dement'ev, S. I. 1982. Sroki lisheniia svobody v zakonodatel'stve, sudebnoi i ispravitel'no-trudovoi praktike (aksiologicheskie aspekty i intensifikatsiia ispolneniia), avtoreferat. Sverdlovsk: Sverdlovskii Iuridicheskii Institut.

Demin, V., and V. Khalin. 1985. "Overreporting: The Lessons of a Court Case." FBIS Daily Report III, no. 005:R4–R7.

Derviz, O. V. 1971. "Rabota ili ucheba vne mesta postoiannovo zhitel'stva—odin iz faktorov prestupnosti nesovershennoletnikh." *Prestupnost' i ee preduprezhdenie.* Leningrad.

Dremin, V. N. 1982. "Izuchenie kriminogennovo vliianiia ranee sudimykh lits na nesovershen-noletnikh." *Problemy sotsialisticheskoi zakonnosti* 9:142–145.

"Events and Opinions: Against Drugs" 1986. *Current Digest of the Soviet Press* 38(40):20–21.

Fedorchuk, V. V. 1983. "Militsiia Day Address." Soviet television 10 November, reported in SU/7491/B/1.

Frank, L. V. 1966. "Ob izuchenii lichnosti i povedeniia poterpevshego (Nuzhna li sovetskaia viktimologiia?)." In *Voprosy ugolovnogo prava, ugolovnogo protsessa i kriminologii,* edited by R. N. Khamrakulov and L. V. Frank, pp. 131–45. Dushanbe: Tadzhikskii gosudarstvennyi universitet.

———. 1971. "O viktimologicheskikh issledovaniiakh." *Voprosy ugolovnogo prava prokurors-kogo nadzora kriminalistiki i kriminologii* 3–4:151–61.

Frank, L. V., and V. P. Knoovalov. 1975. "Viktimologicheskie aspekty khuliganstva." In *Aktual'nye voprosy teorii i istorii prava i primeneniia sovetskogo zakonodatel'stva,* edited by V. G. Melkumov et al., pp. 258–66. Dushanbe: Tadzhikskii gosudarstvennyi universitet.

Frank, L. V., and S. Soboleva. 1975. "Nekotorye napravleniia viktimologicheskikh issledovanii semeino-bytovykh otnoshenii pri izuchenii prestupnosti." In *Aktual'nye voprosy teorii i istorii prava i primeneniia sovetskogo zakonodatel'stva,* edited by V. G. Melkumov et al., pp. 266–94. Dushanbe: Tadzhikskii gosudarstvennyi universitet.

Fuller, Elizabeth. 1980. "Georgian Offical Sentenced to Death for Bribery." Radio Liberty Research 290/80.

Fursev, V. 1968. "Nekotorye voprosy sostoianiia i struktury prestupnosti nesovershennoletnykh v Kazakhskoi SSR." In *Voprosy bor'by s prestupnost'iu nesovershennoletnykh,* edited by U. Dzhekebaev, pp. 3–28. Alma Ata: Nauka.

Gabiani, A. A., and M. Didebulidze. 1981. "O nekotorykh printsipakh sravnitel'nogo analiza prestupnosti v gorodakh i sel'skoi mestnosti." In *Aktual'nye voprosy preduprezhdeniia pravonarushenii,* edited by A. Alapishvili, pp. 106–18. Tbilisi: Izd. Tbiliiskogo universiteta.

Gabiani, A. A., and R. G. Gachechiladze. 1982. *Nekotorye voprosy geografii prestupnosti.* Tbilisi: Izd. Tbiliiskogo universiteta.

Gabiani, A. A., M. Shoniia, O. Mylnikova, and M. Didebulidze. 1981. "O resultatakh konkretno-sotsiologicheskogo issledovaniia uslovii formirovaniia lichnosti podrostkov-pravonarushitelei." In *Aktual'nye voprosy preduprezhdeniia pravonarushenii,* edited by A. Alapishvili, pp. 119–36. Tbilisi: Izd. Tbiliiskogo universiteta.

Gelishchanov, Anastasia. 1979. "Juvenile Crime in the Georgian SSR." Radio Liberty Research 25/79.

Gerasyuk, I. 1985. "Assignment Based on a Letter: A Bottle for a Favor." *Current Digest of the Soviet Press* 37(3):10.

Gernet, M. N. 1924. *Prestupnyi mir Moskvy.* Moscow.

Gertsenzon, A. A. 1928. *Bor'ba s prestupnost'iu v RSFSR.* Moscow.

———. 1960. "The Community's Role in the Prevention and Study of Crime." *Soviet Review* 2, no. 1:14–17.

Greenberg, David F. 1977. "Delinquency and the Age Structure of Society." *Contemporary Crises* 1 (April):189–223.

"Growing Concern over the Drug Scene." 1986. *Current Digest of the Soviet Press*, 38(34):1–4.

Gusev, S. I. 1985. "Raise the Level of the Courts' Judicial Activity." *Current Digest of the Soviet Press* 37(16):13–14.

Gusev, L. N., and A. A. Bakhitov. 1971. "Ob itogakh sotsiologicheskogo obsledovaniia retsidivistov i drugikh lits, ukloniaiushchikhsiia ot obshchestvennogo truda." *Informatsionnye soobshcheniia VNIIOP pri MOOP* 35:21–22.

Iakovlev, A. M. 1971. *Prestupnost' i sotsial'naia psikhologiia.* Moscow: Iuridicheskaia Literatura.

———. 1985. *Teoriia kriminologii i sotsial'naia praktika.* Moscow: Nauka.

Iakovlev, A., and I. Gamaiunov. 1986. "V pol'zu spravedlivosti." *Literaturnaia gazeta*, September 24, p. 13.

Juviler, Peter H. 1976. *Revolutionary Law and Order.* New York: Free Press.

Kafarov, T. M., and Ch. T. Musaev. 1983. *Bor'ba s posiagatel'stvom na obshchestvennyi poriadok.* Baku: Elm.

Kairzhanov, E. I. 1963. "Nekotorye voprosy bor'by s prestpno-nebrezhnym ispolzovaniem i khraneniem sel'skokhoziaistvennoi tekhniki." *Voprosy ugolovnogo prava i protsessa, Akademiia nauk Kazakhskoi SSSR* 7:80–94.

Kalmykov, V. T. 1979. *Khuliganstvo i mery bor'by s nim.* Minsk: Belarus'.

Kaminskaya, Dina. 1982. *Final Judgment.* New York: Simon & Schuster.

Karatygina, T. 1986. "Thoughts to the Point: Victims of Drug Addiction Brought to the Brink." *Current Digest of the Soviet Press* 38(32):3–4.

Kil'g, R. 1982. "Nekotorye dannye, kharakterizuiushchie prestupnost' zhenshchin v estonskoi SSR v 1976–1981 godakh." In *Zadachi iuridicheskkh nauk v svete reshenii XXVI c"ezda KPSS*, edited by V. Kel'der, pp. 99–100. Tartu: Tartuskii gosudarstvennyi universitet.

Konovalov, V. 1986. "Sushchestvuet li v SSSR prostitutsiia." Radio Liberty Research 158/86.

Kormshchikov, V. M. 1981. "Vliianie semeinovo neblagopoluchiia na protivopravnoe povedenie nesovershennoletnykh." *Voprosy bor'by s prestupnost'iu* 35:51–54.

Kudriavtsev, V. N. 1960. *Ob"ektivnaia storona prestupleniia.* Moscow: Iuridicheskaia literatura.

Kurs. 1985. *Kurs Sovetskoi kriminologii.* Moscow: Iuridicheskaia literatura.

Kuznetsova, N. F. 1969. *Prestuplenie i prestupnost'.* Moscow: Iuridicheskaia literatura.

Kvitsinia, A. K. 1980. *Vziatochnichestvo i bor'ba s nim.* Sukhumi: Alashara.

Kydyralieva, S. K. 1981. *Khuliganstvo ugolovno-pravovye i kriminologicheskie voprosy.* Frunze: Ilim.

Leps. A. 1980. "Izuchenie prestupnoi aktivnosti v razlichnykh regionakh respubliki." *Sovetskoe Pravo* 2:123–26.

Los, Maria. 1983. "Economic Crimes in Communist Countries." In *Comparative Criminology*, edited by I. L. Barak-Glantz and E. H. Johnson, pp. 39–57. Beverly Hills, Calif.: Sage.

Marchenko, Anatoly. 1969. *My Testimony.* Oxford, England: Pall Mall Press.

Matza, David. 1964. *Delinquency and Drift.* New York: John Wiley.

McNeill, Terry. 1980. "Battling the Problems of Today with the Weapons of Yesterday." Radio Liberty Research 288/80.

Mel'nikova, Iu. B., T. Iu. Oreshkina, and N. V. Beliaeva. 1984. "Voprosy ugolovnoi otvetstvennosti za vypusk nedobrokachestvennoi, nestandartnoi i nekompletnoi produktsii." *Voprosy bor'by s prestupnost'iu* 40:32–40.

Merton, R. K. 1938. "Social Structure and Anomie." *American Sociological Review* 3:672–82.

————. 1968. *Social Theory and Social Structure*, 2d. ed. New York: The Free Press.

Mostovoi, A. 1986. "Subject for Reflection: When the Poppies Bloom." *Current Digest of the Soviet Press* 38(22):1–3, 23.

Murray, Charles. 1984. *Losing Ground: American Social Policy, 1950–1980.* New York: Basic Books.

"Nekotorye itogi i perspektivy prikladnykh kriminologicheskikh issledovanii v Irkutske." 1980. *Problemy sovershenstvovaniia taktiki i metodiki rassledovaniia prestuplenii.* Irkutsk: Irkutsk gosudarstvennyi universitet.

"New Drive against Drinking Is Launched." 1985. *Current Digest of the Soviet Press* 37(20): 1–5.

Osipenko, P. G. 1985. "USSR Procurator Discusses Grain Embezzlement." *USSR National Affairs,* May 20: R17–18.

Osipov, P. P., ed. 1978. *Kompleksnoe izuchenie sistemy vozdeistviia na prestupnost'.* Leningrad: Leningradskogo Universiteta.

Ostroumov, S. S. 1966. "Study of Criminal Personality." *Soviet Review* 7:13–20.

————. 1970. *Sovetskaia sudebnaia statistika.* Moscow: Iuridicheskaia literatura.

Pankratov, V. V., M. I. Arseb'eva, and N. I. Kulicheva. 1984. "Preduprezhdenie kvartirnykh krazh, sovershaemykh nesovershenoletnimi." *Voprosy bor'by s prestupnost'iu* 40:19–25.

Patiashvili, D. I. 1986. "For a Model City – Exemplary Order in Everything." FBIS Daily Reports vol.3, no.010:R13–15.

Polozov, G. 1984. "The Problem Teenager." *Current Digest of the Soviet Press* 36(31):21–22.

Powell, David. 1985. "The Soviet Alcohol Problem and Gorbachev's 'Solution.'" *Washington Quarterly* 8(4):5–15.

Randalu, Kh. 1977. "EVM ne tol'ko sostavliaet otchety." *Sovetskoe pravo* 1:19–22.

Raska, E. 1978. "Profil' zhiznennykh orientatsii kak sub"ektivnyi faktor prestupnosti molodezhi." *Sovetskoe Pravo* 3:185–91.

Rasputin, Valentin. 1985. "Pozhar." *Nash sovremmenik* 7:3–38.

Reznik, G. M. 1985. "Protivorechiia sovremennoi urbanizatsii i prestupnost'." *Sovetskoe gosudarstvo i pravo* 9:50–57.

Sarkisova, E. A. 1975. *Ugolovno-pravovye sredstva preduprezhdeniia prestuplennii.* Minsk: Nauka i tekhnika.

Serebriakova, V. A. 1979. "Sotsiologicheskie aspekty izucheniia zhenskoi prestupnosti." *Voprosy bor'by s prestupnost'iu* 30:17–26.

Sergeev, I. 1987. "Kto daet im narkotik?" *Literaturnaia gazeta,* January 14, p. 12.

Shelley, Louise. 1980. "The Geography of Soviet Criminality." *American Sociological Review* 45:111–22.

————. 1981. *Crime and Modernization: The Impact of Urbanization and Industrialization on Crime.* Carbondale: Southern Illinois University Press.

————. 1982. "Female Criminality in the 1920's: A Consequence of Inadvertent and Deliberate Change." *Russian History* 9, part 3:265–84.

Shtromas, A. 1977. "Crime, Law and Penal Practice in the USSR." *Review of Socialist Law* 3(3):297–324.

Simon, Rita J. 1976. "American Women and Crime." *Annals of the American Academy of Political and Social Science* 423:31–46.

Smirnov, V. 1985. "Juvenile Crime – Some Statistics and Explanations." *Current Digest of the Soviet Press* 37(6):14.

Smith, Gordon B. 1979. "Procuratorial Campaigns against Crime." In *Soviet Law After Stalin*, Part III, edited by F. J. M. Feldbrugge, G. Ginsburgs, and P. B. Maggs, pp. 143–67. Aphen aan den Rijn: Sijthoff and Noordhoff.

Soldatov, L. L. 1981. "Vliianie rannei kriminalizatsii na prestupnoe povedenie lits molodovo vozrasta." *Opyt kriminologicheskogo izucheniia lichnosti prestupnika.* Moscow: Vsesoiuznyi institut po izucheniiu prichin i razrabotke mer preduprezhdeniia prestupnosti 82–87.

Sootak, Ia. 1977. "Tak nazyvaemoe kvartirnoe khuliganstvo." *Sovetskoe pravo* 1:22–29.

Spitzer, Steven. 1975. "Toward a Marxian Theory of Deviance." *Social Problems* 22:638–51.

Sutherland, Edwin H. 1947. *Principles of Criminology*, 4th. ed. Philadelphia: Lippincott.

Sutherland, Edwin H., and Donald R. Cressey. 1974. *Principles of Criminology*, 9th ed. Philadelphia: Lippincott.

Tension, Andreas. 1980. "Piracy on the Soviet Railroads." Radio Liberty Research 276/80.

Thomas, Charles W., and John R. Hepburn. 1983. *Crime, Criminal Law and Criminology*. Dubuque: Wm. C. Brown Co.

Tobias, J. J. 1967. *Crime and Industrial Society in the 19th Century*. New York: Schocken Books.

United Nations. 1977. *Crime Prevention and Control*. Report of the Secretary General. New York: United Nations.

United States Department of Justice. 1977. *Sourcebook of Criminal Justice Statistics*. Washington, D.C.: U.S. Government Printing Office.

———. 1978. *Myths and Realities About Crime*. Washington, D.C.: U.S. Government Printing Office.

Utkin, M. S. 1980. "Kriminalisticheskaia kharakteristika khishenii." In *Aktual'nye problemy kriminalizatsii i dekriminalizatsii obshchestvenno opasnykh deianii*, edited by L. A. Iantsen, pp. 129–39. Omsk: Omskaia vysshiia shkola militsii.

van den Berg, Ger. 1985. *The Soviet System of Justice: Figures and Policy*. Dordrecht: Martinus Nijhoff.

Volkov, B. S., and M. D. Lysov. 1983. *Pravonarusheniia nesovershennoletnykh i ikh preduprezhdenie*. Kazan': Izd. Kazanskogo Universiteta.

Wilson, James Q., and Richard J. Herrnstein. 1985. *Crime and Human Nature*. New York: Simon & Schuster.

Wolfgang, Marvin, R. Figlio, and T. Sellin. 1972. *Delinquency in a Birth Cohort*. Chicago: University of Chicago Press.

Wolfgang, Marvin, and Franco Ferracuti. 1967. *The Subculture of Violence*. London: Tavistock.

Yakubovich, P. 1986. "Subject for Reflection: 'Lady with a Tip.'" *Current Digest of the Soviet Press* 38(41):21–22.

Zehr, Howard. 1976. *Crime and Development of Modern Society: Patterns of Criminality in 19th Century Germany and France*. Totowa, N.J.: Rowman and Littlefield.

10
Full Employment and Labor Utilization in the USSR

David Lane

On 13 March 1930, Mikhail Shkunov, a Moscow plumber, finally got a job. When he left the labor exchange the doors closed, and Soviet commentators pronounced that this event symbolized the ending of mass unemployment in the USSR. Since that time the provision of regular paid labor and a permanent occupation for all who are able to work has been one yardstick that has been used to legitimate Soviet society as a socialist state. This chapter seeks to discover the extent to which this claim is correct and whether there are any systemic features of Soviet society, in contrast to a capitalist society, that lead to the provision of full employment.

This work is both empirical and theoretical. In the first part, it argues that the Soviet labor market is characterized by the employment of a large proportion of the population, leaving no "reserve army" of unemployed. However, when one turns from the quantity of people at work to their quality in work, study reveals underutilization of labor, or hoarding. This is accompanied by a labor shortage: the labor market is a sellers market. The second part considers three explanations of a full employment economy and develops a systemic model.

In the two decades following the October Revolution, economic development was the major economic objective of the Soviet government to which all other goals were subsidiary. Providing employment, or reducing

Note: This chapter draws on my book, *Soviet Labour and the Ethic of Communism: Full Employment and the Labour Process in the USSR* (Brighton, U.K.: Harvester, 1987).

levels of unemployment, was not a policy priority (Adam 1982, 126; Davies 1985). During the period of War Communism (1918–21) and the New Economic Policy (1921–28), mass unemployment continued at levels comparable to those of Western European countries. The chief cause of such unemployment was the movement of peasants to the town to seek work (Suvorov 1968, 146–7). The draft of the First Year Plan, compiled in 1927, estimated that the unemployment level of 1.9 million in that year would rise to 2.3 million in 1931–32 (Davies 1985). During the First Five Year Plan (1928–32), however, the massive expansion program led to an increase in employment opportunities not only in industry and building, but also in the sphere of government services (hospitals, schools). Despite the growth of the working-age population and the influx of rural emigrants to the towns (1.06 million in 1928 and 2.63 million in 1930), the number of jobs increased at an even faster rate and absorbed the available urban labor power (including a rising proportion of women). In the early 1930s, a seven-hour day was introduced, double and triple shift working was practiced, and no financial restraints on managers were introduced to limit labor recruitment. The expansion in social services and administration provided opportunities for the graduates of educational institutions and entailed a massive increase in the number of nonmanual posts.

From the early 1930s labor shortage became characteristic of the Soviet economy. This does not imply that various types of structural and frictional unemployment did not exist: structural imbalances between regions continued, and frictional imbalances between jobs available and those sought also persisted. But the government felt justified in closing employment exchanges and in October 1930 ceased to pay unemployment benefits. The matching of vacancies with job seekers took place through an imperfect labor market: workers were able to leave their jobs and present themselves for recruitment "at the factory gates." The ending of unemployment pay helped cajole the unemployed to work. However, a large share of the work force was occupied as nonwage labor in agriculture either on individual plots or on collective farms throughout the 1930s. If we calculate the proportion of the able-bodied population working in manual or nonmanual jobs in the national economy, excluding private farmers and collective farm peasants, even in 1939 the figure reached only 33 percent.

Soviet spokespersons regard the ending of unemployment as being coterminous with the abolition of the reserve army of unemployed labor – which in Marxist theory is characteristic of capitalism – and of the ending of the labor market in the USSR. Compared to capitalist market economies, it is the case that wages were not effective in regulating the supply of labor, and the absence of a pool of unemployed made dismissal less effective as a means of labor discipline. But labor supply was not planned. At most, about a quarter of entrants to the labor force came from the official department concerned with labor supply (called *orgnabor*). Most of these entrants were peasants drafted to work in the towns, and they did not necessarily stay in their first jobs. The vast majority of workers were recruited through informal channels and in practice moved from one job to another. Enterprises attempted to maximize the size of their labor force by persuading valued workers to stay and to attract others from outside. In this more limited sense a labor market existed and continues to the present day. Furthermore, labor placement bureaus were started in 1967. However, they do not direct labor and in the early 1980s accounted for only about 10 percent of all hirings (Kotlyar 1984).

The claims that mass unemployment had been ended in the Soviet Union helped legitimate the Soviet government. The absence of unemployment benefits meant that any increase in involuntary unemployment would lead to poverty and possible unrest by the discontented unemployed. The proclaimed ideology of full employment became a constraint on the leadership: people came to expect full employment, and it became necessary for the government to provide it. In its absence the government would lose legitimacy.

The Contemporary Employed Labor Force

All studies of the Soviet labor force concur that a very high proportion of the population is economically active. In 1979 the economically active participation rate for men sixteen to fifty-nine years old (the male economically active cohort) was 88.5 percent; for women sixteen to fifty-four years old (the comparable female cohort) it was 88.2 percent. The total figure for men is not dissimilar from that of advanced European countries, but that for women is much higher. Table 10.1 provides comparative figures for France and West Germany. We must bear in mind that the Soviet Union has a higher participation rate in education during the working ages and also that a large proportion (usually more than half) of employed women in Western Europe are working part time. However, even if the cohort most likely to be involved in education, that is, those under thirty, is excluded from the figures, Soviet women still evidence an extraordinarily high participation rate as compared to French and German women.

One other major difference from advanced capitalist countries is that full employment participation ceases through retirement at a relatively early age. While employees in capitalist countries usually work well beyond age sixty, in the USSR the retirement age is set at fifty-five for women and sixty for men, and in some industries (e.g., coal mining) retirement is five years earlier. On the other hand, as with retirees elsewhere, some continue to work in some form of paid labor. In 1982, for instance, 32 percent of old-age pensioners continued in paid labor (Kostin 1983).

Such high labor participation rates do not preclude involuntary unemployment, particularly structural and frictional. The absence of mass unemployment in the USSR since 1931 has led to the discontinuation of the collection of comprehensive unemployment statistics (Davies 1985; Wheatcroft 1985). Estimates, however, can be made on the basis of labor turnover (*tekuchest'*) and of reports of a localized character. Though the proportion of the work force changing jobs and, thus, subject to frictional unemployment shows considerable regional and sector variation (in 1975 from 18.2 percent of the work force in machine tools to 26.6 percent in the food industry), the average turnover for the USSR is annually about 19 percent according to numerous local studies. Turnover is greater for women than men, for younger workers than older ones, for poorly educated than well educated, for manuals than nonmanuals. In addition, the length of the period of frictional unemployment varies tremendously between geographical areas. Among

Table 10.1
Proportions of the Male and Female Population That Are "Economically Active" in Three Countries.

		USSR[b]	France[c]	W. Germany[c]
Proportions "Economically Active"	Male	88.5%	83.4%	86.9%
	Female	88.2%	50.3%	53.6%
30–44 yrs. (30–39/40–49)	Male	(97.6% /95.9%)	96.9%	97.7%
	Female	(92.7% /90.6%)	60.9%	56.7%

[a] The total "economically active" age cohort includes males between 16 and 59 and females between 16 and 54, including collective farmers. The proportions reported are figured by dividing the number of people in jobs in the given cohort by the total in that cohort. For convenience the proportions are converted to percentages in the table.

[b] Disaggregated data on the Soviet labor participation rate are not regularly included in Soviet statistics. Figures given here are estimates based on employment data and extrapolations of the population by age groups. Soviet figures for the total "economically active" cohort are for 1979. Other Soviet figures are for 1980. *Source:* David Lane, *Soviet Labour and the Ethic of Communism* (Brighton, U.K.: Harvester, 1987), ch. 3.

[c] Figures for the total "economically active" cohort for France and W. Germany are from 1975–78. *Source:* M. Marrese, *Labour Shortage in Hungary* (New York: St. Martin's Press, 1982), p. 103. For the 30–44 cohort, the figures date from 1981. *Source:* ILO, *1982 Yearbook of Labour Statistics* (Geneva: ILO, 1982), p. 29.

studies reviewed, time taken to change jobs ranged from seventy-three days in Armenia to twenty-five days in Moscow. In general, turnover time has declined in recent years, and in the early 1980s it averaged twenty-five to thirty days. Considering all of these factors, a rate of frictional unemployment of between 1.3 percent and 1.5 percent of the work force can confidently be estimated.

Rates of frictional unemployment are similar to those of advanced Western countries, and work time lost through labor turnover is less (based on data in Price 1977, ch. 3). There is a difference here compared to Western societies where turnover varies conversely with the level of unemployment; in the USSR labor shortage does not induce levels of turnover higher than those of full employment in capitalist societies. This is due to (1) the lack of wage incentives for mobility; (2) the poorly developed national labor market; (3) the tendency of enterprises to hoard labor; (4) the use of administrative sanctions against job changers; (5) the greater level of integration of the worker into the structure of the economic enterprise;[1] and (6) high female participation rates that make husband/wife the unit in the labor market and restrict geographical mobility.

Structural unemployment can be defined as a lack of demand for certain types of labor caused by a reduction in demand for particular products, by the introduction of capital intensive production methods, or by an increase in the supply of workers. Demographic changes in labor supply are the principal form of structural unemployment in the USSR, though some industrial concentration (e.g., mining) leads to uneven regional demand for certain types of labor (e.g., male rather than female). The major imbalance has to do with the mismatch between areas of population growth by the indigenous non-Russian ethnic groups in the Central Asian areas of the USSR and the places of labor demand, which are in Siberia and the European industrial areas.

Underemployment

Labor utilization in the USSR is not characterized by mass unemployment. The main disutility is in various forms of underemployment. By underemployment one has in mind conditions in which persons are paid for jobs but their labor is not efficiently used: they may be idle for all or part of the time, or their level of skill is higher than the job they do. The Soviet economy can be characterized as one of labor shortage and underutilization. Shortage may be defined as a state in which effective demand for labor (the number of jobs) outstrips supply. Labor shortage, however, is complicated by considerations of the efficient use of labor, by whether the supply of jobs is inflated, and by whether the requirements of production can be met by fewer workers. Such considerations involve technical, managerial, educational, psychological, and cultural criteria.

Vacancies in the USSR regularly exceed 2 million, including an annual addition of 750,000 to 800,000 new jobs (Myasnikov and Anan'ev 1979). With an employed work force of 112 million in 1980, this figure represents some 2 percent of the work force. This is not particularly high, as one would expect vacancies to approximate this figure with normal turnover and the creation of new jobs. No national figures are available on the duration and frequency of such vacancies. The increase in the numbers of jobs regularly exceeds the numbers planned. In 1975, 101.4 million jobs were planned, and 104.1 million workers were engaged (Myasnikov and Anan'ev 1979); in 1981, regular inflation of the number of jobs by an annual number of 2 million was reported (Manevich 1981, 55).

From the point of view of the operation of the economic system there are two major reasons why an excessive number of jobs is created. First, the level of investment is high, and new investment creates its own demand for labor. Though the total amount of investment is controlled by the State Planning Committee (Gosplan), it (and lower agencies) regularly underestimates the labor implications of new investment. Second, production enterprises have little incentive to economize on labor. The essence of Soviet planning is the fulfillment (and overfulfillment) of production targets in quantitative terms. The wage fund – the money allocated to an enterprise to pay employees – is given by higher authority, and the larger it is, the easier it becomes for the enterprise to meet its production targets. Enterprises have no financial incentives to "shed labor," and they are penalized, rather than rewarded, if the wage fund is not used up.[2] At all levels of the enterprise, from factory manager to foreman, there is no incentive to reduce the level of the labor force. Sanctions could be exercised by the Ministries for exceeding the limit on workers' places, where these are defined. However, in 1981, in 2,000 cases known to the authorities in the Russian Republic (RSFSR), sanctions were applied in only 564 instances (Kotlyar 1983, 155).

Labor is inefficiently employed. Not only is the quantity of labor excessive, but also the organization of the work force depends on an excessive supply of workers. Analyses conducted in the USSR show that Soviet plants use from 30 percent to 50 percent more workers in comparable plants than are used abroad; and in imported plants as many as one and one-half times as many operatives are employed, three and one-half times as many engineering, technical, and administrative staff, and eight times as many auxiliary workers (See Manevich 1978, 78–79). Surveys have indicated that from 15 percent to 20 percent of the work force is often underutilized because of poor organization.[3] Labor reserves are useful for enterprises to make up for shortages and bottlenecks and to substitute for capital. Labor productivity is not only lower than in Western capitalist countries, but the growth in labor productivity also fell from 139 percent in the period 1966–70 to 125 percent in 1971–75, and to 117 percent in 1976–80 (Gavrilov 1982, 25). One must acknowledge that a cost of full employment is a lower level of productivity and mobility than would be the case in a competitive market system with a reserve army of labor. The regime of "soft" labor discipline and the strong bargaining position of labor are effects of a full employment economy.

On the basis of the imperfect empirical data discussed, one can confidently conclude that, in distinction from capitalist societies, a very high rate of labor utilization is a feature of socialist states. And the Soviet labor market is characterized by (1) the employment of a large proportion of the population leaving no reserve army of unemployed or self-employed; (2) underutilization of labor at the place of work – the hoarding or maintenance of labor reserves; and (3) a market shortages of labor (the labor market is a seller's market).

In explaining the labor market in the USSR, one needs to grapple with two distinct dimensions of the labor market: full employment at a macro level and underemployment at a micro level.

Explaining a Fully Employed but Under Employed Work Force

One can distinguish three explanations of the high, though inefficient, labor utilization rate in socialist societies. The first explanation regards full employment as a consequence of government policy. The second interprets the labor market in terms of overfull employment and emphasizes the inefficient underutilization of labor. The third considers the labor market in terms of systemic contradictions. After outlining the first two approaches, this chapter will then discuss the third paradigm.

The structure of the Soviet labor market and its ensuing problems are explained by many writers in terms of government policy. A socialist economy, it is argued, rests on public ownership and planning and ensures the maximum utilization of labor power. Workers are not left unemployed but are utilized gainfully at work. Government policy under planning has a goal of providing work. The political framework, in which the Communist party is legitimated as the expression of the interests of the working class, ensures that full employment is a priority. From this point of view full employment is a consequence of socialist planning.

Shortage of labor and the underutilization of labor are considered by this school of thinkers to be imperfections of planning and are due to "lack of fit" between labor supply and labor demand. Demographic considerations (fluctuating levels of birth rate, mismatch between geographical areas of industrial development and labor supply) lead to shortages of labor. The educational system lags behind changes in technology, and various skills are lacking among the work force: labor discipline and socialization are inadequate. Organizational methods are poor, and enterprises are given too slack a wage fund or fail to improve productivity. Improvements in planning the size, training, and discipline of the labor force are seen as antidotes to the inefficient and wasteful use of labor. This line of reasoning is taken by most economic reformers in the USSR who believe that the existing structures need perfecting rather than changing in any significant way. Some Western writers also explain labor shortage as due to deficiencies in the planning of labor, but they see such deficiencies as an inherent part of the planning system (Oxenstierna 1985, 35–39).

The second approach, adopted by many Western commentators, is to fault the pricing system. Labor shortage and underutilization are caused by wages that are too low and insufficiently differentiated. Overemployment is a cause for sorrow not rejoicing. If the price of labor reflected market forces of supply and demand, there would be no chronic shortage at a macro level (though frictional unemployment would persist): a higher cost to the enterprise would stimulate more efficient use and reduce overstaffing, and higher wage incentives would increase labor productivity. The development of a proper labor market would lead to the shedding of surplus labor and the creation of a pool of unemployed; therefore, the seller's market in labor would become a buyer's one. Implementing these policies would involve major changes in the present economic system. The forces of the market would replace many activities now subject to administrative control. The present high rate of labor utilization would fall; fewer people would be employed, but they would be more effectively used and better paid.

The third explanation of the present labor situation looks to systemic contradictions. Writers adopting this stance reject the assertion that the high levels of labor utilization are an intended result of planning. Planners, they argue, have little control over recruitment and labor supply. They have been unable to eradicate labor shortages and underutilization (unemployment on the job), and their attempts at increasing labor productivity have not been successful. The working of the economic mechanism in socialist states leads to shortages not only of labor, but also of other goods; a feature of the system is its incapacity to supply commodities in relation to effective demand. At the same time, however, resources are not efficiently used – labor and capital are underutilized. The operation of the economy is seen as the unintended consequences of individuals' and institutions' actions. Such writers would seek independent laws of a *socialist* economy in the same way as Western economists and sociologists assume that capitalist economies have their own internal logic leading to depression and underutilization of resources.

It is important to stress that the socialist economy operates in quite a different political, administrative, and ideological environment, and consequently the processes of capitalist economies cannot be applied. The major differences are as follows: (1) public ownership and planning give the socialist government a greater role over the economy and a responsibility to provide work for the citizen; (2) the ideological constraints make chronic unemployment an unacceptable economic and political cost; and (3) demand and supply are not responsive to price as in capitalist economies. Hence, "freeing" the price system (making it more like a Western market one) will not resolve the pathologies of the labor market noted above.

In such an economy a labor shortage concurrent with underemployment at the work place is a systemic contradiction of the system: it is, to quote Kornai, a "consequence of the economic mechanism and of the institutional framework" (Kornai 1982, 103). This school of economists does not make any normative pronouncements about reform of the system; rather, it is concerned in a behavioral sense to expose the operation of the economy (Kornai 1980, 15).

Janos Kornai is the best-known exponent of this approach, contrasting a "resource-constrained" market for labor in socialist states with a "demand-constrained" one under capitalism. The demand for labor is determined by the supply, and the plan for labor is based on the forecast of employment constraints (Kornai 1980, 254). The plan uses up all available labor in the forecast, and this creates a shortage of labor. The system has an "investment hunger" that uses resources and labor reserves (1980, 260). Employers, to counter this shortage, inflate the demands for labor expressed in their labor estimates. This in turn leads to "unemployment on the job": "the more frequent and intensive the labor shortage, the greater will be the internal slack, namely the unemployment on the job" (1980, 255).

Effects of the labor shortage are the loosening of labor discipline, the deterioration of work quality, and the lessening of workers' diligence. The security of employment, determined by the market, gives rise to irresponsibility in anyone susceptible to it. Absenteeism exacerbates the shortage. Output becomes erratic, and supply of commodoties and services falls short of demand. Shortage characterizes the wholesale market as well. Shortage of inputs – supplies, materials, and services – in turn leads to slackness on the job (Kornai 1980, 255) but then creates "storming" (i.e., rushing to complete) when they become available. Securing ample labor reserves, therefore, is a logical response by employers to meet their output targets.

Kornai rejects the view that a pattern of full employment can be explained solely in terms of government policy in socialist states. "It is true that much depends on employment policy ... yet an explanation of the process ... depends on considerations deeper than mere government policy. It follows necessarily from the *system*; for if the system is resource-constrained, an almost unlimited hunger and expansion drive *must* prevail and then the potential reserve labor *must* be absorbed sooner or later" (Kornai 1980, 261).

It is when Kornai analyzes the political and social framework that his explanation is inadequate. He points out that the tolerance level of employment is a "social phenomenon" (1980, 248). Once "given," only marginal changes are possible. Unemployment, he argues, cannot fall much below the minimum level caused by "friction." Employment, he notes, is not just work for a wage but is "a way of life" (1980, 237). Hence, in socialist states there is no fear of "genuine" unemployment, only fluctuations around the normal participation rate (1980, 250). He asserts that the state of the labor market has changed permanently under socialism – the behavior of sellers of labor is *"characterized by guaranteed employment"* (1980, 252, emphasis in original). There is a "control mechanism that drives (the) system ... back to a normal state following deviation from it" (1980, 265). Having dismissed the explanation of full employment as being due "solely to a description of government policy measures," he insists that it be traced to "intrinsic social forces" (1980, 265). It is precisely here that Kornai's argument breaks down. Although he refers in a general way to the institutional framework, he does not analyze the relationship between polity and economy (1980, 13). Kornai emphasizes that "definite social relations and institutional conditions generate definite forms of behavior, economic regularities and norms" (1980, 569). But the role of values, the nature of exchange between economy and polity, and the legitimation process involving loyalty and solidarity are not dealt with in his work. It is precisely these areas, however, that shape expectations and are powerful constraints on the operation of the economy. The following section examines this wider social and political framework.

A Sociological Model

Although Kornai argues that employment and labor shortage are systemic characteristics of state socialism, the account lacks any systemic coherence. It describes the economic mechanism but evades the societal and political dimensions. One reason for this perhaps is that Marxism is a systemic theory of society and, in state socialist societies, a legitimating ideology. If the traditional Marxist model is brought into question by having insufficient power to explain the operation of the economy, then its role as a legitimating theory is cast into doubt. In addition, economists by training have insufficient interest in, and knowledge of, other theories of *society*, rather than models of the economy. When economic models break down, which they must do when applied to activity beyond their frame of reference, analysis relies on making discrete observations of the noneconomic factors. The following outlines a sociological explanation of the socialist labor market. The objective is to highlight the exchanges between the economy and its social and political environment.

Earlier we noted a number of ways socialist and capitalist systems differ. In the contemporary socialist economy:

1. Production is not responsive to price, and price is insensitive to demand; this is the case in all commodity markets.
2. The place of work not only fulfills consumption needs through wages but also fulfills other forms of psychological satisfaction – social conviviality, companionship.
3. A high level of employment is usually "given" and labor is in a strong bargaining position.
4. Inefficiencies are characteristic of the economy and have become an accepted way of life.
5. The economy is publicly owned; it is organized and planned by administrative bodies.
6. There is little institutionalized entrepreneurship.
7. Flows of money (credit) and interest rates do not influence investment or production.
8. There is no payment for risk (profit) and there is no bankruptcy.

Such observations can be analyzed in the framework of a society conceived to be composed of four analytically distinct subsystems. These are: (1) the economy, (2) the polity, (3) the societal community, and (4) the cultural system. The economy needs little comment: it is concerned with production and distribution of commodities and services; labor is the major resource that turns natural objects into use values. The polity's functions are to make decisions for the mobilization of resources, for the defining and attainment of society's goals. The societal community has to do with maintaining social control and integration including norms, law, and coercion; the integration system has the role of coordinating the various parts of the system. The cultural system represents the goals that motivate people in society, and these goals are derived from the overriding values. Following Parsonian practice, the four subsystems can be illustrated by four boxes designated by the letters A (adaptation), G (goal attainment), I (integration), and L (latency). (Parsons 1967) (see Figure 10.1).

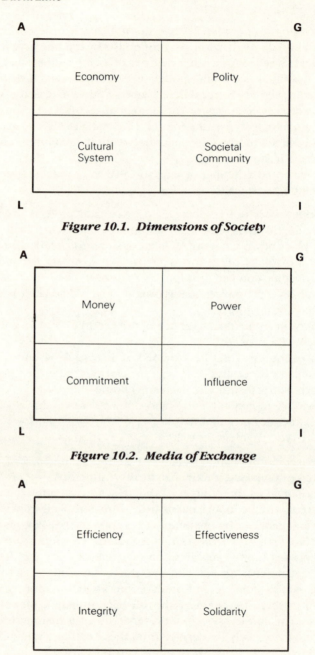

A   **G**

| Economy | Polity |
| Cultural System | Societal Community |

L   **I**

Figure 10.1. Dimensions of Society

A   **G**

| Money | Power |
| Commitment | Influence |

L   **I**

Figure 10.2. Media of Exchange

A   **G**

| Efficiency | Effectiveness |
| Integrity | Solidarity |

L   **I**

Figure 10.3.   Governing Principles

These analytical categories apply to all societies. Complex exchanges take place between these four subsystems. But various societies have different ways of making such exchanges. After considering the interchanges described by Parsons that characterize a market system (he had in mind the United States), I will suggest how this model can be applied to socialist societies. From economic analysis, the notion of moving equilibrium is applied to adjustments that continually happen. Parsons has described his scheme as one of "the analysis of dynamic equilibrating processes." (Note, however, that equilibrium under capitalism does not always occur – exceptions to equilibrium are hyperinflation and chronic shortages). Exchange takes place between these systems in a way analogous to an economic model consisting of inputs (factors of production) and outputs (products between each system). Links are established between the subsystems through media (see Figure 10.2). Money serves as a medium for the economy, power for the polity, influence for the integrative subsystem, and commitments for the cultural system. The principles governing the four systems are efficiency (for the economy), effectiveness (for the polity), solidarity (for the integrative system), and integrity (for the value system). (See Figure 10.3.) There are six systemic sets of exchanges between *A–G–I–L* that characterize all societies, as illustrated in Figure 10.4 (cf. Parsons and Smelser 1956, 68). The detailed categories cannot be described here (see Parsons 1967).

As far as the economy under capitalism is concerned, a few salient points can be highlighted: individual motivation for work is provided by wages; demand has priority over supply; priorities and budgeting are controlled through allocations of money in return for productivity. Such exchanges are performed through differentiated institutions; money is a crucial unit of account and medium of exchange.

These types of exchanges do not occur in socialist states. The values involving motivational commitments are different. Commodity demand is not a prime motivational force under planning. Wage income in return for labor capacity does not have the same salience; moral duty and psychological satisfaction are also considered motivating factors for work. In Parsons's scheme, the medium of money affects all the exchanges into and out from *A*. The budget constraints in socialist societies are extremely weak; money is a unit of account but not a medium of exchange as under capitalism. Companies are not bankrupted. Neither the price of money (interest) nor the amount of money (credit) regulates the level of investment. Accumulation of money does not lead to investment. Entrepreneurship is not rewarded by profit. The price system does not mediate supply and demand as under capitalism. Administrative control is ubiquitous.

In conceptualizing the role of the economy in contemporary socialist

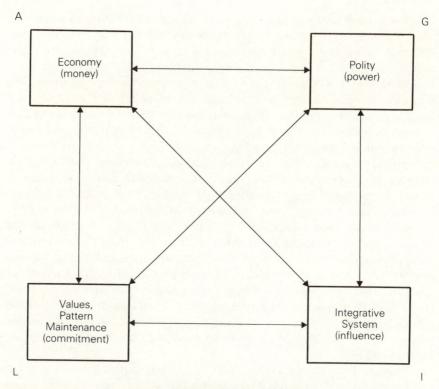

Figure 10.4. Systems of Society

society, however, Parsons's insights should be retained because they provide a conceptual framework. It must be conceded that all societies have four functional dimensions, and differentiated ones need to have forms of exchange to maintain equilibrium. Compared to market-type societies, planned ones of the Soviet type have a deceptively simple appearance. The main structural difference is the absence of differentiated institutions having related autonomy. The Communist party as an institution appears to be omnicompetent, and in practice the functions defined are not clearly differentiated. (See the chapter by Field in this volume.) The inputs, outputs, and media are dissimilar in the capitalist and socialist systems. The motivational commitment system is derived from the value system of Marxism-Leninism, though money and status for the individual also have a role. Integration through planning, law, and education seeks to secure the values of the dominant Communist party: harmony is sought through the notion of a classless society. (The complicating effects of traditional values, procedures, and norms are excluded here, though I have discussed them elsewhere (Lane 1979).) Efficiency and effectiveness, the motivating values of capitalism, have less salience than those of integrity (of ideology) and solidarity.

The socialist system has some notable differences compared to the capitalist. Parsons has made it clear that the United States has the major "collective goal" of the pursuit of economic productivity. The collective goals of the Marxist–Leninist party are much more comprehensive. Motivational commitment stemming from values include full employment and social welfare (the L–I exchange). Commitments as media out of L are retained in this model. The exchange with the economy ($I–A$) involves a commitment to maximum production of goods and services: goals are defined in terms of supply rather than commodity demand, as under capitalism. This has important implications in output terms rather than efficiency ones. The medium of coordination at I under capitalism is "influence"; in socialist societies planning exerts analogous power-like sanctions. Administratively ordered plans characterize the $I–A$ exchange rather than entrepreneurship and the influence of the interest rate, as in market societies.

Legitimation of authority ($L–G$) comes from public ownership and the expression of class interests, which in turn have been derived from the value system of Marxism–Leninism. The economy is not a market-linked network of competing firms, but a system of enterprises controlled by ministries, which in turn are subordinate to the polity and the societal community (I). Money is still a medium out from A, and wages are products that fulfill motivational commitments ($A–L$). However, money is not a means for accumulation.

Socialist ideology legitimates societal integration in terms of a classless society and the meeting of needs; market systems fulfill wants in terms of consumer demands, which in turn may violate norms of equality. Shortages can be a source of strain ($I–L$), but as Kornai conceded, shortages are an accepted part of life (as inflation is under capitalism) and do not have serious destabilizing effects. Consensus is maintained through a combination of social and welfare benefits coupled to the provision of employment in the context of a low productivity economy. The welfare state and full employment are linchpins in the loyalty–solidarity–commitment exchanges between I and L and the political support exchanges between G and I (the polity and the societal community).

Systemic Limitations on Reform

Full employment, labor shortages, and the limitations of economic reforms can be analyzed in terms of the systemic social system model outlined here. The $L–A$ exchange under socialism is a labor–output maximization system. The ideology of Marxism–Leninism is one of maximizing production; commitment is assured partly by monetary reward (wages) for effort but also by psychological and moral satisfaction.

The implication for policy and reform is that a reliance on market wage stimulation will not be effective unless there are reciprocal changes in the other societal sectors. Values, however, are notoriously difficult to alter. The role of the polity is to release resources to maximize output. This is ensured by the public ownership of the means of production and planning (the $G–L$ link). The nature of the political support system that links the G and I sectors is also different than that under capitalism. The polity is much more strongly anchored under the domination of the political party. Political support, to be sure, is necessary, but there are few effective checks on leadership for effective management. This can weaken solidarity and consensus. However, this is compensated by the stabilizing effects of full employment and social security. Under capitalism the allocation of resources and the need for efficiency lead to employment uncertainty; under socialism efficiency in the economy is sacrificed for solidarity.

And unlike capitalist market societies, where the amount of credit and the levels of interest depress economic activities, in socialist societies the "allocative standard system" linking the economy (A) and societal community (I) is weakly developed. Administrative control of claims to resources is weak in the face of the power to invest sanctioned by the polity. The loyalty–solidarity–commitment system ($I–L$) is predicated on the creation of a classless society. The standards of allocation then are in terms of maintaining loyalty. Full employment itself is a priority; under capitalism the striving for efficiency in the economy determines how closely full employment can be attained. It is in this sense that full employment is part of government policy. It would not be impossible to reduce the level of labor utilization through the creation of "redundant" workers in the USSR.

Kornai and other commentators who argue for a systemic analysis of socialist societies are correct in their general standpoint. This chapter outlines the fact that full employment is systemic because it is closely linked to (1) the loyalty–solidarity system, (2) motivational commitments, (3) a supply-resourced economy, and (4) an output maximization and politically determined resources allocation system. Shortages are likely to be a consequence of such a system because integration is not fulfilled through the satisfaction of demands.

Any major change in the system of motivational commitments and integration processes would lead to the breakdown of the complex set of institutional interests and exchanges. This change would have to include greater individual sovereignty, enhanced role to "influence," and the strengthening of standards of allocation involving the use of money as a medium (as a criterion of investment). A thorough use of the price system (affecting wages, capital, and commodities) would destroy the present complicated sets of exchanges established under state socialism. A rise in the levels of involuntary unemployment would undermine the authority legitimation system. It is likely that existing levels of solidarity and consensus would be significantly weakened, as would the integrity of the dominant value system. In other words, the adoption of a Western-type labor market would undermine public ownership and planning, the present forms of social integration, and the legitimacy of the leading role of the Communist party.

From the point of view of practical politics, economic reform is limited by the systemic properties of the socialist system, not by the preferences of individual political leaders. A movement away from a full employment, low wage policy at a macro level would have serious destabilizing consequences for the present political system. Economic reform cannot simply copy Western processes that are organically part of a different socioeconomic infrastructure. If the socialist system is to be maintained, reform has to be within the existing structures and procedures of planning.

Notes

[1] The large size of enterprises creates a primary labor market within them; housing and social benefits are administered through enterprises, and the Party and union provide a personnel function to keep workers in the plant.

[2] This is so even in such economic "experiments" as Shchekino. (Such experiments cannot be described in this summary but are included in Lane 1987.)

[3] There is evidence of people having an awareness of the overstaffing of work posts: of a thousand people who participated in a discussion forum, 80 percent denied the existence of a "real" labor shortage (*Literaturnaia gazeta* 1980).

References

Adam, Jan. 1982. "Similarities and Differences in the Treatment of Labour Shortages." In *Employment Policies in the Soviet Union and Eastern Europe*, edited by Jan Adam, pp. 123–144. New York: St. Martin's Press.

Davies, R. W. 1985. "The End of Mass Unemployment in the USSR." In *Labour and Employment in the USSR*, edited by David Lane, pp. 19–35. New York: New York University Press.

Gavrilov, R. 1982. 'Tempy faktory i novye pokazateli rosta proizvoditel'nost' truda.''*Voprosy ekonomiki* (3)23–32.

ILO. 1982. *1982 Yearbook of Labour Statistics*. Geneva: ILO.

Kornai, J. 1980. *Economics of Shortage*, vol. A. Amsterdam: Elsevier.

Kornai, J. (interview with A. Jutta-Pietsch). 1982. "Shortage as a Fundamental Problem of Centrally Planned Economies and the Hungarian Reform." *Economics of Planning* 18 (3):103–113.

Kostin, L. A. 1983. *Pravda*, Jan. 4: p. 3.

Kotlyar, A. 1983. "Polnaya zanyatost' i sbalansirovannost' faktorov sotsialisticheskogo proizvod-stva." *Voprosy ekonomiki* (7):106–117.

———. 1984. "Sistema Trudoustroistva v SSSR.' *Ekonomicheskie nauki* (3): pp. 50–59.

Lane, David. 1979. "Towards a Sociological Model of State Socialist Society." In *The Soviet Union and East Europe into the 1980s,* edited by Simon McInnes, pp. 27–58. Ontario: Mosaic Press.

———. 1987. *Soviet Labour and the Ethic of Communism: Full Employment and the Labour Process in the USSR.* Brighton, U.K.: Harvester.

Literaturnaia gazeta. 1980. *Literaturnaia gazeta,* December 24, p. 7.

Manevich, E. 1978. "Defitsit i reservy rabochei sily." E.K.O. no. 2 1978. pp. 75–86.

———. 1981. "Ratsional'nee ispol'zovanie rabochey sily." *Voprosy ekonomiki* (9)55–66.

Marrese, M. 1982. "Labour Shortages in Hungary." In *Employment Policies in the Soviet Union and Eastern Europe,* edited by Jan Adam, pp. 96–122. New York: St. Martin's Press.

Myasnikov, A., and A. Anan'ev. 1979. "By Skills. Not by Numbers." *Trud,* July 17. Abstracted in *Current Digest of the Soviet Press,* vol. 3. no. 29 (1979) pp. 4–5.

Oxenstierna, Susanne. 1985. *Labour Shortage in the Soviet Enterprise.* Stockholm: Institut for Social Forskning.

Parsons, Talcott. 1967. "On the Concept of Political Power." In *Class, Status and Power,* edited by R. Bendix and S. M. Lipset, pp. 240–265. London: Routledge.

Parsons, Talcott, and Neil Smelser. 1956. *Economy and Society.* London: Routledge.

Price, James L. 1977. *The Study of Turnover.* Ames: Iowa State University Press.

Suvorov, K. I. 1968. *Istoricheskii opyt KPSS po likvidatsii bezrabotitsii (1917–1930).* Moscow.

Wheatcroft, S. 1985. "A Note on the Sources of Unemployment Statistics" (with R. W. Davies). In *Labour and Employment in the USSR,* edited by D. Lane, pp. 36–49. New York: New York University Press.

11
The Armed Forces and Soviet Society

Ellen Jones

The Soviet Armed Forces represents one of the most intriguing, if perhaps the most frustrating, object of sociological inquiry. Because military institutions everywhere share a unique and highly specialized mission – national security – they also share many key characteristics in common. But militaries are not just instruments of organized coercion; they are also social institutions reflecting the societies in which they are embedded. Armies everywhere, for example, have to devise ways to procure manpower; but how a given army goes about procuring personnel mirrors values, social organization, and historical experience specific to that society. Virtually every military organization faces the common problem of turning civilians into soldiers, but the methods of handling this problem vary widely. Examination of the social dimension of the armed forces represents, then, a potentially valuable avenue of sociological research for the Sovietologist.

Military sociology examines the human perspective of the military (Harries-Jenkins and Moskos 1981). How are the armed services manned? How is the military elite recruited? Military sociology is also concerned with the emergence of professionalism: To what degree do members of the officer corps share a corporate identity? It also examines the extent to which the military is insulated from other institutions, asking, in effect, How permeable are military–civilian boundary lines? To what degree do military values converge with or diverge from civilian values?

Military sociologists are also concerned with the pattern of personnel problems within the military and how these problems are handled. To what degree does the experience of military service result in shifts in values? Are these value changes (if any) the intended result of a deliberate socialization program or the unintended (and unwanted) result of the service experience itself?

Another key focus of inquiry for the military sociologist is the treatment of specific social groups within the military. Are certain ethnic, regional, or socioeconomic groups excluded? Are military roles assigned by gender?

Military sociologists interested in the Soviet Armed Forces face a special set of problems in applying these questions to the Soviet military. There are several basic sources of evidence on the Soviet military, all of them flawed. One important source is the Soviet media, but evidence drawn from the media suffers from several biases. The most obvious is that the media are state owned and controlled. The Soviet political leadership routinely uses the media, including the military press, to manipulate public opinion both at home and abroad. Much of the media reporting on the Soviet military, moreover, is done by military journalists. In effect, Defense Ministry officials are reporting on their own ministry. This means that press coverage tends to be incomplete, and military journalists are more concerned with presenting the Armed Forces in the most positive light than with uncovering weaknesses and social pathologies. These problems are compounded by the secrecy that shrouds most military issues. There are entire areas of interest to the military sociologist that are simply not covered in the press. And the traditional Soviet penchant for secrecy means that many issues receive only anecdotal coverage. Articles on alcohol abuse within the officer corps, for example, describe individual cases but provide no statistics on how widespread the problem is (Andruyshkov 1984).

Countering all of these negative points is the fact that the media are rich sources of material on Soviet military life. They are after all some of the main mechanisms by which Soviet military officials communicate policy to and discuss problems with the officers and NCOs who run the army on a day-to-day basis. Whereas many strategic issues are totally off-limits for military journalists, many personnel-related issues are not. Although individual articles may present an overly optimistic picture of the army's human dimension, careful scrutiny of a broad sample of the military press yields a more realistic appraisal. For example, the press contains graphic descriptions of corruption, inefficiency, and abuse of position by military officials (Ye. Sorokin 1983). It describes draftees who sneak off post at night and officers who conceal the offenses in order to protect their own careers (Levitskiy 1976). All of these problems, of course, are dealt with as isolated cases, but the frequency with which a given issue surfaces in the press and the level of attention devoted to remedial measures provide two indicators of how widespread the problem might be. The press also provides the researcher with some tantalizing, if highly censored, results of in-house military sociological surveys on such issues as attitudes toward military service and conscript adjustment problems.

It bears adding that the nature of the Soviet media has changed significantly since Gorbachev became General Secretary. Under the banner of *glasnost*, topics previously avoided completely are now dealt with more openly. The extensive Soviet media coverage of the December 1986 riots in the Soviet republic of Kazakhstan is one example of *glasnost* in action (*Kazakhstanskaya Pravda* 1986, 2). Even though media treatment of military issues has so far been less affected by *glasnost*, the policy has resulted in fuller coverage of negative events such as instances of ineffective management and corrupt on in the military and draft avoidance. This trend is a positive one for sociologists interested in the Soviet military because it means a fuller, richer portrait of military life. It also means that greater caution must be used in interpreting shifts in media attention to a specific problem. Greater media coverage of, say, alcohol abuse in the armed forces may reflect changes in media policy rather than a change in the seriousness of the problem.

The second major source of information on the Soviet military – the comments of former Soviet citizens – also suffers from some weaknesses (Jones 1985). The most obvious is that this commentary, like the Soviet press, is quite apt to present a biased portrait of the military. Most Soviets who left the USSR, whether as defectors or legal emigrants, did so at some personal cost, and many view the Soviet system in an extremely negative light. In some cases this attitude produces an image of the Soviet military in which pathologies are magnified; in others it leads to an exaggerated image of Soviet military strength. Evidence drawn from Soviet emigres also tends to be incomplete, because people who served in certain types of units (for example, construction) tend to be overrepresented, whereas those who served in others (for example, submarines) tend to be underrepresented. Emigre evidence is also, by its nature, anecdotal. The most valuable information provided by emigres consists of their personal experiences in the individual units in which they served. Because conditions vary so much from unit to unit, it is dangerous to generalize from the comments of a few individuals.

The major strength of emigre data is the extent to which it serves as a valuable supplement to the material drawn from the Soviet press, filling in some of the gaps created by the Soviet military's traditional reluctance to discuss problems openly in the press. For example, the military media speaks obliquely of the need for junior officers and warrant officers, who deal directly with conscripts, to exercise tact when interacting with the draftees in their charge; eyewitness accounts of military life suggest that this remark is aimed at career soldiers who frequently resort to unauthorized physical punishments to maintain order within their units (Jones 1985, 134–35).

It is important to note that both the Soviet media and the accounts of former Soviet soldiers provide contradictory information. For example, most emigre accounts of Soviet military life note the existence of an informal seniority system that places second-year soldiers in a position of authority over newly arrived conscripts (Suvorov 1982, 222–23). Some see this as a strong point for the Soviet military system (it assists officers and warrants in maintaining control), whereas others portray it as a serious morale problem, undermining unit solidarity. Similarly, some military journalists portray the system in negative terms, warning of the potential threat it poses to healthy personnel relations within the unit, whereas others detail the ways in which a skilled commander can use it to his benefit for unit control and socialization (Volkogonov 1976; Chistyakov and Maslov 1973).

Much of this material, then, points to conflicting conclusions about Soviet military life. Without the ability to perform on-site surveys, we can make few definitive statements, for example, about the level of given disciplinary infractions. We know – because both the military press and Soviet emigres tell us – that some Soviet teenagers try to avoid service. We do not know how widespread the problem is, whether service avoidance has increased over the past decade, and (if so) what this means in terms of public attitudes toward the military and toward the regime itself. Many conclusions presented in this chapter represent judgements based on incomplete and sometimes contradictory information.

Permeability of Military–Civil Boundary Lines

All military organizations face the common problem of procuring manpower; how they solve this problem has a significant effect on the degree of permeability in military–civil boundary lines. Voluntary recruitment of military personnel tends to accentuate the differences between military and civil life for several reasons. First, recruits are self-selected. Those who volunteer for military duty and make it through the military's own filtration system tend to be more attracted to military life styles and more sympathetic to military values than is the general population. Their presence in the armed forces tends to reinforce those aspects of military life that set it apart from the civilian world.

Second, reliance on recruitment to procure manpower can sometimes result in a much narrower social base. In those cases in which manpower is in short supply and military careers are perceived as less appealing (for monetary or status reasons) than those in the civilian economy, the armed forces may find itself drawing a disproportionate percentage of its recruits from regions and socioeconomic groups with lower access to high-status occupations (Janowitz 1973). Similarly, in instances in which military careers are well rewarded relative to civilian occupations – and this is particularly likely in the case of careers in the officer corps – the primary recruitment pool might narrow to encompass only the upper socioeconomic strata.

Third, volunteer systems frequently entail longer service terms than those based on the draft. In this case, there are fewer individuals cycling through the military, and the longer service tenures allow for more complete socialization than would be the case for short-term draftees. A larger percentage of military personnel view their service as a lifelong career and way of life, a factor that tends to increase their personal commitment to the military as an institution and cements their personal identity as a member of the armed forces.

Conscript armies, by contrast, tend to be dominated, numerically at least, by *citizen soldiers*, civilians in uniform who are called up for relatively brief duty tours. They bring with them civilian values and life styles that may be incompatible with military life, and the military must devote a large share of its attention to attenuate these conflicting values and make effective soldiers out of civilians. Similarly, a draft system generally involves a large number of demobilized draftees returning to the civilian world, bringing with them the results of their conscript experience. These factors tend to increase the permeability between the military and civilian world (Dabezies 1982).

In the USSR, conscription is the primary mode of manpower procurement. The Soviet leadership experimented briefly with a volunteer system but then switched over to the draft in May 1918. Their current manning system (embodied in the 1967 universal military service law) is based on an explicit link between citizenship and military service (Prezidiuma verkovnogo soveta SSSR 1982, 181–202). Teenage boys are registered at age seventeen through a network of military commissariats (a combination of draft boards and recruiting stations) and conscripted at age eighteen or nineteen for a two- to three-year service hitch.

The Soviet intent is to make the obligation to serve as universal as possible. Deferments, which are provided for family hardship, health, and education, are relatively limited and becoming more so. The largest loophole is the educational deferment. The 1967 service law provided deferments for all full-time students at higher and specialized secondary educational institutions. This was pared back in the early eighties to those students at selected institutions. Although the Soviets have not yet published a list of deferment-granting institutions, indications are that the net effect of the change has significantly reduced the number of young men receiving educational deferments. The cutback in educational deferments was primarily a response to changing demographic realities: the supply of eighteen-year-old males peaked in the late seventies and will decline by 25 percent to its projected low point in 1988 (Jones 1985, 57–58). But the change also dovetailed well with the Soviet ideological commitment to the concept of military service as a corollary of citizenship (*Programma KPSS* 1986, pt. IV). As a result, a large proportion of the eighteen-to-twenty-one-year-old male pool – perhaps as high as 80 to 85 percent – is drafted, compared to perhaps 65 to 70 percent in the mid- and late seventies, when the supply of young males peaked and educational deferments had not yet been cut back.

The commitment to universality in military service means that the conscript contingent of the Soviet Armed Forces represents the larger civilian world. Virtually the entire range of socioeconomic classes and ethnic and regional groups are represented in the biannual intake of new conscripts. In contrast to an army that relies on more selective recruitment, the Soviet military cannot filter out individuals unsuited or unattracted to military life. Many young men who have physical or mental disabilities that would exempt them from military service in most other national settings are called up to serve. As a consequence, the Soviet military cannot insulate itself from broader social trends. The civilians in uniform who numerically dominate the USSR Armed Forces bring with them into the military both the strengths and weaknesses of the civilian world.

It is not surprising, then, that several of the military's major personnel problems reflect the pathologies of the larger social setting. The obvious example is alcohol abuse, a problem widespread both inside and outside the armed forces. Alcohol consumption increased significantly in the 1970s (Zaigrayev 1986, 8). Most troubling to Soviet authorities were results from studies revealing dramatic increases in alcohol consumption among Soviet teenagers (Zaigrayev 1986, 110; 1985). Many problem drinkers begin drinking as children or teenagers, and these individuals bring their drinking problem with them into the military when they are drafted (Fedotov 1976). Moreover, because a higher proportion of males of all ages than females in the USSR drink and drink to excess, the personnel problems associated with alcohol are magnified in the all-male environment of military units (Tedder and Sidorov 1976). The stress and boredom of military life, particularly for conscripts, make them especially susceptible to alcohol problems. These factors help explain why alcohol abuse is a serious discipline issue for the military. To cope with the alcohol problem, Soviet military authorities have tried to limit availability for conscript personnel by barring its use, but draftees frequently get around these restrictions by drinking alcoholic beverages smuggled on post or sent by indulgent parents or by consuming various home brews concocted from shoe polish or strong tea (Sokolov 1983).

The negative economic and social effects of alcohol abuse, both inside and outside the military, have prompted the Gorbachev leadership to adopt a strenuous anti-alcohol campaign. The campaign involves measures to decrease both the availability of alcohol and what has apparently been an official tolerance toward alcohol abuse (*Izvestiya* 1985, 1–2; *Pravda* 1985, 2). Nearly two years into the campaign, Gorbachev claimed major successes for the program, including a drop in alcohol-related crime and workplace accidents (Gorbachev 1987). The anti-alcohol campaign has also been applied to the armed forces. As in civilian life, there has been a general crackdown on alcohol abuse, particularly while on duty (*Krasnaya Zvezda* January 1986, 2; February 1986, 2). The likely result will be at least a short-term decline in alcohol availability, consumption, and abuse in the Armed Forces (*Krasnaya Zvezda* April 1986, 4). The extent to which the anti-alcohol program results in long-term shifts in traditional patterns of alcohol use will depend largely on continued leadership attention and commitment to the program.

Official corruption is another social malady, widespread in civilian life, that has affected the military as well. Corruption can take the form of deception – falsifying official reports to avoid rebukes from above. Civilian factory managers routinely pad production figures. Their military counterparts underreport disciplinary infractions (*Krasnaya Zvezda* October 1985 2). Misuse of official position – pilfering state property, using state assets for personal gain, or outright bribery – is even more widespread (*Krasnaya Zvezda* August 1985, 2). A typical example in the military context is a military commissariat official or examining doctor who accepts a bribe to give a physically fit teenager a health deferment. Nepotism is another common problem – officials who arrange sought after assignments for relatives or friends (*Krasnaya Zvezda* February 1987, 2).

Although the Defense Ministry has clearly not been immune from corruption, there are no indications that this problem is particularly acute in the Armed Forces. One factor is the existence of redundant oversight networks, set up originally to exert political control, that probably also operate to discourage fraud and misreporting as well. These networks include the military's political officers (who, theoretically at least, have a separate reporting chain for such abuses) and, more importantly, the KGB's Special Departments, which are completely independent of the military hierarchy and provide a separate channel of information on illegal activity. These oversight mechanisms have apparently operated to keep corruption in the Defense Ministry from assuming the huge proportions it has in certain other Soviet agencies (e.g., the Ministry of Foreign Trade) and regions (e.g., Kazakhstan).

This discussion suggests that the Armed Forces are by no means exempt from the social pathologies that trouble the civilian world. The military must also cope with unique social problems that reflect the behavioral problems of postadolescent males combined with the predictable challenge of adjusting to military life. Probably the most common disciplinary violation is disobedience of orders: improper wearing of uniforms, being late for formation, failing to salute properly. Most of these offenses, not surprisingly, are committed by newly arrived soldiers or soldiers about to be demobilized (Volkov, Prilepskiy, and Cherkasov 1968). Another common offense is unauthorized absence, typically committed by draftees who sneak off post at night to the nearest town in search of alcohol and female companionship. Fist fights between draftees are also common in some units.

Soviet military authorities have several mechanisms for dealing with these problems. Disciplinary infractions are discouraged by a series of disciplinary punishments, whereas more serious incidents are subject to criminal prosecution (Prezidiuma verkhovnogo soveta SSR 1982, 463–94; Gorniy 1983, 167–74). Public censure is also used as a control mechanism. Conscript misconduct is publicized at unit meetings where the culprit is publicly chastised. Misconduct by officers and nonofficer career personnel is subject to public censure in comrades' courts of honor (Prezidiuma verkhovnogo soveta SSSR 1982, 515–22). These measures reflect larger Soviet efforts to harness peer group pressure to enforce official behavioral standards.

Corporate Identity of the Career Military

Another focus of interest for the military sociologist is the corporate identity of the career military. The Soviet career force consists of several groups: nonofficer career personnel and commissioned officers (Iovlev and Storozhenko 1977). The USSR Armed Forces does not have a well-developed career enlistee/NCO corps like many Western militaries. There are very few career enlistees (who may enlist for two-to-six-year service hitches after completing conscript service), and these individuals serve in a relatively limited number of menial posts. A second category of nonofficer career personnel is represented by warrant officers. The warrant officer program, which was only set up in the early seventies, was expanded in the early eighties. Warrants serve in both command and technical–administrative support positions, including posts (like platoon commander) that may also be assigned to junior officers.

The bulk of the military career force is composed of officers who fill many military roles allocated to the NCO force in Western militaries. One key issue for the military sociologist is the extent to which the officer corps is characterized by a strong corporate identity, a core of common values that sets the group apart from the rest of society.

In the Soviet case, the development of a strong corporate identity within the officer corps was delayed for many decades. The early Bolshevik political leaders were very distrustful of military professionals, and for good reason: many Tsarist officers were strongly opposed to the Bolshevik revolution. Yet the new regime was forced to rely on former tsarist officers to provide many of the command cadres for the new Red Army. To ensure reliability and counter political sabotage, the Bolshevik leadership established a system of political watchdogs – military–political commissars who cosigned the commander's operational orders (Kolychev 1976). As the former tsarist officers were replaced by politically reliable Red commanders, the need for the commissar system declined, and it eventually evolved into the contemporary political officer hierarchy, whose primary missions are not political control but socialization and motivation.

However, the heritage of party leadership mistrust of the officer corps was to have a significant impact on the development of professionalism within the career force (Jones 1985, 79–82). Traditional military ranks, which the Bolshevik leadership had abolished in December 1917, were not reestablished until 1935, and then only partially. The officer corps was also hit hard by the Stalinist purges in the late thirties. Many of the losses sustained by the Soviets in the early years of World War II were due in part to ineffective command. The war itself, however, set in motion a series of events that were eventually to produce an officer corps in the true sense of the word. The Soviets finally adopted a unified military rank structure in 1943. The officer corps as an institution was given wide and positive publicity, and military hierarchy and discipline were more strongly emphasized. After the war the Soviets embarked on a program to upgrade the educational qualifications of their officers and, simultaneously, to enhance the political, economic, and social status of the officer corps. All of these developments furthered the sense of professionalism within the officer corps.

The emergence of a stronger corporate identity within the postwar Soviet officer corps was also facilitated by increasing social homogeneity. The early officer corps was a heterogeneous group of former tsarist officers, untrained but politically reliable Red commanders, and virtually illiterate, blue-collar workers and peasants. The huge number of fatalities during World War II created rapid turnover among command cadres and hence operated to maximize the regional and socioeconomic heterogeneity among officers.

The postwar period, however, has brought with it a narrowing of the social base. A larger proportion of officers are products of the officer commissioning school system, rather than "direct commisions" or reserve officers. Admission to one of the extensive network of Soviet military commissioning schools is through a series of competitive exams and is theoretically open to any male of appropriate age who can pass the exam

(Provorov and Porokhin 1976). In practice, however, those who are better educated and those who are native Russian speakers are greatly advantaged in the selection process. There are indications, moreover, that officer careers are more popular with blue-collar families, and less popular with individuals from well-educated, white-collar families. Soviet surveys also suggest that military families tend to pass the preference for a career in the officer corps on to their sons (Yefimov and Deryugin 1980; Levanov 1979). This means that the offspring of military professionals are probably overrepresented in the officer corps. Non-Russians (who are disadvantaged because the exams are conducted in Russian) are almost certainly underrepresented.

These factors are likely to result in an ever narrowing social base in the officer corps. Moreover, the increasing reliance on military commissioning schools as a source of officer recruits means that the vast majority of Soviet officers are individuals who have made a long-term commitment relatively early in life to a military career – another factor facilitating the growth of a corporate identity.

Countering these considerations are factors that operate in the opposite direction. The Soviet military, as indicated earlier, is not insulated from the civilian community in the sense of being able to filter out individuals not open to accepting military values and life styles. Moreover, development of a strong corporate identity in many militaries is linked to the existence of a uniquely military value system. In the Soviet Union, as detailed in the following section, there is a great deal of overlap between approved values in military and civilian institutions. These factors mean that the gulf that separates the military officer from his counterpart civilian is much narrower in the USSR than in many other modernized societies.

Civilian and Military Values

In many societies, the military has not only a unique way of life, but also a unique ethos that sets it apart from the civilian world. In general, armies tend to be more rigidly hierarchical than analogous civilian organizations. They also tend to be more authoritarian and place greater emphasis on discipline, teamwork, and procedure than on creativity, democracy, and individualism. In sum, there tends to be a greater stress on the need to sacrifice personal interests for the needs of the larger organization.

To a large degree, the Soviet Armed Forces has embraced these traditional military values. There is much less divergence, however, between these values and those held up as ideal in the civilian world. Soviet society itself is also authoritarian and hierarchical. The values of civilian society also place strong emphasis on the importance of sacrificing individual rights to the needs of the group. These considerations mean that there is much more convergence between official military and civilian value systems in the USSR.

One example of the convergence between military and civilian values is the compatibility between the ideal Soviet citizen and the ideal Soviet soldier. The ideal Soviet citizen – the New Socialist Man – is someone who is patriotic, well informed, and hard working. He takes an active role in community and civic affairs and is strongly supportive of the Communist system, willing to fight and die for it if necessary (*Programma KPSS* 1986, pt. V). The ideal Soviet soldier is a minor variation on this theme (Sobolev 1984, 103–15). In addition to the qualities that distinguish the New Socialist Man, the ideal Soviet soldier accepts his duty to serve, respects and obeys his commanders, likes his combat comrades and military unit, and keeps military secrets.

In contrast to many Western societies, where the social norms and values of the military may clash with those of civilian society, in the Soviet Union approved military values are compatible with officially approved values in the civilian world. In fact, the draftee's military experience is viewed by Soviet socializers as a unique opportunity to instill pro-Soviet values, because the conscripts are physically isolated from family and community and the environment is more regimented and strictly controlled.

Another example of shared values is the congruence between the value system of military officers and civilian managers. The qualities prized in a Soviet officer are quite consistent with those prized among civilian managers. Both are judged on a combination of political and professional characteristics (Shkadov 1982). Both must operate in an authoritarian, hierarchical system that gives lip service to the virtues of initiative and flexibility but rewards rigidity and subservience. The major difference is the military's greater emphasis on teaching ability, a natural outgrowth of the military organization's preoccupation with training and socializing young draftees.

Given the strong convergence between official military and civilian values, it is not surprising that the military as an institution, judging by the comments of Soviet emigres, seems to enjoy a relatively positive image within Soviet society. It is apparently viewed as one of the few organizations in the USSR that works efficiently – a view that probably stems partly from the contrast between the Soviet Union's achievement of parity with the West in the strategic sector and its inability to compete with Western civilian economies.

The relatively positive image enjoyed by the Soviet military is also due to the existence of a comprehensive "military–patriotic" socialization program designed to instill both a high level of respect for the military and broad acceptance of the need to perform active duty military service (Mosolov and Kolychev 1976). Child-care manuals lecture parents on the importance of teaching their preschoolers to love the motherland. The socialization program continues in a more systematic fashion in the school system, where both formal lessons and extracurricular programs depict the military in a positive light. The military also benefits from the exploitation of World War II as a technique to instill patriotism. The officer corps itself also receives a strong positive image in the Soviet media.

Closely related to the military's overall image within Soviet society is the attitude of draft-age youth toward conscription. Again, the evidence on this issue is incomplete, consisting primarily of Soviet emigre comments and the occasional published results of Soviet public opinion surveys. These data suggest that even though the typical Soviet teenager does not look forward with any great enthusiasm to his two-year service obligation, he accepts it as an unpleasant, but inevitable, interruption of his life (Yefimov and Deryugin 1980).

Acceptance of the military service obligation has probably decreased somewhat since the sixties and early seventies. Media discussion of service avoidance is on the increase (*Krasnaya Zvezda* March 1986, 4). Although this trend may be partly due to an increased willingness to discuss the problem openly, there are several other factors that suggest that the incidence of draft dodging has increased in the last decade or so. One is Soviet military involvement in Afghanistan and the possibility of being assigned to a unit involved in combat. Another is the shift in youth attitudes consequent to socioeconomic modernization. The proportion of draftees from small, consumer conscious, and relatively well-off urban European families is on the upswing. These youngsters are more materialistic and less acceptant of hard work, discipline, and self-sacrifice than were previous generations. They are also less acceptant of the two-year service obligation – a phenomenon attributed at least partly to the passage of time since World War II (Ogarkov 1982, 65; Sorokin 1983). All of these factors help explain what is probably a real increase in service avoidance, as indulgent parents (concerned about the possibility of an Afghanistan posting) seek to buy their sons out of the draft or at least to ensure an assignment outside of Afghanistan. The probable increase in illegal cases of service avoidance is also due to the cutback on legal deferments associated with the cutback in educational deferments.

Soviet authorities are rightly concerned about these trends. They are trying to counteract them by more sophisticated socialization efforts. These efforts include programs to revive the memory of World War II and to ameliorate adverse public reaction to military casualties in Afghanistan by expanding media coverage of the war and linking the activities of Soviet soldiers assigned there with the heroic exploits of their fathers and grandfathers in World War II. Afghanistan veterans are also being tapped to lecture prospective draftees on military life, taking the place of the World War II veteran as role models of heroism and sacrifice (*Sovetskiy Patriot*

1986, 1; Yegorov 1986). The success of both efforts is far from assured, but thus far public resistance to the draft and individual instances of draft dodging appear to be well within manageable limits.

Ethnic Soldiers

Another issue of concern to the military sociologist is the relationship between ethnic trends and military developments. The USSR is a multiethnic state with more than one hundred nationalities separated by language, religious and cultural traditions, economic level, and life styles. The Russians, as well as two related Slavic groups (the Ukrainians and Belorussians), are the dominant groups from both the numerical and political standpoint; together these groups comprise 73 percent of the Soviet population. Another large cultural grouping (comprising about 17 percent of the population) consists of less-modernized Islamic minorities from the USSR's southern periphery. These groups are particularly important because they are the fastest growing component of the Soviet populace. In contrast to the European north and west, where families of one and two children have become the norm, large families are still very popular in the Islamic southern tier. In many parts of this region, women have only just recently begun to practice family limitation. As a result, the ethnic composition of the conscript pool has been shifting in favor of Islamic minorities, whose share increased from 13 percent in 1970 to 24 percent in 1985, with further shifts in the same direction to continue to the end of the decade and beyond.

Coping with ethnic diversity is one important component of Soviet domestic policy (*Programma KPSS* 1986, pt. III). The solution that has emerged over the nearly seven decades of Soviet rule is clearly a compromise, a mix of programs that encourage ethnic convergence in both socioeconomic level and values, as well as programs that give less-modernized minorities preference in order to promote social mobility. In short, the Soviet leadership has tried to balance the ideological commitment to upward mobility for historically disadvantaged minorities with the practical need for efficiency.

A similar balance is evident in the Armed Forces' treatment of ethnic minorities. The commitment to ethnic equality means that all minorities must be endowed with full citizenship. Because the obligation to serve is a corollary of Soviet citizenship, this means that all ethnic groups are subject to military service on an equal basis. Similarly, the commitment to equality requires that assignment policy be ethnically neutral and that all minorities have equal opportunities within the military career force. However, applying these principles to minorities with low levels of Russian fluency or relatively low educational levels directly conflicts with the military's need for efficiency.

The history of ethnic soldiers in the USSR is essentially one of ongoing efforts to balance the two conflicting goals of equality and efficiency (Jones 1985, 182–88). The tsarist military manpower system had excluded many minorities from military service. Bolshevik leaders were committed ideologically to reversing this policy, but their heavy reliance on army veterans as a source of military manpower during the Civil War, coupled with the open hostility of many ethnic groups on the Soviet southern periphery, meant that many minorities continued to be exempt from the draft during the Civil War. To help overcome the language barrier and maximize minority military participation, the Bolshevik leadership set up nationality units consisting of volunteers from among the more pro-Bolshevik socioeconomic groups. Muslim minorities from the Soviet southern tier presented a particularly difficult challenge to Bolshevik authorities, because of their low educational attainments, low levels of Russian fluency, and deep-seated resistance to military service. The draft was not extended to these areas until the late twenties and early thirties. The nationality units were phased out in the mid-1930s, only to be resurrected during World War II, when (despite sporadic problems with minority reliability) minority soldiers played a significant role in combat.

Nationality units were once again phased out after the war, and the current policy is one of ethnic integration. Minority draftees, like their Russian counterparts, are assigned on the basis of individual qualifications to multiethnic units. Access to a career in the military is also, at least in theory, ethnically neutral.

In practice, however, these ideals have frequently been sacrificed in the interests of military efficiency. The assignment of minority draftees provides one example. Soviet military authorities clearly try to ensure an ethnic mix in military units. But many non-Russians, particularly Islamic minorities, are selected out of conscript assignments requiring fluency in Russian (the command language). Minorities with low levels of Russian fluency or low educational levels tend to be underrepresented in units with a high proportion of posts requiring technical training and overrepresented in more menial posts. Conversely, ethnic. Russians tend to be overrepresented in those units, such as the Strategic Rocket Forces and certain naval units, where demands for Russian fluency (i.e., to absorb technical training or to understand technical manuals) are high.

A similar compromise between nationality considerations and military requirements is evident in trends affecting military professionals. Ideally, the cadre of military professionals should reflect the ethnic composition of the pool of draftees (Nikitin 1982; Bel'kov, 1981). Pressures to recruit minority officers were particularly strong during the twenties and thirties, when many minority soldiers were assigned to nationality units. Special native-language schools were set up to train minority officers, who were not forced to compete with their better-educated Russian counterparts.

The complete phase-out of nationality units after the war has meant that non-Slavs and Slavs are recruited through the same process – one that places a high premium on Russian fluency. Acceptance into a military commissioning school, the main avenue for entry into the contemporary officer corps, involves examinations conducted in Russian, covering Russian language and in some cases Russian literature. Clearly, even well-educated non-Russians are disadvantaged in the selection process (Melkunyan 1980). As a result, the limited data providing insight into the ethnic composition of the officer corps suggest that non-Russians are significantly underrepresented, particularly in the upper reaches of the officer corps.

The increased proportion of Islamic groups among Soviet draftees has resulted in increased pressures to recruit more Islamic officers. Special remedial Russian courses for officer commissioning school applicants have been set up in several republics; and some republics have experimented with preferential admission policies assuring minority youths a small number of slots in officer commissioning schools. These developments suggest that Soviet military authorities, while sensitive to the need for an adequate representation of minorities within the officer corps, are hesitant to lower admission standards to achieve it. The preferred solution is to help upwardly mobile minority individuals to adjust (e.g., through remedial language programs) to the requirement for a Russian-fluent officer corps.

The military roles assigned to ethnic minorities in the USSR represent one response to the problems and opportunities posed by distinct linguistic and cultural groups. Despite the problems posed by diverse languages and life styles, despite the potential threat to combat cohesion posed by interethnic friction, Soviet leaders have sought to maximize minority participation in the military and to minimize or limit the use of mechanisms, such as nationality formations and preference in officer commissioning schools, that categorize by ethnic origin. This approach reflects the way nationality policy has been applied in the civilian world. Soviet leaders recognize the need for minority or regional preferences in the short term, but they recognize the social divisiveness of minority quotas, which tend to alienate the dominant Slavs and other minorities excluded from preferences. Minority preferences, as demonstrated by the rioting that broke out in Kazakhstan when a Russian outsider replaced a Kazakh party chief, can also be politically volatile; the young Kazakh students who took to the streets did so because they correctly concluded that the party personnel change presaged a decrease in the ethnic preferences that had ensured preferential access to education, jobs, housing, and consumer items. The long-term goal is to make such preferences unnecessary by equipping non-Slavic groups with the linguistic and educational skills they need to compete effectively for economic and political rewards. The goal of integrating non-Slavs into the Armed Forces, then, reflects the larger leadership goal of integrating them more fully into mainstream civilian society.

Women in the Military

Women, by contrast, are almost totally excluded from the peacetime Soviet military. The military roles assigned to women in the USSR provide an interesting case study in female roles and values associated with them. Prerevolutionary Russian peasant society was patriarchal (Dunn and Dunn 1967, 8–13). Roles were assigned on the basis of gender. Even though females were an important part of the agricultural labor force, they were assigned subordinate social and political roles; and women were virtually excluded from the prerevolutionary military. The Bolshevik revolution brought with it a major transformation in female roles, granting women full legal equality. The Bolshevik commitment to female labor force participation, however, was a continuation of prerevolutionary trends. Women moved into a wide variety of modernized occupations, including many harsh, physically demanding jobs that have been (until recently at least) virtually closed to women in many Western industrial societies. Despite high labor force participation rates, however, women were largely excluded from the upper reaches of management and the political elite, as well as from the military.

Not until World War II were women employed in large numbers in the Armed Forces (Murmantseva 1979). Nearly a million women saw service during the war, primarily in a support capacity but also in combat roles. Soviet willingness to employ women in combat was partly a function of military necessity and partly a function of the fact that broad social acceptance of females in jobs involving hard menial labor may have facilitated social acceptance of women in combat.

After the war, however, Soviet women were demobilized, and female military roles were again restricted. Women are not subject to the peacetime draft. They can volunteer, as both officers and nonofficer career personnel, for an extremely limited number of occupational specialties, primarily in the medical, communications, and clerical fields. Although information on the extent of female employment in the Armed Forces is limited, it seems clear that the number of Soviet servicewomen is very small (perhaps 10,000 or so out of a force of five million).

There is no evidence to suggest that demographic trends in the eighties and nineties will result in any major shift in this policy. To be sure, the downturn in the supply of draft-age males has resulted in a stepped-up recruitment campaign. Opportunities for servicewomen are being better publicized, and Soviet authorities have made some effort to improve benefits. However, this development is part of a larger program to upgrade the nonofficer career force and does not appear to have resulted in anything other than marginal increases in recruitment of women. Females remain limited to a very small number of military specialties, and job advancement opportunities continue to be severely restricted. There is, in short, no Soviet analogue to the dramatic increase in female military roles that has occurred in the United States, and to a lesser extent in Great Britain and France.

The continued virtual exclusion of women from military roles in the USSR contrasts with their high level of labor force participation in the civilian world and with the use of servicewomen during World War II. There are several explanations for this anomoly. First, Soviet support of the legal equality of the sexes is linked to constitutional recognition of the continued existence of gender-based role differences. Moreover, the theoretical support for sexual equality has always been tempered in practice by a large residue of traditional patriarchal values toward women that have resulted in their virtual exclusion from positions of power and authority. Women are almost totally absent from the top reaches of state and party management and from the real centers of power in the USSR. For example, Central Committee Secretary Alexandra Biryukova is the only female on the Politburo or Central Committee Secretariat, and her responsibilities – consumer goods, trade, and services – are in areas traditionally accorded a low priority by Soviet policy makers. Exclusion of women from the security field can therefore be viewed as an extension of their exclusion from other areas of power.

Another explanation for the limited role servicewomen play in the USSR Armed Forces is the apparent perception among Soviet socializers that young Soviet males need an all-male environment to counteract the feminizing effects of an overprotective and female-dominated home life. Military service is viewed as providing positive male role models and in instilling masculinity (Deryugin and Yefimov 1981). Extending the draft to women or employing females on a large scale in the career force would dilute the masculine environment within military units and thus undermine a key aspect of the military's socialization role.

The virtual exclusion of females from the Armed Forces has some important social and political consequences. Exempting women legally from the draft provides an official recognition of their status as a special class of citizens. This, in turn, serves to legitimize informal gender stereotyping that operates to exclude women from positions of authority. Moreover, security issues, which play an important role in most industrialized political systems, are especially important in the Soviet decision-making process. Excluding women from the Soviet military perpetuates their exclusion from related fields and severely impedes their access to political elite status.

Conclusion

The Soviet Armed Forces represent the chief justification for the USSR's claim to superpower status. In no other arena have the Soviets been able to compete effectively with the West. The USSR's great power status has been purchased at a price: the high priority accorded the military and its needs has its corollary in the low priority accorded consumer goods, services, and housing. Still, the investment in military power has bought the USSR a key place in the world diplomatic community – a status that is an important point of pride for many Soviet citizens and a critical source of legitimacy for their leaders. Soviet willingness to make these sacrifices, a decision taken by a handful of political leaders but accepted with little overt protest by the majority of the populace, is reflective of cultural values.

Although the Soviet Armed Forces have surely benefited from preferential status in the political and economic system, the military is by no means isolated from civilian life. Despite the uniquely military characteristics that the USSR Armed Forces share with other armies, it is a peculiarly Soviet institution, reflecting the values, strengths, and weaknesses of the larger social setting. Neither the draftees who cycle through the system nor the career military men whose job it is to turn them into soldiers are exempt from the patterns of deviance and social cleavages that characterize the civilian world. The military's problems with alcohol abuse and corruption, for instance, are merely subsets of larger social pathologies, although the tight control characteristic of military life probably renders both problems more manageable. The linguistic and cultural problems faced by military authorities trying to meld soldiers from diverse ethnic backgrounds into a cohesive fighting force reflect the multinational character of Soviet society. The higher level of regimentation, harsh discipline, and austere living conditions within the Soviet military mirror the regimentation and low living standards of Soviet civilian life. The virtual exclusion of women from peacetime military roles reflects the ambiguity of women's roles in the Soviet system as a whole. In short, the sociologist who focuses inquiry on the USSR Armed Forces finds in it an institutional reflection of the larger society.

References

Andryushkov, A. 1984. "The Knot: On the Subject of Ethics." *Krasnaya Zvezda* 25 (January): 2.

Bel'kov,O. 1981. "An Army of Friendship and Fraternity of Peoples." *Kommunist Vooruzhennykh Sil* 12: 9–16.

Chistykov, N., and V. Maslov. 1973. "Persuasion and Compulsion in the Struggle against Legal Violations in the Army and Navy." *Voyennaya Mysl'* 5.

Dabezies, Pierre. 1982. "French Political Parties and Defense Policy: Divergence and Consensus." *Armed Forces and Society* 2 (Winter): 239–56.

Deryugin, Yu. I, and N. N. Yefimov. 1981. "Socializing Role of the Soviet Armed Forces." *Sotsiologicheskiye Issledovaniya* 4: 104–09.

Dunn, Stephen P., and Ethel Dunn. 1967. *The Peasants of Central Russia*. New York: Holt, Rinehart & Winston.

Fedotov, A. V. 1976. "Social Problems of the Struggle Against Alcoholism." *Sotsiologicheskiye Issledovaniya* 5: 26–9.

Gorbachev, Mikhail. 1987. "On Reorganization and the Party's Personnel Policy." *Pravda*, January 28, pp. 1, 2.

Gorniy, A. G., ed. 1983. *Komandiru o Voyenno-ugolovnom Zakonodatel'stve*. Moscow: Voyenizdat.

Harries-Jenkins, Gwyn, and Charles C. Mosko, Jr. 1981. "Trend Report: Armed Forces and Society." *Armed Forces and Society* 29 (3):1–82.

Iovlev, A. M., and V. Ye. Storozhenko. 1977. "Kadry voyennyye." *Sovetskaya Voyennaya Entsiklopediya*, vol. 4: 25–26. Moscow: Voyenizdat.

Izvestiya. 1985. May 17, pp.1–2.

Janowitz, Morris. 1973. "The Social Demography of the All-Volunteer Armed Force." *Annals of the American Academy of Political and Social Science* 406 (March): 86–93.

Jones, Ellen. 1985. *Red Army and Society: A Sociology of the Soviet Military*. Boston: Allen & Unwin.

Kazakhstanskaya Pravda. 1986. December 19, p. 2.

Kolychev, V. G. 1976. "Voyennyy komissar." *Sovetskaya Voyennaya Entsiklopediya*, vol. 2: 268–69. Moscow: Voyenizdat.

Krasnaya Zvezda. 1985. August 22, p. 2; September 17, p. 2; October 11, p. 2.

Krasnaya Zvezda. 1986. January 29, p. 2; February 9, p. 2; March 19, p. 4; April 15, p. 4.

Krasnaya Zvezda. 1987. February 11, p. 2.

Levanov, Ye. Ye. 1979. "Family Socialization: Status and Problems." *Sotsiologicheskiye Issledovaniya* 1: 115–18.

Levitskiy, V. 1976. "Commander and the Law: Behind a Convenient Wording." *Krasnaya Zvezda*, August 1, p. 2.

Melkunyan, A. 1980. "To Raise Defenders of the Motherland." *Kommunist* (Yerevan), February 17, p. 2.

Mosolov, G. K., and V. G. Kolychev. 1976. "Voyenno-patrioticheskiye vospitaniye." *Sovetskaya Voyennaya Entsiklopediya*: 254–56. Moscow: Voytenizdat.

Murmantseva, V. S. 1979. *Sovetskiye Zhenschiny v Velikoy Otechestennoy Voyne, 1941–1945*, 2d ed. Moscow: Mysl.'

Nikitin, Ye. 1982. "The Triumph of Leninist Nationality Policy." *Agitator armii i flota* 23 (December): 10–14.

Ogarkov, N. V. 1982. *Vsegda v Gotovnosti k Zaschite Otechestva*. Moscot: Voyenizdat.

Pravda. 1985. May 17, p. 2.

Prezidiuma verkhovnogo soveta SSSR. 1982. "On Universal Military Service." *Svod Zakonov SSSR*, vol. 9: 181–202. Moscow.

————. 1982. "Disciplinary Regulations of the USSR Armed Forces." *Svod Zakonov SSSR*, vol. 9: 463–94. Moscow.

————. 1982. "Statute on Comrades' Courts of Honor for Officers in the USSR Armed Forces." *Svod Zakonov SSSR*, vol. 9: 515–22. Moscow.

Programma KPSS. 1986. *Pravda*, March 7: pp. 3–8.

Provorov, K. V., and A. D. Porokhin. 1976. "Voyenno-uchebnyye zavedeniya." *Sovetskaya Voyennaya Entsiklopediya:* 255–56. Moscow: Voyenizdat.

Shkadov, I. 1982. "Professional Qualities of the Officer." *Krasnaya Zvezda*, August 20, p. 2.

Sobolev, M. G. 1984. *Partiyno-politicheskaya Rabota v Sovetskoy Armii i Flote*. Moscow: Voyenizdat.

Sokolov, A. 1983. "A Father's Opinion: Such Are the Parcels." *Krasnaya Zvezda*, November 25, p. 2.

Sorokin, A. I. 1983. "The Armed Forces of Developed Socialism." *Voprosy Filosofi* 2: 3–17.

Sorokin, Ye. 1983. "With Someone Else's Hand." *Krasnaya Zvezda*, November 13, p. 2.

Sovetskiy Patriot. 1986. December 17, p. 1.

Suvorov, Viktor. 1982. *Inside the Soviet Army*. New York: Macmillan.

Tedder, Yu. R., and P. I. Sidorov. 1976. "Influence of the Family on Children's Attitudes toward Alcohol Use." *Zdravookhraneniye Rossiyskoy Federatsii* 7: 10–12.

Volkogonov, D. 1976. "Moral Conflict." *Sovetskiy Voin* 12: 32–33.

Volkov, I., D. Prilepskiy, and L. Cherkasov. 1968. "Theoretical Questions of Military Discipline." *Voyennaya Mysl'* 3.

Yefimov, N. N., and Yu. I. Deryugin. 1980. "Ways to Increase the Effectiveness of Military-Patriotic Socialization of Youth." *Sotsiologicheskiye Issldovaniya* 1: 60–66.

Yegorov, G. 1986. "To Prepare Youth for Military Service." *Kommunist Vooruzhennykh Sil* 18 (Septmber): 31–37.

Zaigrayev, G. G. 1985. "The Alcoholic Situation – an Object of Preventative Measures." *Sotsiologichskiye Issledovaniya* 4: 47–54.

Zaigrayev, G. G. 1986. *Bor'ba c alkogolizmom*. Moscow: Mysl'.

About the Contributors

MICHAEL PAUL SACKS is Professor of Sociology at Trinity College. He received his Ph.D. in sociology from the University of Michigan in 1974, and is the author of two books that focus on gender, regional, and ethnic differences in the Soviet work force: *Work and Equality in Soviet Society: The Division of Labor by Age, Gender and Nationality* (1982) and *Women's Work in Soviet Russia: Continuity in the Midst of Change* (1976). Professor Sacks is also co-editor of *Contemporary Soviet Society* (1980).

JERRY G. PANKHURST is Associate Professor of Sociology at Wittenberg University. He received his Ph.D from the University of Michigan in 1978. His research and publications have focused on religion in the USSR and the more general topic of religion and politics. He is also co-editor of *Contemporary Soviet Society* (1980) with Michael Paul Sacks.

RALPH S. CLEM is currently Professor of International Relations at Florida International University, Miami. He is the author or editor of several books and articles on population trends and ethnicity in the USSR, including *Research Guide to the Russian and Soviet Censuses* (1986). He received his Ph.D in geography from Columbia University.

WALTER D. CONNOR is Professor and Chairman in the Department of Political Science at Boston University, and a Fellow of the Russian Research Center at Harvard. He is the author of *Deviance in Soviet Society* (1972), *Socialism, Politics and Equality* (1979), and co-author of *Public Opinion in European Socialist Systems* (1977), as well as many articles in scholarly and policy journals here and abroad. His chapter in this book is a revision of a study originally done on an unclassified contract basis for the Bureau of Intelligence and Research, U.S. Department of State.

MARK G. FIELD is Professor of Sociology at Boston University, and a Fellow in the Russian Research Center and Lecturer in the School of Public Health at Harvard University. Professor Field is also an Assistant Sociologist in the Department of Psychiatry at Massachusetts General Hospital. His major professional interests are Soviet society, Soviet socialized medicine and psychiatry, and medical sociology – particularly the comparative study of health systems. He is the author, co-author, or editor of five books and over one hundred papers in professional literature. He has visited the Soviet Union eleven times since 1956.

CAROLINE HUMPHREY is a Lecturer in the Department of Social Anthropology at Cambridge University. She has done field work in the USSR, Mongolian People's Republic, Nepal and India, and is the author of *Karl Marx Collective: Economy, Society and Religion in a Siberian Collective Farm* (1985).

ELLEN JONES has worked as an analyst for Soviet military/political affairs at the Defense Intelligence Agency since 1976. She received her Ph.D in history from Syracuse University in 1975, and is the author of *Red Army and Society: A Sociology of the Soviet Military* (Allen & Unwin, 1986); and co-author of *Modernization, Value Change and Fertilization in the Soviet Union* (1987). She has published numerous articles in the areas of Soviet military manpower, military/political leadership, and decision-making structures and processes.

DAVID LANE is Professor of Sociology at the University of Birmingham, England. He was educated at Birmingham and Oxford Universities, and has been on the faculty at the Universities of Essex and Cambridge. He has written extensively on Soviet affairs and communist studies. His most recent books include *Soviet Labour and the Ethic of Communism*, *State and Politics in the USSR*, and *Soviet Economy and Society*.

ROBERT A. LEWIS is Professor and Chairman in the Geography Department at Columbia University. His research has concentrated on population change in Russia and the USSR since the end of the nineteenth century and its impact on society. At present, he is working on the third and final volume of a series on Soviet population change since 1897. Professor Lewis holds a Ph.D from the University of Washington.

THOMAS F. REMINGTON is Associate Professor of Political Science at Emory University. He received a Ph.D in Political Science from Yale University in 1978. He is the author of *Building Socialism in Bolshevik Russia, The Truth of Authority: Ideology and Communication in Soviet Society*, and with Fredrick B. Barghoorn, *Politics in the USSR* (3rd Ed.), and a number of articles on Soviet politics, history and ideology.

LOUISE I. SHELLEY is a Professor in the Schools of Justice and International Service of American University. She is the author of numerous articles as well as *Lawyers in Soviet Work Life* (1984) and *Crime and Modernization* (1981). She is presently completing a book on the Soviet police.

Index

261

DATE DUE			
	DATE DUE		